THE MEASUREMENT OF COMMUNICATION PROCESSES
Galileo Theory and Method

HUMAN COMMUNICATION RESEARCH SERIES

PETER R. MONGE, Editor

Monge and Cappella:
MULTIVARIATE TECHNIQUES IN
HUMAN COMMUNICATION RESEARCH 1980

Cushman and McPhee:
MESSAGE-ATTITUDE-BEHAVIOR
RELATIONSHIP 1980

Woelfel and Fink:
MEASUREMENT OF COMMUNICATION
PROCESSES 1980

THE MEASUREMENT OF COMMUNICATION PROCESSES
Galileo Theory and Method

JOSEPH WOELFEL
Department of Rhetoric and Communication
State University of New York at Albany
Albany, New York

EDWARD L. FINK
College of Communication Arts
Department of Communication
Michigan State University
East Lansing, Michigan

ACADEMIC PRESS

A Subsidiary of Harcourt Brace Jovanovich, Publishers

New York   London   Toronto   Sydney   San Francisco   1980

ACADEMIC PRESS, INC.
111 Fifth Avenue, New York, New York 10003

United Kingdom Edition published by
ACADEMIC PRESS, INC. (LONDON) LTD.
24/28 Oval Road, London NW1 7DX

Library of Congress Cataloging in Publication Data

Woelfel, Joseph.
    The measurement of communication processes.

    (Human communication research series)
    Bibliography: p.
    Includes index.
    1. Interpersonal communication—Testing.
2. Psychology—Methodology. I. Fink, Edward L.,
joint author. II. Title. III. Series.
BF637.C45W63   153.6'028'7   80-19833
ISBN 0–12–761240–8

CONTENTS

PREFACE

The study of "mental" experiences has a long history. The Greek philosophers considered mental processes, both on the individual and group level, and were preceded in this by eastern savants. In modern times, each emerging new social and behavioral science has addressed anew the question of cognitive and cultural processes and their causes and effects. Thinkers have differed sharply about this class of experience; some believe that the thoughts of individuals govern their behavior. Western ethical thought in particular depends on the belief that mental activities govern behaviors, since the notion of praise, blame, and responsibility depend on the belief that thought can influence action.

Others, particularly sociologists and anthropologists, have emphasized the extent to which the beliefs, attitudes, and cognitive processes of individuals depends on the beliefs, attitudes, and cognitive processes of the larger culture to which the individual belongs. Even in this "two-staged" model, however, abstract cultural patterns like aggregate beliefs and attitudes are thought to exercise real impact over the actions of individuals and whole cultures.

Another group, probably the smallest numerically, would hold that both individual beliefs and attitudes and cultural beliefs and attitudes are epiphenomena which have their origins in daily events but which do not influence them.

Regardless of the position of individual scholars and groups of scholars on these issues, the study of individual cognitive processes and aggregate cultural processes has almost always been accorded a lower epistemological status than investigations of material motions, for example, because attitudes, beliefs, and cultural processes are usually thought to be insubstantial and abstract, too evanescent and flimsy to be caught and measured precisely. For this reason, most workers in the area of cognitive processes have held lower expectations for the results of their work than for the work of the "physical" scientist. By the same token, it is widely believed that lower standards of precision and evidence are appropriate for studies of the mental, the cognitive, and the cultural than might be required of the student of "physical reality."

The development of communication as a separate field of study has led to a renewed interest in cognitive and cultural processes, since most writers agree these bear a profound relation to human communication processes. In the case of two persons communicating, most writers would probably agree that the attitudes and beliefs of the participants would influence the communication process between them, and in turn the participants would be influenced by the communication. On an intercultural level, theorists generally agree that the aggregate beliefs and attitudes of each of the communicating cultures influence communication with each other culture, and in turn the cultures are influenced by that communication.

The past 15 years have seen the development of a new orientation to communication processes, one that draws heavily on theory and research primarily from sociology, psychometrics, and physics as well as from the field of communication itself. This new tradition draws its primary model of communication processes from the works of Emile Durkheim, George H. Mead, and empirical social psychologists like A. O. Haller and William H. Sewell who established these models on firm empirical grounds.

This theoretical model, often called the "Galileo" model, defines cognitive and cultural processes as changes in the relations among sets of cultural "objects" or concepts. The interrelationships among these objects are themselves measured by magnitude estimation pair comparisons, and the resulting dissimilarities matrices are entered into metric multidimensional scaling programs. The result of this work is that each of the cultural objects is represented as a point in a multidimensional Riemann space. Cognitive and cultural processes may be defined within this framework as motions of these objects relative to the other objects within the space.

Although the theory is completely general in its application to individuals or groups and cultures, most workers in this new tradition concern themselves primarily with cultural processes, and so typically work with averaged dissimilarities matrices of very high precision and reliability. For this reason, they generally shun nonmetric multidimensional scaling routines and prefer instead the classical or metric form of multidimensional scaling developed by Young and Householder (1938) and Torgerson (1958). As a result, the past decade in particular has seen a great concentration of experience with metric scaling in the field of communication, and, in fact, it is fair to say that more research concerning multidimensional Riemann surfaces typical of metric multidimensional scaling has been done by communication researchers than by most other workers. Little is known of this work outside the field of communication, and this book may serve as an introduction to it for those as yet unfamiliar.

Most of the work done by communication researchers deals with how one operates on the multidimensional coordinate system yielded by the metric scaling algorithm rather than with how the coordinate system is generated. In particular, researchers have capitalized on the resemblance of the coordinate system to conventional practice in physics to develop a theory of the cognitive and cultural processes modeled by these methods, which is itself based on the principles of thermodynamics and information theory, and for these reasons is a straightforward generalization of Newtonian and relativistic dynamics. In fact, research has shown generalized equations from these theories to conform to observed outcomes to within closer tolerances than theories written specifically to deal with human behavior alone.

This book serves the important task of compiling some of this early work within the framework of a general theory. In this book we try to outline a consistent philosophy of science which leads specifically to the development of the substantive theory presented in this volume. Since the theory is quite specific about its associated measurement operations, a great deal of space is devoted to measurement procedures, and several new methods of establishing validity and reliability particularly for these measures are set forth here.

Since a primary advantage of the present model is its easy translation into mathematical form, effort has been made to translate generalizations into mathematical form wherever possible, although the nonmathematical reader will find the same propositions put forward verbally in the text.

The application of mechanical and mathematical principles to any area of knowledge often gives rise to the possibility of engineering applications. In the case of the current theory, specific methods are presented for modifying cultural processes in planned ways. Applications of these methods are discussed, and examples of both experimental and commercial applications are presented.

A final purpose of this book was to be the comprehensive review of work already produced in this tradition. While we have tried to be as inclusive as possible, it became clear during the writing of the book that a complete discussion of the work already done in the area is beyond the scope of a single work. Indeed, during the writing of the book at least as much work was performed as was available before we began. Nonetheless, the present work may serve as a useful introduction to the literature in the area.

While we expect this book to be of special interest particularly to communication researchers working within the theory, the book also may serve as a theoretically grounded introduction to this work for those who have found the scattered trail through journal articles and convention papers too unwieldy to follow without some guidance. Sociologists and anthropologists interested in culture and cultural processes may find both the theory and the methods described here useful to their own concerns. Psychometricians and mathematical psychologists may find something interesting in the treatment of processes by means of multidimensional scaling methods, particularly since these fields have seen an increase in attention to Riemann manifolds along with a resurgence of interest in metric multidimensional methods in the past several years. For similar reasons, we hope some of the ideas in this book might interest physicists, engineers, and other scientists interested in the application of scientific method to investigations of human experiences.

Since the methods described here yield a very powerful applied capacity to manipulate cultural belief systems which have been well supported by research, workers in business, marketing, and advertising may find the book interesting and useful. Chapter 11, in fact, has been devoted to discussing both previous and possible future applications in a variety of contexts.

Finally, in part because the methods presented in this book do show unusual effectiveness in manipulative campaigns, but also because the general approach modifies many basic epistemological premises common to social science, we have taken some pains to explore our philosophical foundations fairly carefully. Moreover, since the approach is thoroughly relativistic in its foundations and methods, we have considered the problem of ethics within a relativistic and empirical framework.

ACKNOWLEDGMENTS

Many people and organizations have helped to make this book possible. Much of the text was written while the senior author was a Senior Fellow at the Communication Institute of the East-West Center in Honolulu, and the opportunity to communicate with scholars from the United States, Asia, the Pacific Basin, and the rest of the world has had a major impact on the thinking in the book. In particular, we are indebted to D. Lawrence Kincaid, first for major contributions to the philosophy and theory presented here, and second for his generous and unselfish support. So many others from the East-West Communication Institute contributed that it is impossible to mention each by name, but special thanks are due to June Ok Yum, Barbara Newton, Chung Ying Cheng, Tulsi Saral, Betty Buck, Wilbur Schramm, Jack Lyle, Godwin Chu, and Vera Hong. We are also indebted to the Computing Center of the University of Hawaii for extraordinary help, and in particular to Ginger and Helen Carey for programming assistance. Thanks also to Walter Yee who allowed us priority status for mounting the Galileo™ computer program at the University of Hawaii, and to the many users who waited a little longer for outputs due to our emergencies.

No Galileo-based work can be written without thanks to Richard A. Holmes, who wrote most of the code for the IBM, CDC, and UNIVAC versions of the Galileo program. Rick's unwillingness to tolerate lower standards for social science work than for standard engineering practice has been vitally important to us all. Donald P. Cushman has been a friend, advisor, and critic for so long that he serves as a permanent mental audience, and much of this book is a conversation with him. George A. Barnett has been one of the most ingenious and productive workers in this area, and his influence over this book is very substantial. James R. Gillham, John Saltiel, Michael Cody, Kim Serota, Donald Hernandez, and Gail Wisan all played a very important role in developing these ideas, as did other students too numerous to mention. John Woelfel has done extensive work in this area and has shared his results and advice freely to our great advantage. Mary Woelfel has had an important impact on the thinking in this book, quite apart from her support as a human being. Varda Fink has been a great influence on us all. We owe a very special debt to Archie Haller and hope this book repays some small part of it.

The final preparation of the manuscript was done while the senior author was at the State University of New York at Albany, and we have accumulated a great debt to both faculty and students, particularly in the Rhetoric and Communication Department at SUNYA. Thanks particularly to Robert Pfeiffer, John Tuecke, and Peg Carr at the SUNYA computing center. Overall, we have never been served better by any computing facility anywhere in the world, and we are deeply grateful. Thanks especially to Phil Tompkins, Bob Sanders, Kathleen Kendall, T. J. Larkin, Richard Wilkie, Brandt Burleson, David Kaufer, Maria Rudden, John Shoemaker, Barbara Towslee, Jean Slezak, and William Hedberg for support in the last stages.

This book would not exist except for the kind efforts of Peter Monge, whose work in our behalf can never be fully repaid. The staff of Academic Press has been more helpful than we deserve. And without Cherylene Hidano, there would be no manuscript at all.

CHAPTER 1

SCIENCE
AND HUMAN PHENOMENA

Introduction

In the period from A.D. 1500 to the present, human understanding of our environment has changed extensively and fundamentally. Those processes by which we accomplished these changes have generally been called *science*, and the last five centuries particularly have seen many phenomena previously discussed and accounted for by older systems of knowledge increasingly falling within the purview of science. It is neither possible nor necessary here to describe the remarkable changes in social organization which have followed from the development of science, but it is enough to point out that the increase in our collective ability to describe, anticipate, and control phenomena encompassed by science is so manifest that it is seldom disputed even by those who, for whatever reasons, oppose the continued expansion of science.

Not all domains of inquiry have yet fallen within the system of scientific knowledge, however, and most significant among those excluded areas are human individual and social processes, particularly human thought processes. This is not to say that many workers (if perhaps not a majority) within the human discipline have not eagerly and earnestly attempted to treat human thought in the same general way that physical scientists have approached nonhuman processes, but is simply meant as the recognition that there still remains a substantial gap between the

1

theories, procedures, and results of social and physical scientists. Although millenia of intense and profound human inquiry have been devoted to the study of human individual and social processes from theological, philosophical, artistic, and political perspectives, and while the study of human behavior in the present century has even renamed itself social *science* in preference to older names, nothing remotely resembling Newton's Laws of Motion or Maxwell's field equations can be found in the realm of social scientific thought. Moreover, a fair assessment of current opinions among scholars would probably show a large number who do not believe such laws will ever be shown to apply to human mental or behavioral phenomena except possibly in a metaphorical way.

Many writers both in the social sciences and elsewhere have attributed the differential development of physical science and social science to inherent differences in the phenomena studied by physical and social science (Sorokin, 1928). Among those who hold this view, physical phenomena are generally held to be relatively observable, objective, simple, and law-governed, while social or human phenomena are thought to be relatively unobservable, subjective, complicated, and spontaneous. One of the central beliefs of modern social science holds that the meanings of phenomena are not simply characteristics of the phenomena, but rather are constituted out of an interaction between observer and observed. These meanings, therefore, which constitute a main focus of social science, are internal to the observer and quite variable depending on characteristics of the observer, the observed, and the observational context. As a consequence, therefore, the primary phenomena of social science are both unobservable and subjective. Moreover, since none of the phenomena under study have meanings which are independent of other aspects of the observational setting and history of the observer, a complete understanding of any single phenomenon requires an understanding of all those other phenomena to which it may be related. As a result, the phenomena of social science are thought to be very complicated—too complicated to be understood by any relatively simple laws and principles such as those which characterize physical science.

As a direct result of our failure to encompass cognitive or human behavioral phenomena within a scientific theory, many events within the social and psychological domain appear to occur spontaneously and without apparent cause. Many writers quite explicitly assume that human events are not completely causally determined, and the notion of "free will" is a popular and historical expression of the spontaneous or "acausal" character of human activity.

While this argument is repeated frequently in many different forms, and while it is relatively widely accepted both within and without the social sciences, it contains two important flaws. The first of these flaws results from an incomplete application of the first principle of the argument itself—that meaning is composed of the interaction between observer and observed. Taken literally, this principle means that nothing can be said about an object itself, but that all statements about objects are simultaneously statements about the object, the observer, and the observational situation. If this is true, then all the statements on the preceding pages are not statements about human phenomena at all, but rather are statements about human phenomena as we have observed and understood them in the past. But if we include human phenomena within the framework of science, this means that we agree to adopt a different way of observing those phenomena. The characteristics of such phenomena may well be quite different when observed within a scientific context. In fact, a clear hope of science is certainly that the inclusion of a set of phenomena within the observational framework of science will make those phenomena appear to be more observable, objective, simple, and law governed than they appear when observed by less scientific procedures. That human phenomena, when observed through traditional observational frameworks, appear unobservable, subjective, complicated, and spontaneous might just as well be taken as an indictment of the traditional observational framework, rather than as a statement about the "nature" of human phenomena. Viewed in this light, a primary goal of science might well be to devise observational frameworks such that the phenomena under study are rendered as observable, objective, simple, and law governed as possible.

The second major objection to the argument is that it rather seriously misunderstands the extent to which the phenomena of physical science may be thought of as observable, objective, simple, and law governed. The idea that physical theory may be described by a simple, mechanical model has become pretty much a straw person argument, since no physical scientists have believed this for a long time. As early as 1934, Bohr wrote: "The great extension of our experience in recent years has brought to light the inefficiency of our simple mechanical conceptions and, as a consequence, has shaken the foundation on which the customary interpretations of observation was based [Capra, 1975, p. 42]." First of all, many of the most important variables in physical science are not observable at all, even in theory. In fact, of the primitive or fundamental variables of physical science—usually considered to be distance, time, force (or mass), and temperature (and sometimes angle)—neither force, mass, nor temperature are directly observable at all, but rather are measured indirectly by the aid of arbitrary (but consensual) stipulations and premises. Even the measurement of the primitive descriptive variables distance, time, and angle depends entirely on arbitrary conventions and formal stipulations to which scientists agree to adhere. The extent to which the observability of these variables depends on such conventions can be made clear by realizing that even today force, mass, and temperature are measurable by the layperson only with the aid of scientifically developed instruments, and, without scientific instruments, even our perceptions of distance and time are very crude and will differ substantially from person to person and from culture to culture.

Even in physical science, the dependence of observation on arbitrary stipulation of measurement rules and procedures implies an inherent subjectivity to such observations. That this is quite evident to modern physicists is evidenced by Heisenberg (1971) in a remark he attributes to Pauli: "(T)he idea of material objects that are completely independent of the manner in which we observe them proved to be nothing but an abstract extrapolation, something that has no counterpart in nature [p. 85]."

The implications of this reasoning are twofold: First, no object is observable independent of some method of observation. All observations we obtain represent the outcome of applying a method of observation to some observational situation. Applying different methods of observation to the "same" object will result in different outcomes. Thus every observation we make, even observations of what we have been accustomed to call physical objects, contains subjective components. Second, what we call objectivity is clearly the result of a consensus among observers concerning the methods of observation to be used. Whenever two or more independent scientists observe what they consider to be the same object or process yet obtain different observational results, the first question that must be raised is the extent to which the different outcomes can be attributed to differences in the methods of observation used by each.

Acceptance of the dependence of observation on the initially arbitrary methods of observation clearly precludes the possibility that we can make judgments about the inherent characteristics of objects or events on the basis of observation alone. With this in mind it follows rigorously that phenomena, whether physical or human, cannot be said to be simple or not, or even law governed or not, in and of themselves. We may only consider objects, processes or other phenomena to be simple or complicated, law governed or spontaneous, *as we observe them*. Should phenomena we hope to be simple appear complex, or those we hope to find law governed appear spontaneous, then we must at least be open to the possibility that, observed another way, they may indeed be found to be simple or law governed.

If we agree to call the set of symbols, definitions, and stipulations which define our observational procedures *theory*, then we might agree with Einstein (as cited by Heisenberg, 1971) when he says: "But on principle, it is quite wrong to try founding a theory on observable magnitudes alone. In reality the very opposite happens. It is the theory which decides what we can observe [p. 63; see also Kuhn, 1970]."

Viewed in this light it does not make sense to ask whether a theory is correct or incorrect, but rather theories must be evaluated on their ability to define measurement procedures whose outcomes are as objective, simple, and law governed as possible. Rather than being correct or incorrect, therefore, theories are either better or worse. They are better to the extent that they render the phenomena of interest objective, simple, and law governed.

Two very important considerations follow from these arguments that deserve special attention. First, no actual theories (apart from ideal theories) are ever complete or completely satisfactory, regardless of the range of phenomena to which they are meant to apply. The degree to which any theory and its associated measurement or observational procedures renders phenomena objective, simple, and law governed is always incomplete, particularly early in its life. Throughout the history of science, every scientific theory has always been in some state of relative disarray, and this is true of the most sophisticated of contemporary theory in physical science. Every scientific theory should be thought of as a process tending toward objectivity, simplicity, and lawfulness.

Physicists aptly refer to this mode of theorizing as "bootstraps" theory, recognizing the underidentified and iterative character of the process involved. The initial steps involve the creation of some observational procedures and measurement rules, along with a set of fundamental premises or general principles which the scientist would like the observations to satisfy. The next step is to accumulate a series of observations within the observational framework to determine the extent to which such observations satisfy the general principles. Failure to satisfy such principles results in adjustments in the measurement rules and perhaps even in the principles, to make the observations fit the principles to ever-increasing approximations.

What is not apparent from the foregoing, however, is the scope and magnitude of this "bootstraps" process. The first step in the process requires establishing measurement rules and observational frameworks such that the phenomena in question at least may be observed. It is not sufficient, however, to develop idiosyncratic rules and frameworks which apply only to single individuals; rather, some consensus must be achieved so that the phenomena become observable to many independent observers. Clearly the criterion of objectivity requires multiple observers, for objectivity by definition requires that observations be independent of any specific observer. As Einstein (1956) suggests, "We are accustomed to regard as real those sense perceptions which are common to different individuals, and which therefore are, in a measure, impersonal [p. 1]." Clearly the requirement that an experience (observation) be considered "real" for Einstein is that multiple observers, having applied the same measurement rules within the same observational system, observe outcomes which may be communicated, compared, and found to be the same to within some tolerance. As Bohr puts it (Heisenberg, 1971), "science is the observation of phenomena and the communication of the results of others, who must check them [p. 130]."

All of this clearly implies that science is a social phenomenon, regardless of how highly we may value the individual accomplishments of great scientists. The development of initial measurement rules, observational frameworks, and founding principles is never the individual work of a set of individual scientists, but rather the *social* accomplishments of an organized body of scientists. Like other social phenomena, the development of science is dependent on social and organizational factors which play themselves out over large spans of time. How long such processes may take is dependent on many factors, few of which are well understood, but it is clear that the time required for the development of initial measurement principles and observational procedures is in general vastly greater than the amount of time required to make discoveries and verify hypotheses within a scientific theory after such preliminary work has been accomplished.

The second important consideration to follow from the dependence of observation on previously stipulated measurement rules and observational procedures is equally vital: Since the character of events observed in a measurement frame is dependent on the measurement frame, failure to record observations which are objective, simple, or law governed in one or more frames can never provide affirmative evidence that those phenomena will not seem objective, simple, and law governed in another frame. Put another way, this means that no matter how many times we fail to construe the phenomena of interest in such a way that they appear objective, simple, and law governed, we can never conclude that such a construction is impossible. Such a conclusion would require that we know something about the phenomena that is independent of the way in which we have observed it, and this would contradict the principle which led us to question the possibility of our inquiry in the first place. Failure to include phenomena (such as human phenomena) within rigorous scientific theory in the past, therefore, can never be taken as secure evidence that such inclusion is not possible in the future.

Brief though it has been, this discussion should at least lead us to question the force of the argument which suggests that some phenomena (such as physical phenomena) are sufficiently observable, objective, simple, and law governed to allow their inclusion within scientific theory, whereas other phenomena (such as social or human phenomena) are too unobservable, subjective, complicated, and spontaneous to be encompassed by scientific theory. It is now clear that respected and thoughful physical scientists believe that even the "phenomena" which make up the subject matter of physical science have properties which are a consequence of the way we construe them. Yet this has not been an insuperable barrier to the development of present-day physical theory. One might even turn the argument around and suggest not that observable, objective, simple, and law-governed phenomena have been found easy to fit into the confines of scientific theory, but rather that phenomena become observable, objective, simple, and law governed to the extent that they have been successfully fit into scientific theory.

The Sociology of Science

If we grant the plausibility of these arguments, we are left to deal once again with the question of why human phenomena have not as yet been included within the realm of well-formed scientific theory, and why some are skeptical of such efforts even today. Furthermore, since these same writers would assume, rightly or wrongly, that such suspicions are themselves based on previous observations of human phenomena, a satisfactory answer to the foregoing questions will require a careful examination of the observational framework of social science to determine what there is about it that leads to such conclusions.

The Observational Framework

So far we have described the observational situation as including an observer (or set of observers), a method of observation, and a set of phenomena to be observed. Out of the interaction of these elements come observations which are dependent on the characteristics of all three basic components. Modern high-energy physicists generally consider the first two of these—the observer(s) and the observational method—to be the "observing system," and the phenomena to be the "observed system": "The starting point of the Copenhagen interpretation is the division of the physical world into an observed system ("object") and an observing system. The observed system can be an atom, a subatomic particle, an atomic process, etc. The observing system consists of the experimental apparatus and will include one or several human observers [Capra, 1975, p. 119]." The "experimental apparatus" which Capra mentions is itself considered to be composed of two basic components: a preparation process and a process of measurement:

> If we want to observe and measure such a [subatomic] particle, we must first isolate it, or even create it, in a process which can be called the preparation process. Once the particle has been prepared for observation, its properties can be measured, and this constitutes the process of measurement. . . . The properties of the particle cannot be defined independently of these processes. If the preparation or the measurement is modified, the properties of the particle will change, too [Capra, 1975, pp. 121–122].

Figure 1.1 represents a block diagram of the process by which scientific observations are generated. First, an observer or observers create an "apparatus" (the apparatus need not, of course, be physical machinery, but simply a setting for observation) within which (and in interaction with which) the phenomenon of interest will exhibit certain properties. These properties are recorded within a measurement system. The properties observed and recorded will themselves be functions of the measurement system as well as the phenomenon. These recorded observations must then be communicated to another independent observer or observers who will check them in a similar way. As Einstein suggests, those observations about which the observers agree will be considered "real." Since all observations are the result of interactions between the observing system and the observed system, an understanding of the observations of social scientists will require an analysis of the characteristics of the observing system as well as the observed system. If it is the case (as stated here) that the observations made by physical scientists seem to fit reasonably and usefully within the confines of well-formed scientific theory, while the observations of social scientists do not, we must examine the differences both in the observing systems and in the observed systems of these scientists before being able to conclude

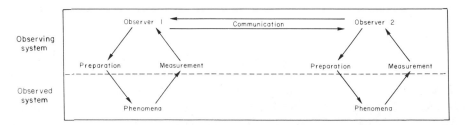

FIGURE 1.1   Diagram of the process of scientific observation.

that it is the phenomena observed which give rise to the differences in outcome.

The Observing System   The notion of an observing system is based on the understanding that nature, apart from human observation, has no meaning. As Heisenberg puts it, "natural science does not simply describe and explain nature; it is part of the interplay between nature and ourselves [Capra, 1975, p. 126]." But the interplay between nature and ourselves is itself not independent of our method of investigation, and we should expect a single observer using different methods of observation to obtain different results. Again Heisenberg puts it clearly: "What we observe is not nature itself, but nature exposed to our method of questioning [Capra, 1975, p. 126]." An inquiry into the character if any observing system, therefore, will require a discussion of the observer(s) and the method of observation employed by them.

The Observer   Our analysis up to this point has stressed the collective or social nature of science. Bohr's suggestion that science is "the observation of phenomena and the communication of the results to others who must check them" indicates clearly enough that the observer we speak of in this context is not an individual but an organized body of observers. Consequently, an analysis of the characteristic of observers in science needs to focus on the sociological characteristics of the aggregate field rather than on characteristics of single observers. Thus, although social scientists who are individually similar to physical scientists can be found, on a collective level there exist several significant and substantial overall differences between the average social scientists and physical scientists.

The first of these aggregate differences, already discussed in part, lies in the attitude each group holds toward their respective phenomena. Physical scientists in general have a much more optimistic notion of the possibility of placing their phenomena within well-formed scientific theory. While exceptions can of course be found, many social scientists are skeptical about fitting cognitive or human behavioral phenomena within a framework of science as it is practiced by physical scientists.

There are two basic types of such skepticism. The first type represents a combination of metaphysical and epistemological skepticism, which assumes that human phenomena cannot be contained within the confines of science, at least not in exactly the same way as physical phenomena are included. The second type of skepticism may be seen as ethical or esthetic. Even within this second type of skepticism divisions exist: One view would argue that the development of scientific understandings of human phenomena would result in an increased capacity for establishment forces to control and manipulate people, with un-desirable consequences for the overall good of humanity. In this regard, these scientists do not differ radically from those physical scientists who hold fears and reservations about the uses to which the fruits of their science may be put. But a second group, not completely distinct from the first, argues further that the inclusion of human phenomena within a scientific framework would result inherently in a serious change in the way the phenomena are viewed. Rather than observing people as mor-ally responsible agents each of whom has an ethically valid definition of self and reality which may differ from the views of all others, a scientific understanding would objectify human phenomena, describing them from the objective viewpoint of a collective scientific perspective. Such a view is frequently described as "dehumanizing" or "reducing people to numbers" which is itself thought of as ethically or esthetically unfor-tunate.

Without argument at this point as to whether or not human processes may be included within science in its normal sense, it is at least appro-priate to point out that the fact that a large number of social scientists do not believe their discipline can or should be scientific must have impor-tant consequences for the likelihood that these same investigators will produce a science of human processes. Moreover, when persons who disbelieve the possibility of genuine scientific study of social phenom-ena occupy important disciplinary positions such as journal editors or officers of professional associations, they must, as a consequence, exer-cise control over the publication and evaluation of research aimed at developing such understandings.

These attitudes, moreover, are quite deeply rooted or massive, and strongly resistant to change. As Durkheim (1915) pointed out at the beginning of this century, when members of a culture engage in collec-tive activities, particularly ritual activities, a cultural force is generated which exercises control over the activities of the participants in a way which is compelling, internal, and generally inexplicable to the partici-pants. The source of this force is the society itself, or the interaction of the members of the society. The compelling and mysterious character of the force gives rise to feelings of awe on the part of those influenced by it, and it takes on a sacred character, as do those symbols and represen-tations which are associated with it. Only members of the society are affected by this force, however, and it becomes coterminous with the society itself in the minds of the participants. Thus the society and its associated signs and representations take on a sacred character which is fundamentally connected with the society in the minds of the members. This sacred quality diffuses itself throughout those objects associated with the society, but the source of the sacred character itself remains the society. Durkheim believes these dynamics constitute the origins of religious belief, and consequently the conception individuals hold of their own societies and human persons in general ultimately may be seen to be religious in character.

If, as Wilson (1952) suggests, "the primary aim of pure science is not the laying of foundations for future inventions but the pushing back of the wall of ignorance and superstition which surrounds the human race [p. 9]," then the fundamental nature of the conflict becomes clear: ethical and esthetic opposition to the scientific transformation of our conception of human phenomena are rooted in the conservative social forces of society and are religious in character, while science is radical and disruptive of older social forms, and is irreligious or even antireligious in character. The conflict between science and religion is prehistoric and has been fundamental, and it is reasonable to expect that, however intense were the feelings generated when sacred conceptions about physical objects such as the stars and the earth were transformed into scientific understandings, the feelings attached to conceptions about society and humanity ought to be even more intense, since these phenomena lie so much closer to the generating locus of the idea of the sacred. We should not be surprised, then, if human phenomena are among the last to be included within the domain of science.

If social scientists differ from physical scientists in their collective attitudes toward the phenomena, they differ as well in the orientations they hold toward science. This should not be unexpected, since the recruitment patterns into social and physical science are quite different and the formal training procedures for each of the fields also differ greatly. Most obvious among these differences are the differences in orientations toward mathematics. (Figures 12.4 and 12.5 show this gap between social science and mathematics graphically.) Although individual exceptions can always be found, those who choose to enter the physical sciences are generally more favorably disposed toward mathematics and are better able to do mathematical work than social scientists. Many current social scientists in fact attribute part of their motivation toward the social sciences to a dislike for or lack of facility with mathematical work. These differences are substantially increased by the virtual absence of required mathematics in the curricula of most of the social sciences. It is probable that the majority of practicing social scientists both in the United States and the world have had no higher mathematics; even required statistics courses usually require no calculus. So substantial is the lack of mathematics within most social sciences that those social scientists whose work is mathematical often complain that they are cut off from the main body of their discipline, while others claim that the quantitative methodologists within social science (i.e., those whose work is at least partly mathematical) are remiss in failing to find ways to make their work accessible to the bulk of the larger non-mathematical audience.

If social scientists are socially distant from mathematics, they are also widely separated (in a communication sense) from the bulk of physical science as well. For example, virtually no undergraduate program in any social science in the United States requires any physical science course beyond the general university requirements for any degree, and these usually consist of one or two introductory courses at most. As a result, social scientists are at a real disadvantage when they try to understand the role mathematics plays in modern science. Having only elementary arithmetic, some geometry, and elementary algebra available to them, many social scientists are unaware of the subleties of expression possible in the mathematical language; many feel, quite erroneously, that vernacular language is capable of more sublety and fineness of discrimination than is mathematics. Being so widely separated from the actual works of physical science, it is easy to fail to realize that physical scientists have in fact found the opposite to be the case: a continuing source of dispair to the atomic physicist, for example, is the difficulty if not the impossibility of expressing in the vernacular language what is clearly stated in mathematics: "The problem of language here are really serious. We wish to speak in some way about the structure of atoms. . . . But we cannot speak about atoms in ordinary language." And, "here we have at first no simple guide for correlating the mathematical symbols with concepts of ordinary language; and the only thing we know from the start is the fact that our common concepts cannot be applied to the structure of atoms [Heisenberg, both statements from Capra, 1975, pp. 32–33]."

Perhaps most significant is the nearly complete absence of the calculus from the working vocabularies of most social scientists. Although a few of the more mathematical branches of social science, such as mathematical economics, econometrics, mathematical sociology and communication, and psychometrics, routinely include concepts from the calculus, very few social scientists have used any calculus in their work. The significance of this fact flows from the understanding that most social scientists define the phenomena of interest to them as processes, and the emphasis on the processual character of human phenomena in the social sciences is very heavy; however, the description of the process in vernacular language is very tedious and imprecise. It is very difficult for the worker without any knowledge of the calculus to grasp the extent to which description of process is made possible by concepts from the calculus like the differential element and the time derivative. In this regard, social scientists lack the apparatus available for descriptions of process that were available to Newton, and as a result, the overwhelming bulk of research in social science is what physical scientists would call comparative statics. Time series models of processes are virtually the exclusive domain of a small group of econometricians whose work is largely incomprehensible even to mainstream economists; it is even more incomprehensible to other social scientists.

Although there are many other differences between the characteristics of physical and social scientists, one last difference is of importance here. As a result of long historical processes and a heavy reliance on the essentially discrete vernacular language, social scientists tend more so than physical scientists to divide up the flow of social phenomena into discrete elements and discrete events. The continuous flow of individual human activity tends to be subdivided into a series of discrete acts, and long-term social processes tend to be broken into stages. We are presented with stages in the process of socialization of individuals; the continuing process of association and disassociation among persons is broken into discrete groups and societies and systems. To be sure, social scientists are aware of the violence done to the phenomena by these discrete classifications, since the problem of defining boundaries around these systems is continual and well known, but the extent to which these problems are caused by the discrete character of ordinary language as an encoding system has not been fully grasped by the discipline as a whole. While some social scientists seem clearly aware of this,[1] fewer social scientists are in a position to be aware of the extent to which language like the calculus might alleviate the problem.

These generalizations, like most generalizations, admit of important exceptions and qualifications. Many individual social scientists and even associations of social scientists, such as groups of psychometricians, econometricians, and mathematical sociologists, have fewer reservations about the possible inclusion of human phenomena within the realm of science, and they also have considerably more acquaintance with physical science and mathematics than their less scientifically oriented colleagues. Some of these social scientists are excellent mathematicians with backgrounds in physical science. Some whole disciplines, such as the field of communications, overlap engineering and physical science on one side and social science on the other, and it seems clear that the possibilities for communication between physical and so-

---

[1] See, for example, the statement by Whorf (1956) on p. 33 of Chapter 2.

cial science are greatest within these areas. Nonetheless, it is clear that, on the whole, the attitudes of social scientists toward their subject matter differ in many important ways from the attitudes of physical scientists toward theirs. They are, in general, little acquainted with the conception of and work in modern science, and are cut off from communication with physical science by the fact that most social scientists do not speak the language—mathematics—within which physical scientists communicate about their work. At least part of the difference in the character of observations made by these two groups, then, might well be accounted for by these differences in the characteristics of the two broadly conceived disciplines. This should warrant some additional caution, therefore, in attributing differences in the *perceived* characteristics of physical and social phenomena to the *inherent* characteristics of the phenomena.

Observation Method   Given the substantial differences in characteristics of social and physical scientists, it would be reasonable to suspect some differences in the observational methods used by the two groups. These differences can be found in both the preparation process and the measurement process which constitute the observation method.

The Preparation Process   The preparation process, as we have described it so far, refers to those operations whereby conditions are established such that the phenomena to be observed will manifest themselves, while at the same time other competing phenomena which might contaminate the phenomena or alter them importantly are held in abeyance. In physical science the preparation process can range from the extremely extensive operation required to assemble the apparatus needed to bring about atomic collisions to the simple act of waiting until nightfall so that celestial events may be observed free from the contamination of daylight. Similarly, in social science, we may distinguish between elaborate experimental rituals in which subjects are assembled and exposed to well-planned stimuli which are hypothesized to produce an effect (such as a change in attitude), and the far simpler unobstrusive observational schemes such as going to a bowling alley to observe bowling teams interact with each other. In any event, the preparation process always involves either creating or discovering circumstances under which the phenomena in question are expected to be manifest and relatively uncontaminated by other factors which might interfere with or obscure the resulting manifestation. This process is in general well understood both by physical and social sciences. Nonetheless there are important differences in the actual procedures used by both.

The most significant of these differences is a general but important one. The preparation process involves creating a situation (or identifying a preexisting situation) in which the phenomena of interest are likely to occur. Clearly, the ability to do this is itself dependent on previously developed theory, since one must have an idea as to what conditions give rise to the phenomena. To the extent that social or psychological theory is as yet less well developed than physical theory, the collective ability of social scientists to generate precise observational situations will be necessarily lower. The results of social or psychological experiments, therefore, should be expected to be less precise and secure in part for this reason.

Since very little truly dynamic theory exists in the social sciences, most of the events that interest social observers are conceived of as static, and experiments are constructed to yield static analyses as outcomes. In a typical experiment on cognitive processes, for example, social scientists may randomly divide a set of experimental subjects into two groups, administer stimuli which are expected to produce cognitive changes, and expect to find subsequent differences in the cognitive structures of the two groups that cannot be accounted for on the basis of chance alone. The experimental situations in social science in general, and of those interested in cognitive processes in particular, tend to be structured to yield comparative static information rather than continuous change data.

The absence of dynamic theory has had similar consequences for survey research as well. A typical survey consists of one mailing of questionnaires (or one wave of interview data) which may or may not be broken into a series of static comparisons between groups within the mailing. When time-ordered data are collected (as is sometimes the case in political studies such as those which might be done prior to an election, for example), the time process is almost always broken into two, three, or four "waves" of data. Analyses of these data sets again consist of a set of comparative static analyses to determine whether data at each of the time points are statistically different from those at the foregoing point. Most often, even when a set of observations is sequenced in time, the real time characteristics of the data set are ignored, and each successive time point tends to be described only by its ordinal rank in the series, that is, time 1, time 2, etc.

It is not the case that this discrete bunching of real time is required or justified by the logistics of social data collection, since it is probably more tedious and expensive to gear a research program to peak efforts at data collection points with a corresponding reduction of effort during intervening periods, and in fact several methodologies within the social sciences have very recently begun to attend to the implications of the lengths of the time intervals between measurements when investigating processes such as those underlying changes of attitude (Heise, 1975). Moreover, some groups of social scientists have moved strongly toward real time analysis of social data recently, particularly in the area of econometrics. It is interesting to note, though, that the data which provide the basis for econometric analysis are in general not collected by econometricians at all, but rather are made available by business, government and industry, whose concern about the role of real time in social and economic processes has been greater than that of social scientists. Moreover, these same investigators have found it increasingly necessary to utilize such mathematical techniques as differential equation models, and related computer programs that have been developed in departments of physics and engineering.

The implications of this comparative static orientation found in the typical social science data collection process cannot be overestimated. Because social science theory almost never includes time as a variable or variable index, and because it is traditional among social scientists to think of social and individual activity discretely rather than continuously, the observational methods of social science tend to obscure the role of time in cognitive and other human processes. Thus data which could lead to a truly processual theory of human processes are seldom obtained by normal social science procedures. Finally, even "questions posed in comparative statics ordinarily cannot be answered without an explicit dynamic formulation [Blalock, 1969, p. 138]"; we cannot avoid dynamic theory by simply ignoring it.

The Measurement Process   The measurement component of the observation process consists of those rules (operations) by which attention is selectively focused on certain aspects of the phenomena and by which the resulting impressions are encoded into symbols to be communicated to other observers "who must check them." It is in the realm of measurement that social scientists, particularly those whose focus of attention is on cognitive processes, differ significantly from their counterparts in the physical sciences. A primary reason for these differences flows from the fact that the phenomena of interest, that is, cognitive processes, take place within the minds of persons and are not directly observable by the scientist. Scientists must therefore enlist the aid of nonscientists—that is, the very persons in whose minds the cognitive processes are to be found—to perform the actual observations. In the case of attitude change experiments, for example, scientists may design observational situations which are expected to give rise to changes in attitudes, but must rely on experimental subjects for introspective reports on these processes or their outcomes. Clearly, therefore, attitudes or attitude changes are never observed directly, but are always measured indirectly either through verbal reports of subjects or, less frequently, by means of other behaviors thought to be related to attitudes or attitude changes by some theory.

It is not the indirect observational status of these phenomena which is unusual, since many phenomena of physical science, such as force, mass, and energy, are themselves indirect measures whose existence and character follows from theory. The difference flows from the near universal presence of untrained nonscientists as observers in the process. As a direct consequence of their concerns over the capabilities of the average human observer (rather than the scientist observer), most social scientists universally and routinely restrict themselves to the simplest (and least informative) measurement procedures they can devise.

Two schools of thought have arisen in response to this issue. A first school, related closely to those discussed earlier who see the adoption of a uniform scientific viewpoint on human activities as dehumanizing, argue that the observational systems of the lay observers should be left intact, and that every effort should be made to observe the phenomena from the point of view of the nonscientist—that is, from the point of view of the actor in the situation. Within this perspective, measurement takes on a quasi-journalistic cast, since the observers are attempting to describe processes (such as attitude change or cultural change) as they are seen by those who are experiencing them and as encoded and expressed in the vernacular language of the observers themselves. Such an approach has most recently been called "ethnomethodological," and has had important historical and political ramifications within social science, particularly sociology, within the last decade (Garfinkel, 1967). Regardless of its value as a method of analysis, it is very different from science as practiced within physical science, since its purpose is to yield multiple, equally valid perspectives which are nonpredictive, nonquantitative, and nonmanipulative in character. Moreover, the inherent subjectivity of such procedures works strongly against objective, repeatable observations. Without denying the possibility that different observers using such procedures might reach similar conclusions, it is clearly the case that it is impossible for one observer to verify the results of another by replication, since it is virtually impossible that any two observers will make the same observations. Each investigation is meant to be a unique study, and a second study of the same phenomena by a second observer could be said to be a replication only by a serious extension of the term.

Ethnomethodological measures (along with others of the same type) are characterized by the use of vernacular symbols rather than a special-ized scientific coding system, which furthermore tend to be categorical and nonnumerical. A second school of thought, having its roots in psychometrics, in fact usually defines measurement as the process of establishing correspondences between observations and numbers ac-cording to some rule (Stevens, 1951; Togerson, 1958; Suppes & Zinnes, 1963). Traditionally, those who have investigated scaling procedures within the social sciences have been among the most mathematically sophisticated and the most similar to their physical science counterparts of all social scientists, but nonetheless important difficulties have prevented the development of measurement systems equivalent to those in use in the physical sciences, with the exception of a few impor-tant psychophysical scales. In general, measurement specialists in the social sciences are found almost exclusively in psychology and educa-tion within the area called psychometrics, and there in very small num-bers. Outside psychology, specialists in measurement are very nearly nonexistent. The extensive mathematics involved in psychometrics has furthermore virtually isolated the small cadre of psychometricians from the rest of social science, since their work is largely incomprehensible to the nonmathematical social scientist. As Stevens (1951) has pointed out, even in physical science, the study of measurement has been scant, and it is probably fair to say that the preponderance of physical scientists are themselves unacquainted with the philosophical and historical un-derpinnings of their own measurement systems. These difficulties are further compounded by the fact that many psychometricians themselves exhibit tendencies to think of human phenomena discretely rather than continuously, while at the same time being required to produce mea-surement systems of sufficient simplicity that untrained nonscientist observers may be trained to use them reliably within a few moments. All these difficulties have led to the development of measurement sys-tems for the social sciences which are radically different from those used by physical science. As Coleman (1964) says,

> time and again the same obstacle has been evident in the path of quantification in social science: the lack of adequate measurement. . . . The paucity of quantitative theories, and the primitive nature of those which do exist, testify to the crippling effect of lack of measurement. Quantitative laws and theories seem to require more in the way of measurement than social phenomena are prepared to give. Even the weakest theories, those based on qualitative generalizations, impose measurement requirements which are seldom met by the kinds of measurement which exist today in social science [p. 55].

The basis of measurement in the social sciences is unquestionably given by the fourfold classification set forth by Stevens (1951). That classification system begins with the existential assertion that there exist phenomena which manifest attributes to a greater or lesser degree. Scaling or measurement is the act of assigning numbers (Stevens, following Russell, uses the term *numerals*) to these phenomena in correspondence to the extent to which each manifests the attribute(s) in question. When the phenomena may be distinguished from one another but not ranked or quantified, the resulting scale is called *nominal*, since the phenomena are distinguished and named. When they can further be arrayed in order of the extent to which they manifest the attribute(s), the resulting scale is termed *ordinal*. When they can be established up to an additive constant, the resulting scale is called an *interval* scale. When the magnitudes can be established completely, the result is called a *ratio* scale. This classification system determines the range of measurement types possible to the social scientist and is accepted with unusual unanimity by social scientists in virtually every discipline. In spite of the near-unanimity with which the paradigm is accepted, there are important difficulties associated with its use. The basis of these difficulties is the initial existential assumption that phenomena exhibit differential possession of attributes independent of the human act of observing and measuring them. This proposition is clearly contrary to the fundamental notion both of social and modern physical scientists that the properties of phenomena are manifestations of both the phenomena and the act of observation and encoding; the properties represent interactions between the measured phenomena and the observing system, which includes the scale as a component. Consequently it is not permissible to speak of the accuracy with which phenomena are mapped onto a scale independent of an alternative mapping onto an alternative scale. We may say that the two alternative mappings agree or fail to agree, but we may never adjudge one or the other correct or incorrect. Two scales may be linearly or nonlinearly related to one another, but it is inappropriate to question whether a set of phenomena are linearly related to a single scale of measurement, since any answer to the inquiry presupposes a knowledge of the "actual" array of phenomena independent of any scale of measure.

Psychometricians have attempted to come to grips with this problem by distinguishing those psychological phenomena (usually perceptual phenomena, such as perceived loudness or perceived brightness) which are themselves related to some already well-measured physical phenomena (such as acoustical energy or light intensity) from those for which no related physical continuum is known (such as happiness or affection). In either case, the psychometric scales are invariably accorded a lower epistemological status than the physical scales; whenever psychometric scales are found to be nonlinearly related to physical scales, it is common practice to transform one or both scale values until the transformed values are linearly related. This is good practice, since it is entirely appropriate to attempt to bring new measures into correspondence with an already established system of measure, but the language which usually accompanies such transformations frequently suggests that the original nonlinearity should be thought of as inaccuracies in the psychometric device or peculiarities of human perceptual apparatus. That the related physical measures are themselves artificial constructions of human observers whose epistemological status is identical with the psychometric scale is seldom made clear, however.

This lack of clarity is carried over when levels of measurement are defined: it is seldom clear in psychometric work (and less so in the general literature) that scales should not be thought of as interval or ratio alone, but may only be shown to be linearly or nonlinearly related to yet other scales. This is often seen as a serious problem in the development of scales to measure internal psychological phenomena, such as cognitive processes, since most workers continue to think of the establishment of interval or ratio scales as a goal, but find the problem of achieving such measures without related physical continua to be insuperable. As a result, a great deal of pessimism exists concerning the ability to develop psychological scales which are like those prevailing in physical science; this pessimism even characterizes the psychometricians.

The outcome of all this is the existence of a class of psychometric devices typified by the Likert-type scale, or its close relative, the semantic differential scale (Osgood, Tannenbaum, & Suci, 1957). These are questions whose response alternatives are typically represented by line segments placed at equal physical intervals. Because of the requirement that these scales be used reliably by untrained observers based on only a few moments of (usually written) instructions, the number of intervals marked off is usually small, typically between 5 and 11. While more sophisticated scales than these are known to psychometricians, Likert-type and semantic differential scales, along with occasional rank ordering tasks, are by far the predominant scales used in actual social science research, and have been virtually the exclusive choice of researchers in the field of cognitive processes and attitude change for the last quarter century. While the question of whether these scales are ordinal, interval, or ratio in character is moot, nevertheless they exhibit important properties as formal coding systems which render them considerably less than optimal for such uses. In an information-theoretic sense, these scales have only a very small capacity to carry information. Since the information carrying capacity of a coding system (assuming equally likely alternatives) is given by

$$H = \log_2 x = (\ln x)/\ln 2,$$

where H is the information content in bits and x the number of possible different values the coding system may take, the amount of information such scales can carry (in bits) ranges between 2.32 and 3.46 bits per scale, which is quite small. (By comparison, a 5-digit Arabic number can carry 16.61 bits of information, while a 5-letter English word can carry 22.91 bits of information.)

This means, of course, that the typical encoding procedure of social science, and the resulting measurements (the language in which observations are encoded so that they may be "communicated to others who must check them"), exercises an extremely limiting effect on the information obtainable from even the most sophisticated research. Within this context it is perhaps easier to understand the tendency of so many social scientists to retain the vernacular language as a vehicle for encoding and reporting research findings, since ordinary English, while far less standardized, is capable of conveying immensely more information than the typical scaling procedure adopted by the body of quantitative researchers in the field.

It is not difficult, in fact, to understand the conventional use of Likert- and semantic differential-type scales as an important impetus toward the belief that numbers are dehumanizing, since both lay subjects in experiments and sophisticated and sensitive social scientists are easily able to discriminate more information in a typical observational setting than may be recorded on one of these scales. The complaint from even naive subjects that "my view doesn't fit any of these boxes" is a familiar one, and should be taken as evidence of the deficiencies of these coding systems even from the point of view of the untrained observer.

Hence, it is easy to see why cognitive phenomena, as viewed through the typical coding devices of social science, do not exhibit properties like those of physical phenomena when viewed through the far more informative and well-developed measuring systems of physical science. It is even obvious, in fact, to see that if the results of careful physical observations of what are called physical phenomena were to be encoded onto 5- to 11-point scales, the phenomena would exhibit vastly different characteristics, and it would not be at all surprising if they were to seem as subjective, complicated, and spontaneous as social phenomena now appear to us.

First Principles

The implication of what has been said up until now is that the failure of social science to develop as satisfactory a system of knowledge as has been developed in physical science cannot be attributed to inherent differences in the subject matter of the two branches of knowledge, but rather can be attributed to an inconsistent application of the basic principles of science by social scientists. If this is so, then decisive improvement in the quality of social scientific knowledge must follow from a more explicit compliance with the principles of physical science. In what follows we shall describe five fundamental principles which we believe are necessary to generate a body of scientific theory which is consistent in all major respects with theory which has been so useful in physical science. The first four of these principles provide a basis for the selection of observational frameworks, while the fifth is required to introduce the notion of causality into the resulting system of knowledge. (For the first three of these principles, we rely on an account by Born, 1965.)

1. **Principle of Relativization**   The principle of relativization states that no concept has absolute significance, but rather each concept can only be defined by comparison with some other arbitrarily designated concepts. Thus, even the fundamental concept "length" takes on meaning only by comparison with some arbitrarily designated length, just as the fundamental concept "time" takes on meaning only when compared to an arbitrarily designated interval. The first component of the principle of relativization is that the *standard of comparison* is philosophically arbitrary; that is, there is no unit or perspective in experience which is inherently more satisfactory than any other. The second component of the principle of relativization is that the rule for comparison with the standard is arbitrary. We might adopt a "same versus different" rule, or a "smaller, the same or larger" rule, or the ratio comparison rule typical of physical science. Changes in the standard or the rule for comparison will result in changes of the meaning of the concepts compared to it. Thus, "as long as the earth was regarded as a flat disk, the 'up–down' or vertical direction at a place on the earth was something absolute. Now it becomes the direction towards the center of the globe and this [is] defined only relative to the standpoint of the observer [Born, 1965, p. 2]."

2. **Principle of Objectivization**   The principle of objectivization, according to Born (1965), "aims at making observations as independent of the individual observer as possible [p. 2]." The principle of objectivization is deeply related to the principle of relativization, since observers who choose different arbitrary reference standards and different comparison rules will in general not agree on the results of their observations. The principle of objectivization, therefore, requires that observers *formulate an agreement* about standards of comparison and observational

procedures such that the results of performing observations do not depend on who made them.

3. Principle of Empirical Verification The principle of empirical verification states that "concepts and statements which are not empirically verifiable should have no place in a physical theory [Born, 1965, p. 3]." This principle should not be confused with positivism, which implies that only immediate sense impressions should be regarded as real, since the adoption of the first two principles implies that there are no immediate sense impressions, but rather all sense impressions are mediated by concepts of an arbitrary character. Rather, the principle of empirical verification should be taken to refer to observations made within and contingent upon the arbitrary but consensual framework of reference standards and observational rules established under the first two principles. Thus the principle of empirical verification adopted here requires that theories make statements about the relationships among observations made within the arbitrary but consensual framework adopted by the body of scientists. Following from this principle, statements which do not refer to observations possible under these restrictions are inappropriate to well-formed scientific theory.

These three principles are sufficient to allow the development of an infinity of alternative descriptive schemes for any subject matter. Insofar as all these theories remain logically consistent internally, the first three principles are themselves insufficient to allow us to choose among them. Thus, for example, we could choose as an arbitrary standard of length the distance between the shores of an arbitrary river, and as a standard of time the interval between periodic floods of the same river, and based on these standards, construct a science as defensible on epistemological grounds as our current science. Most scientists would immediately reject such a science, however, but might be harder pressed to specify the principle on the basis of which it should be rejected. Implicit in the rejection of such a science would certainly be dissatisfaction with the complexity of the observations that would result from such initial definitions, since the variability of the standards relative to other processes in time would require very complex correction formulas to render comparisons over time informative, so a "simplicity" criteria certainly underlies such a choice. But simplicity alone is insufficient, since a simple model could easily be developed by the crude expedient of encoding the observations into a language so imprecise that fluctuations in the standards were not noticeable. While physical scientists would immediately reject such a program (and, when stated so starkly and abstractly, most social scientists would reject such an idea as well), in fact this is exactly the process social scientists have traditionally used by expressing measurements on 5- or 7-point scales. While simplicity may serve as a partial criterion for the acceptability of a theory, it is not itself sufficient. Two further principles, therefore, seem required. The first of these we can call the principle of maximum information, and the second, the principle of minimum information or the inertial principle. Both principles have their roots in information theory, and are meant to generate the maximum amount of information with the minimum cost.

4. Principle of Maximum Information   The principle of maximum information suggests that all components of the (arbitrary) science, such as the initial standards, measurement rules, and communication code by means of which observers communicate their observations, should be chosen such that the potential amount of information which can be carried by the system is a maximum. This principle would require, among other things, that the standards chosen be sufficiently accessible so that the maximum number of observers could use them, or, when specially restrictive procedures that limit the access of observers are used (such as special apparatus or special training), that the amount of information potentially realizable from the restricted set of observers should be larger than the amount realizable in principle from a larger set of observers using more accessible standards. The principle would also require that the code or language which carried the information should be capable of carrying the maximum amount of information in the minimum code, and at least as much information as can be obtained from the measurement procedures. (This principle would also be sufficient, for example, to specify the number of significant digits carried in a computation.)

5. Principle of Minimum Information (Inertial Principle)   The inertial principle, which is closely related to the principle of maximum information, requires that the components of the science be established such that the *actual* amount of information required to specify the state of the system of observations along any interval of time be at a minimum. This is the same principle which leads scientists to select a reference frame which minimizes the total magnitude of residual forces which must be postulated to account for the behavior of the system. As such, it is also the principle which gives meaning to the notion of causality within any observational framework (J. D. Woelfel, 1980). The inertial principle may be seen as specifying a "normal" or "natural" state of the system, that is, a state in which it would be most likely to be found if no factors external to the system had impinged on it. Departures from this state require explanations, and so the inertial principle would suggest that the "natural" state of the system be chosen such that the amount of "explaining" required for any set of observations be at a minimum.

We do not mean to suggest that these five principles are sufficient for the formation of a successful science, since certain obvious additions are needed. Science without honesty, for example, seems impossible, as does science without dedication and industry, wealth and leisure, and so on. We do believe these principles are necessary to science as it is understood in the twentieth century. Moreover, while efforts to attribute the inadequacies of social science to inherent characteristics of its subject matter seem doomed to fail, evidences of violation of all five of these principles characterize common social science practice. We have described some of these in this chapter. The belief in the absolute significance of human phenomena, particularly attitudes, beliefs, and other internal cognitive states, is both commonplace and in violation of the principle of relativization, as is the notion that a scale is to be evaluated in terms of its functional relation with the phenomena it measures. Similarly, the notion that the task of the social scientist is to explicate the world view of groups from their own perspectives violates the principle of objectivization, as does the almost total absence of conventional standards of measure among social scientists. The 5- and 7-point scales are clear violations of the principle of maximum information since they place inherent limits on the amount of information which can be communicated among scientists.

We will discuss these principles in the context of specific issues in what follows, and they will serve as a rough guide for the theory presented. We do not mean them as indispensable to any human knowledge, however, but rather believe that they describe the underpinnings of the specific system we call science.

Summary

In this chapter, an attempt has been made to demonstrate both the inappropriateness and futility of considering physical science as qualitatively different from social science. We have focused on the study of cognition in social science, but the arguments presented have been quite general. Phenomena have no inherent characteristics independent of observation, and observation is a process that reflects the interaction of observers and that which is observed. Arbitrary but consensual agreements among scientists allow measurement of highly abstract variables. The communication process plays a key role in measurement: it allows observers to specify the preparation and operation of their measurement systems, and to compare observations one time and across observers. This is the social construction of reality (Berger & Luckmann, 1967) in science, which results in the "objectification" of scientific knowledge. The socialization of social scientists often excludes higher mathematics, and often includes attitudes expressing the difficulty or impossibility of human behavior being explained within the confines of scientific theory. Partly as a result of this, studies often are conducted without any guiding theory, and they are conducted in such a way that processual conceptions of behavior often are ignored or obscured. Measurement in the social sciences has historically been premised on the idea that a scale can be validated independently of other scales or of theory. We also find that the amount of information transmitted by scales typically found in the social sciences is very small. The implication of all this discussion is that it is not at all surprising to find that social scientists have largely failed to achieve the level of theoretical development as have physical scientists, and it is asserted that the principles of science as currently understood have generally not been applied consistently in the social sciences. Five principles are provided, and they will be used in developing a theoretical structure to study cognition, culture, self, social organization, and behavior.

CHAPTER 2

FUNDAMENTAL CONCEPTS

The Context of Cognitive Processes

The world of contemporary science is a holistic, organic, and relativistic world. While points, objects, and events may be segregated from the whole for analytic purposes, many modern physicists are inclined to believe these distinctions are artificial, and that each element of ponderable matter has properties which are determined only in relation to the rest of the universe. This world is moreover thought to be a process which is unfolding continuously. Any event or series of events can only be arbitrarily set apart from the single cosmic process whereby unevenly distributed or unbalanced accumulations of energy flow toward the balance of increasing entropy. Increasingly, scientists have come to see the separation of humanity from this universal process as similarly artificial, and the single most important thrust of twentieth century physics has been to establish human observers fundamentally as an organic component of the world system, sensitive to certain ranges of the energy flows but separable from them and from each other only for analytic purposes.

Individuals communicate with their environment and with each other exclusively by means of flows of energy, and science is itself inextricably bound up in this multifaceted communication process in a way which is not fundamentally different from what we call ordinary human communication. In fact, we may suggest that the term "science" has been applied to a historically recent segment of that communication process during which the range of continua of energy flows to which we are sensitive, the fineness of discrimination of which we are capable, and the precision and consensus with which we intercommunicate about the experiences have grown relatively rapidly.

The flow of energy through individuals and sets of individuals gives rise to what we call consciousness or cognition, and we assume, following Durkheim (1951), that there is no consciousness independent of this flow: "On the one hand, all internal life draws its primary material from without. We cannot reflect on our own consciousness in a purely undetermined state; in this shape it is inconceivable. Now consciousness becomes determined *only* when affected by something not itself [p. 279]."

In this sense the single human individual separate from the world and from others may be seen as a convenient psychological fiction which has no real ontological status, but which may nonetheless serve a convenient organizing function for our thinking in the same way as the fictitious "mass point" or "field of force" serves for physical theory. It is in this sense and for these purposes that we introduce the concept of the individual as a starting point for further inquiry (cf. Sullivan, 1953).

We define the human individual initially as a biological organism connected to the world of experience and to other individuals through the ordinary sensory mechanisms as they are understood by psychophysics; that is, an organism sensitive to variation in energy within restricted segments of the spectra of electromagnetic radiation such as sound, light, and pressure. Each of the senses of the individual is capable of discriminating variations of different segments of the spectrum of radiation, with the ear capable of distinguishing pressure variations from about 15 hertz to 20 kilohertz, the eye variations of electromagnetic vibrations from about 4.3×10^{13} to 6.9×10^{13} Hz, and so on. Moreover, as is well known, none of the human senses can respond to a steady state, that is, sensory apparatus can distinguish only *changes* in energy within their respective ranges. At the starting point of our inquiry, therefore, we may isolate two primitive or fundamental variables which rest at the basis of what follows. The first of these is *difference*, or, as psychometricians usually refer to it, *dissimilarity*. What we mean by a sensation, therefore, is a perceived difference between two levels of energy over a finite time interval.

The second primitive or fundamental term on which the theory is founded, inextricably bound up with the notion of difference, is *time*. Difference and time, as fundamental variables, are usually considered to be defined in term of themselves, that is, they may not be reduced to still more fundamental variables. Einstein (1961) gives the following description of the measurement of distance, which may be seen as a special case of difference, that is, difference in spatial location:

> For this purpose (the measurement of distance) we require a "distance" (Rod S) which is to be used once and for all, and which we employ as a standard measure. If, now, A and B are two points on a rigid body, we can construct the line joining them according to the rules of geometry; then, starting from A, we can mark off the distance S time after time until we reach B. The number of these operations required is the numerical measure of the distance AB. This is the basis of all measurement of length [p. 5].

Similarly, Michels' (Michels, Malcolm, and Patterson, 1968) definition of time (i.e., that which is measured by a clock) can be seen to be logically identical to Einstein's definition of distance, "[a clock is] any device which emits signals such that the interval between any two signals is the same [p. 23]," where the "interval between signals" serves the function of Einstein's Rod S.

Although widely accepted, neither of these definitions is completely satisfactory, since in fact each definition does make implicit reference to variables other than itself: The definition of time as a multiple of some subset of itself requires a reference to distance (or change of distance) inherent in the notion of "signal," since the meaning of signal is dependent on the notion of "no signal," and the signal–no signal conditions imply a difference in energy states. Similarly the laying end-to-end of rods is a process which is extended in time, that is, it requires the transport or motion of rods, and motion implies change of distance over time. This interrelation between time and motion was recognized in antiquity, as Aristotle (McKeon, 1941) says: "Not only do we measure the movement by the time, but also the time by the movement, for they define each other [Physics, IV.II, 220[b] 15-15; see also 218[b] 19-20]." The interdependence of time and distance was reaffirmed in the late nineteenth and twentieth centuries by relativity theory, which led in turn to the new concept of space–time. As Minkowski said in 1908, "henceforth space by itself, and time by itself, are doomed to fade away into mere shadows, and only a kind of union of the two will preserve an independent reality [Einstein, 1952, p. 75]." Different events are called different insofar as they appear separated in space-time for some observer. While we may separate space and time for analytic purposes, we need to emphasize the organic unity of the two concepts in human perception and we do so by adopting as a fundamental concept the idea of *separation* (Whitehead & Veblen, 1932). For a single observer we may distinguish perceived differences in energy level at a point in time, or two similar or identical energy states across an arbitrary interval of time, or different energy states across aribitrary time intervals, and all these will constitute examples of what we intend by *separation.*

With the aid of these definitions we may establish a model of individual cognition as a multidimensional space–time continuum. The space–time continuum of human perception is more general, however, than the space–time continuum of relativity physics in that our notion of space is made up of differences in sensation of any sort, such as, for example, pitch, color, pressure, rather than only differences in spatial and temporal location. It is in this sense, too, that the continuum is multidimensional, since a separate vector will be required for each type of energy perceivable by the sensory apparatus (such as frequency and amplitude) (see Descartes, 1964).

Any point in this continuum will represent a set of values, one for each of the attributes of perception at each point in time. The time path of attention or consciousness will be represented by a curve in the continuum, and lapses of attention (such as those resulting from blinking or sleeping) will be seen as discontinuities in the curve. While it is not possible to draw a picture of this multidimensional perceptual space on the two-dimensional page, it is possible to represent the perceptual continuum in a simple yet complete mathematical notation. First, we define as a set of coordinates the unit vectors e_i but we will require n such coordinates, one for each of the attributes perceivable by the human senses, so that i will range from 1 to n. These coordinates will not in general be mathematically independent, that is, the scalar product $e_i \cdot e_j \neq 0$ for all values of i and j.

All of the energy flows to which the human organism is sensitive are measurable, both in theory and practice, by physical science, and in fact are routinely measured by scientists and engineers to more precise tolerances than may be achieved by unaided human sensory apparatus. If we were to place sensitive measuring instruments very near to the appropriate sensory inputs for any individual—a difficult but not impossible task—we would be able to measure the energy flows to which that individual is exposed with excellent precision. The result of these measurements over an interval of time would be set of projections on the e_i basis vectors which would describe a continuous curve in the manifold as a function of time. Figure 2.1, for example, shows an individual exposed to a sound of frequency f varying between .5 and .7 kHz over an interval Δt. The curve of this phenomena is given by the function $C_f = f_1(t)$, where e_t is the unit basis vector for time, and C_f is the conventional measure of frequency and e_f is the unit basis vector frequency. Similarly, if the amplitude of the sound varies over the same interval, we can represent this by Figure 2.2 where the horizontal axis

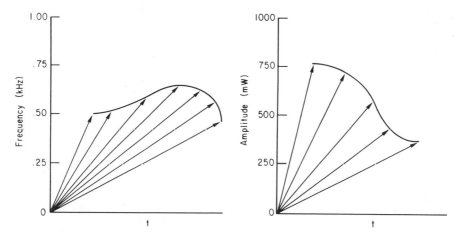

FIGURE 2.1   Frequency of a tone over time.   **FIGURE 2.2**   Amplitude of a tone over time.

remains the same (time), but the vertical axis now represents the amplitude of the sound and the curve of phenomenal experience for this attribute is given by the function $C_a = f_2(t)$, where C_a is the conventional measure of amplitude, and e_a is the unit basis vector for amplitude. We may combine the two functions simply to yield the three-dimensional curve for the complete phenomenal sound function C_s as

$$C_s = C_f + C_a = f_1(t) + F_2(t) = (f_1 + f_2)(t),$$

and, letting $g = f_1 + f_2$, we have

$$C_s = g(t),$$

showing that the phenomenal sound field is given as a function of time, that is, as a curve in a three-dimensional continuum. In this manner, by adding in each of the individual attributes of energy to which the individual is sensitive, we may build up a curve of phenomenal experience in the multidimensional space–time continuum, which can be designated by the multidimensional curve

$$C = f(t).$$

This curve, however, will represent the result of measurement by scientific instruments. As psychologists have shown clearly, however, human sensory apparatus are very seldom calibrated in the same way as conventional scientific apparatus (Stevens, 1951; Hamblin, 1974). Phenomena experienced by the individual will be some transformation of this measured curve, and we may write

$$E = f(C)$$

to show this. We must distinguish two continua, therefore, at the outset: one which represents the time path of results of measurement by conventional scientific instruments, which we will call the conventional continuum and which we may designate as C, and another which represents the time path of phenomena as *experienced* by the individual, which we will designate as E. Moreover, although the form of the function which maps C onto E for most individuals may be similar, the parameters of these trnasformations are known to differ from person to person, so we must designate a set of individual experience continua $E_{(i)}$, where each of the $E_{(i)}$ represents the experiential continuum of a single individual. Similarly, we can designate a common or collective experiential continuum $\bar{E}$ which represents the common space-time of the set of individuals, where

$$\bar{E} = f_i(E_{(i)}).$$

$\bar{E}$ represents the continuum of experiences about which we as individuals agree, and which, according to Einstein (1956), we therefore declare to be real.

> By the aid of language different individuals can, to a certain extent, compare their experiences. Then it turns out that certain sense perceptions of different individuals correspond to each other, while for other sense perceptions no such correspondence can be established. We are accustomed to regard as real those sense perceptions which are common to different individuals, and which therefore are, in a sense, impersonal [p. 1].

As Einstein suggests, it is the function of communication, as aided by language, to construct this continuum of social "reality."

Cognitive and Cultural Processes

It should be noted, however that the set of perceptual continua E_i or even the collective continuum $\bar{E}$ represent the world of perceptions, and the mapping of the world of perceptions has generally been conceded to the realm of physical science. Physical scientists attempt to give substance and order to this realm by constructing common encoding systems and common observational procedures followed by the empirical discovery of transformation rules which bring the individual experiential manifolds $E_{(i)}$ into correspondence with each other while conserving separations within each $E_{(i)}$ (see J. D. Woelfel, 1980). This has been a very fruitful experience, and particularly in the last 400 years considerable order has been brought into the realm of experience by these methods.

But the world of sensory experience is too rich in an information-theoretic sense to be grasped in its totality by any individual and even by the collection of all individuals. As Poincaré (1946) says, this is in a way equivalent to trying to include the whole within the part. Even science finds it necessary and desirable to concentrate on only a small subset of the manifold of experience, which in turn is still beyond the conceptual capacity of any scientist. Rather than cataloging experiences, science develops *rules* for cataloging experience, which may be applied as the occasion demands. In nonscientific or everyday life, we also find individuals and whole cultures "sampling" from the continuum of experience certain components which are retained as a partial representation which (hopefully) serve as a sufficient representation for the adequate conduct of daily life while not overtaxing our cognitive information storage and processing capability. Information provided by each of the attributes of experience is weighted as a function of immediate needs and past experiences, and this weighted aggregate over a finite interval of time is designated as a single unit of experience or recollection represented by some symbol. This process represents a "chunking" or "chopping up" of the continuum of experience according to the interests of the persons or cultures involved, as Whorf (1956) points out in his definition of *lexation*:

> or giving words (names) to parts of the whole manifold of experiences, parts of which are thereby made to stand out in semi-fictitious isolation. Thus a world like "sky" which in English can be treated like "board" leads us to think of a mere optical apparition in ways appropriate only to relatively isolated solid bodies. . . . Each Language performs this artificial chopping up of the continuous spread and flow of existence in a different way [p. 150].

Moreover, the symbols chosen have no significance other than the arbitrary designating function of any sign or symbol, as Einstein (1956) suggests: "The only justification for our concepts and system of concepts is that they serve to represent the complex of our experience; beyond this they have no legitimacy [p. 2]."

On an individual level, though, the subsets of experience designated by these symbols take on great significance, since they represent the set of *concepts* by which the individual represents his or her experience not only to others but also internally in memory and thought. As such they provide the basis of individual cognitive processes, which can be represented as changes in the interrelations or separations among these concepts over time.

On the cultural level, the averages or aggregates of experiences designated by the symbols, we assume to represent social experience of sufficient social importance that they have been set aside and symbolized by words or symbols on a cultural level. These we take to represent Durkheim's *social facts,* the basic elements of the collective consciousness. "Currents of opinion, with an intensity varying according to the time and place, impel certain groups either to more marriages, for example, or to more suicides, or to a higher or lower birth rate, etc. These currents are plainly social facts [Durkheim, in Simpson, 1963, pp. 26–27]."

Changes in the aggregate relations among the collective experiences symbolized by these words or symbols we take as *cultural processes.*

In an important sense, then, we see the manifold of individual and social experience to be continuous, and every point in the continuum represents a meaningful and designatable idea or experience. Not all such points are so designated however, because a complete linguistic representation of this manifold is beyond even the collective cognitive capacity of all present humanity. For this reason, symbols designate regions of the continuum and serve as "marker variables" (see Cushman & Pierce, 1977), not only for scientific purposes, but for the purposes of rendering the overall manifold of experience comprehensible to those who participate in it. Changes in the relations (separations) among these markers indicate the processes.

When we said earlier that this process represents a "chunking" or "chopping up" of the continuum of experience "according to the interests" of persons or cultures, we obscured somewhat the extent to which we are ignorant of the basis of such categorization. In general, however, we understand that the basis of the categorization is usually if not always some "similarity" among the collapsed sensations. We class together a contiguous subset of electromagnetic frequencies and refer to them as the discrete class "light," although we know the set of visible radiations is neither discrete nor undifferentiable. Similarly, we bind together diverse sensations on the basis of their closeness in time and designate them as an *event.* As Bruner (1958) suggests,

the first, and perhaps most self-evident point upon reflection, is that perceiving or registering on an object or an event involves an act of categorization. We "place" things in categories. That is a "man" and he is "honest" and he is now "walking" in a manner that is "leisurely" with the "intention" of "getting some relaxation." Each of the words in quotation marks involves a sorting or placement of stimulus input on the basis of certain cues that we learn how to use [p. 92].

For this reason we may suggest that such categorical words or phrases (usually rendered by nouns or noun phrases) may be thought of as designating or refering to small domains or "neighborhoods" in the experiential continuum. Nouns which are similar in their vernacular meanings we assume to refer to neighborhoods which are close to each other in the overall continuum, and exact synonyms (if there are indeed such) are assumed to be alternative designations for the same neighborhood. Each of these neighborhoods may itself be subdivided into subneighborhoods, just as the domain of light can be subdivided into the various named colors. Different individuals and cultures, it goes without saying, will be differentially capable of fineness of gradation in different domains, and on the smallest level only specialists in a particular domain will be in possession of the specialized vocabulary which designates the most minute subregions of a specific neighborhood. In fact, we assume that learning involves a process of increasing the fineness of gradation of neighborhoods in the experiential continuum and this process is aided and perhaps even rendered possible by acquiring words to designate the subregions within a neighborhood. (This concept is very close to the intent we see in the topological psychology of Lewin.)

As we have described the development of consciousness so far, individuals experience differential flows of energy along independent dimensions of experience which lead to a multidimensional space–time continuum of experience. Major neighborhoods or regions or domains of this continuum are then indexed by symbols like nouns which then serve as marker variables for recollecting and communicating the gross aspects of experience. This process may be thought to describe accurately the historical development of the collective social consciousness, but does not strictly hold for any individual. Each individual is born into a culture which already exists—a point whose full implications began to become clear recently, as evidenced by the works of Mead and the symbolic interactionists in the first half of this century. None of the individuals in society have experienced any but a small portion of the collective social experience, and even the collective social experience is itself but a small part of the manifold of potential experience. Moreover, due to the symbolic character of the socialization process, individuals frequently learn symbols which designate neighborhoods in the experiential continuum they have not yet encountered. Indeed, in the case of historical experiences, such direct contact is unavailable. As a consequence of this fact and the unavoidable failures of symbolic communication which inevitably occur, a dissociation between the continuum of the concepts and the continuum of experience seems inevitable. It is in this sense that we believe Durkheim sees the conceptual world of the social facts becoming dissociated from its substratum and taking on an independent life of its own (Durkheim in Simpson, 1963, p. 26).

For this reason, we find it convenient to designate one final continuum, what we will call the representational continuum, designated as R. It, too, we see as a multidimensional continuum, one dimension of which is always time, and in which the other dimensions represent attributes of distinguishable experience, together represented as the set of covariant vectors e_μ, where μ ranges from 1 to r. Each of the concepts designated by a culture has a meaning which is determined by its separation relations with all other concepts (thus all meaning is relational in this continuum). This set of interconcept separations may be projected on the r basis vectors, and the meaning of any designatable concept will be represented therefore by a contravariant position vector R^μ. Like the topological representation of Lewin, each individual will possess a different "version" of this space, more or less differentiated, and presumably growing more differentiated with increasing experience, both social and physical. Cognitive processes, in fact, will be represented by changes in the structure of the space over time. Moreover, in addition to a set of n such spaces $R_{(1)}, R_{(2)}, \ldots, R_{(n)}$, one for each person in culture, we will designate an aggregate or overall space for the whole culture (which we represent as $\bar{R}$) which is a composite of all the individual spaces. This space we take to be a representation of the domain of social facts or collective representations of Durkheim. It is our purpose to establish a metric on these spaces so that the separations among the concepts and the changes among them representing cognitive and cultural processes can be measured in a theoretically and pragmatically useful way.

Procedures for Mapping
the Representational Continuum

While the elements of the representational continuum R (i.e., the concepts or neighborhoods of the experiential continuum) are ultimately based in collective human experience, the linkages between the experience and its representation are lengthy and obscure to us. For this reason they present special measurement difficulties, since they may not at present be calculated solely through transformations made on the outcomes of scientific measurements of the electromagnetic continuum. They are located within the individual members of the society and are not directly accessible to the scientist. Moreover, the individual's own access to his or her own cognitive processes is somewhat obscure, and there is respectable empirical evidence that individuals do not know how they call up concepts or reason to conclusions based on them (Nisbett & Wilson, 1977). Nonetheless, people do express separation or dissimilarity relations among concepts, and frequently with considerable definiteness and apparent confidence, as when we say that communism is very different from capitalism, or that the Soviet Union is becoming more capitalistic (i.e., "closer" to capitalism), or when we say that sadness is different from happiness, but that despair is further yet from elation, and so on. Each of these concepts—that is, capitalism, communism, the Soviet Union, happiness, sadness, despair, elation, and even "me" or the self—are neighborhoods or domains of the collective experiential continuum, and statments about their similarities and dissimilarities are, in the most fundamental sense, *measurements* of their separation relations. When we communicate with others we are endeavoring to present to them measurements of the separations among our concepts in the domain of our conversation and to learn from them about the separation relations among their concepts in the same domain.

This process is always and only a comparative process, whereby we try to convey lesser-known separations by comparision with better-known separations through simile and metaphor. We may iterate through many such comparisons until we are satisfied we have reached a sufficient precision of understanding (or until we give up the attempt). In the case of persons who share a common base of experience and who have communicated a great deal in the past, a satisfactory comparative standard might occur promptly. "The stranger I met yesterday is as friendly as Uncle Fred." In the case of strangers with little overlapping experience, no such standards may be ready to hand: "What do you mean by 'friendly,' and who is Uncle Fred?" In the latter such cases, communication may well depend on continued interaction in the same environment until shared comparative standards emerge out of shared daily experience, as is the case of a pioneering anthropological study of a previously alien culture.

In any event, so long as the encoding system remains the vernacular language system and comparative standards must emerge freshly in each encounter, communication must always remain indeterminate and ambiguous. It is also important to note that, while considerable precision can frequently be obtained in this manner, the process of developing and iterating through multiple arbitrary comparative standards is inherently uneconomical and time-consuming. In contradistinction, science generally proceeds by establishing much more highly standard-ized encoding systems (such as numbers) and arbitrary but conven-tional comparative standards (such as the meter or the gram) along with standardized rules for comparisons, so that all communicators in a do-main of inquiry compare new experiences to standardized units in standard ways: "the stranger I met yesterday is 1.7 meters tall and weighs 70 kilograms." The result is a communication at once more precise and *much more rapid*.

It is important to understand that neither the coding systems, the comparative standards, nor the rules for comparison are discovered, but come about from the much more prosaic process of conventional agree-ment, and the word "conventional" is especially meaningful since these agreements are often actually made at *conventions,* that is, at convoca-tions of scientists gathered specifically to establish such standards.

The procedures for measuring separations among concepts in the rep-resentational continuum we will present here are precisely conventions in this sense rather than discoveries. As such, they describe conven-tional practices among the group of researchers who have adopted the procedures described here. Every argument, and indeed every bit of experimental evidence presented in this book, should therefore not be considered to be descriptions or explanations of the nature of cognitive and cultural processes, but rather descriptions of the advantages to be gained by the scientist who decides to adopt these conventions.

CHAPTER 3

PRINCIPLES
OF MEASUREMENT

Introduction

The idea that cognitive and cultural processes might be represented as motions in a multidimensional continuum is not a new one. René Descartes, the inventor of the coordinate system, seems to have had such a model in mind in the sixteenth century: "By dimension, I understand nothing else than the mode and aspect in respect of which a subject is considered to be measurable. Thus, it is not only length, breadth and depth which are dimensions; gravity is also a dimension, speed is a dimension of motion . . . and so on with innumerable other dimensions of this sort [Descartes, 1967, p. 31]. Henri Poincaré describes the process of mathematical discovery in graphically spatial terms at the beginning of the present century:

> If I may be permitted a crude comparison, let us represent the future elements of our (thought) combinations as something resembling Epicurus' hooked atoms. When the mind is in complete repose these atoms are immovable; they are, so to speak, attached to the wall. This complete repose may continue indefinitely without the atoms meeting, and, consequently, without the possibility of the formation of any combination.

> On the other hand, during a period of apparent repose, but of unconscious work, some of them are detached from the wall and set in motion. They plough through

space in all directions, like a swarm of gnats, for instance, or, if we prefer a more learned comparison, like the gaseous molecules in the kinetic theory of gases. Their mutual collisions may then produce new combinations [Poincaré, 1946, p. 61].

The appeal of the multidimensional continuum as a device for representing human cognition is powerful, and these developments were accompanied by great enthusiasm among those acquainted with them. Multidimensional scaling (MDS) techniques even came to have important commercial applications in politics and marketing, and even today plots of subspaces of multidimensional scaling solutions awaken considerable excitement among those newly introduced to them. In order to understand the promise of current MDS practice, it is necessary to examine in some detail both the founding presuppositions and technical procedures on which these procedures rest.

As does all empirical knowledge, every MDS procedure begins with measured differences or dissimilarities among some set of perceptions or concepts. Once these measures have been obtained, they are projected onto a set of coordinate axes. Multidimensional scaling routines differ both in the process by which initial measures of distances are made and in algorithms by which these measured discrepancies are projected on coordinate axes.

The Measurement of Separation

Separations among concepts in the representational continuum, as we have defined them here, refer to the extent to which neighborhoods or concepts in the continuum are conceived to be different or distant from one another. These overall differences are themselves presumed to be functions of differences among concepts along specific attributes, such as favorability, height, color, recency, or whatever attributes may be relevant for the concepts in question. Measurements of separations fall into two major types, depending on whether the separations among pairs of concepts are measured directly (e.g., how different are A and B?) or are measured indirectly as functions of differences measured along individual attributes (How different are A and B *in length?* How much do you like A? How much do you like B?) The familiar semantic differential scales, that is, line segments, intersected by a number (usually 7) of tick marks drawn between words thought to be "opposite," such as

Good ├─┼─┼─┼─┼─┼─┼─┼─┼─┼─┤ Bad

are examples of the latter type, since, in a typical format respondents are asked to rate concepts on a set of bipolar attribute scales, and aggregate separations among concepts are determined as a function of the differences over all the attributes (Osgood *et al.*, 1957).

Indirect Measurement

While there is no inherent reason to prefer one or the other types of measurement—choice of either procedure may be made differently under different circumstances—nonetheless there are two essential conditions which must be met before the indirect procedures can be used to best advantage. First, the attributes along which the concepts of interest are differentiated by the population under study must be known in advance. While this is an obvious requirement, since leaving out an attribute over which respondents do routinely differentiate concepts can result in substantial errors in estimating their overall separations, it is a requirement that is very difficult to fulfill at our present stage of knowledge. This problem is further compounded by the twin facts that individuals may differ among each other and over time in the set of attributes along which the same set of concepts are differentiated.

The second requirement for proper use of indirect methods is that the function which relates the overall generalized separation between any two concepts to the set of individual attribute differences must be known. This is an even harder condition to fulfill at our present stage of knowledge. This can be illustrated with a simple mathematical example. Suppose an individual is exposed to two persons A and B, who differ from each other in terms of their friendliness and generosity. Let us further assume (unrealistically) that: (a) the attributes of friendliness and generosity are uncorrelated in the respondents minds; and (b) that they are equally salient for each individual and equally salient across all individuals in the sample. Under these restrictions, the results of measurements may be represented as Figure 3.1. In this case, since friendliness and generosity are uncorrelated, they may be shown as orthogonal axes x_1 and x_2 in Figure 3.1. Since they are equally salient, the markers on the axes may be placed at equal intervals, that is, a unit in the x_1 direction is equal to a unit in the x_2 direction. We may then represent the projections of A and B on these coordinates as the position vectors $R^{\mu}_{(A)}$ and $R^{\mu}_{(B)}$, where (A) and (B) are placed in parentheses to represent the position vectors A and B, and the Greek superscript[1] μ is allowed to range from 1 to 2, indicating that each concept has projections on both

---

[1] This superscript does not mean R is raised to the μth power, but is rather a contravariant tensor index which designates the projection of R on the μth axes. This notation will prove very helpful later. The reader is referred to McConnell (1933) for a description of this notation.

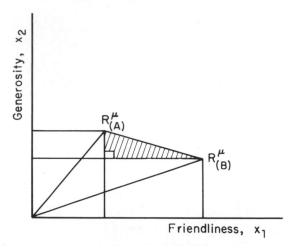

FIGURE 3.1   Two persons on a plane spanned by orthogonal attribute vectors.

x_1 and x_2. We now have the shaded right triangle in Figure 3.1. The base of this triangle is the difference in level of friendliness (x_1, so $\mu = 1$) between persons A and B, which is

$$\left| R^1_{(A)} - R^1_{(B)} \right|,$$

and the height (altitude) of the shaded triangle is the difference in level of generosity (x_2, so $\mu = 2$) between persons A and B, or

$$\left| R^2_{(A)} - R^2_{(B)} \right|.$$

Since this is a right triangle, the total separation between persons A and B, $S_{(AB)}$, is given by the Pythagorean theorem, that is,

$$S_{(AB)} = [(R^1_{(A)} - R^1_{(B)})^2 + (R^2_{(A)} - R^2_{(B)})^2]^{1/2}, \qquad (3.1)$$

and we say equation (3.1) is the function which relates the attribute differences to the overall separation. Equation (3.1) may be written in a very simple and compact form if we adopt a few simple conventions. First, we may define the vector $S^\mu_{(AB)}$ as the difference between $R^\mu_{(A)}$ and $R^\mu_{(B)}$ as

$$S^\mu_{(AB)} = R^\mu_{(A)} - R^\mu_{(B)}, \qquad (3.2)$$

where μ obeys the same range conventions wherever it appears. (In our present example, μ ranges from 1 to 2.) The components of $S^\mu_{(AB)}$, therefore, are given by the differences in the components of $R^\mu_{(A)}$ and $R^\mu_{(B)}$. The length of this vector $S^\mu_{(AB)}$ can now be given as

$$S_{(AB)} = \left| S^{\mu}_{(AB)} \right| = \left(\sum_{\mu=1}^{2} S^{\mu}_{(AB)} S^{\mu}_{(AB)} \right)^{1/2}. \tag{3.3}$$

It is possible to simplify this notation even further if we adopt the Einstein convention that repeated indices are to be summed over. Thus, since μ is a repeated index, we have

$$S_{(AB)} = (S^{\mu}_{(AB)} S^{\mu}_{(AB)})^{1/2}. \tag{3.4}$$

Since the term $S_{(AB)}$ contains no tensor index (subscripts or superscripts in parentheses are not tensor indices), it may be thought of as a tensor of the 0th rank, or a *scalar*. We will frequently also follow the physical convention and refer to scalars as *invariants*.

Equations (3.2) and (3.4), therefore, express the function by which the overall separation or dissimilarity between the two persons may be established from their differences on the separate attributes. In words, they say that the overall difference between two concepts is equal to the square root of the sum of the squares of their differences on each attribute.

But this is true only if the foregoing very unrealistic assumptions—that is, that the attributes are equally salient and uncorrelated—are also true, and it is rare that they are even approximately true. If generosity and friendliness are correlated, for example, they may no longer be represented as orthogonal reference axes, as in Figure 3.1, but must be represented as axes at an angle θ to one another, where $\cos \theta = r$, and r is the product–moment correlation between friendliness and generosity, as in Figure 3.2.

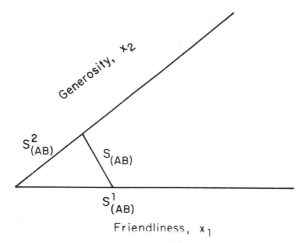

FIGURE 3.2 Two persons on a plane spanned by nonorthogonal attribute vectors.

Notice that the triangle given in this figure is not a right triangle, and so the ordinary Pythagorean theorem as given in equations (3.1) and (3.4) will not suffice to give $S_{(AB)}$. Rather we require

$$S_{(AB)} = [(S^1_{(AB)})^2 + (S^2_{(AB)})^2 - 2S^1_{(AB)}S^2_{(AB)} \cos \theta]^{1/2} \tag{3.5}$$

which is the generalized theorem of Pythagoras. Similarly, if the sizes of the units in which generosity and friendliness have been measured are not the same, then further adjustments will need to be made, since a *scale correction factor* w_μ will need to be included for each attribute, as

$$S_{(AB)} = [(w_1 S^1_{(AB)})^2 + (w_2 S^2_{(AB)}) - 2w_1 w_2 S^1_{(AB)} S^2_{(AB)} \cos \theta]^{1/2}. \tag{3.6}$$

This can be very easily summarized in a compact and useful notation by constructing the matrix $g_{\mu\nu}$, where

$$g_{\mu\nu} = w^i e^i_\mu w^j e^j_\nu. \tag{3.7}$$

The reader can easily verify by working through the indices that the $g_{\mu\nu}$ will represent a matrix of weighted scalar products of the basis vectors (attributes) e_μ which leads directly to a much more compact expression for equation (3.6),

$$S_{(AB)} = (g_{\mu\nu} S^\mu_{(AB)} S^\nu_{(AB)})^{1/2}, \tag{3.8}$$

which is the generalized equation for the separation or distance between two concepts projected on correlated attributes not measured in the same scale. (When the scales are the same and the attributes are uncorrelated, then the reader can easily verify that

$$g_{\mu\nu} = w^i e^i_\mu w^j e^j_\nu = \sigma^\mu_\nu = \begin{cases} 0, & \mu \neq \nu, \\ 1, & \mu = \nu, \end{cases} \tag{3.9}$$

where σ^μ_ν is the symbol for Kronecker's delta or the identity matrix.)

Even equation (3.8) assumes that the relationships among the basis attributes are linear, which is usually only approximately true. When the relationships among the basis attributes are nonlinear, equation (3.8) is *approximately* true for small differences, becoming exactly true in the limit as distances become vanishingly small. Thus, even in the most difficult situations we may use the expression

$$dS_{(AB)} = [g_{\mu\nu} \, ds^\mu_{(AB)} \, ds^\nu_{(AB)}]^{1/2}, \tag{3.10}$$

where $ds_{(AB)}$ is the differential element and $ds^\mu_{(AB)}$ the coordinate differentials in small neighborhoods of the overall space with good results.

Equations (3.8) and (3.10) are important equations both because they give the exact functional relations between overall separations and differences along attributes for the linear and nonlinear case, and because they make clear how much information needs to be available in order to make use of indirect attribute-by-attribute measures of the separations among concepts in the representational continuum. All this information is contained within the matrix $g_{\mu\nu}$, and consists of the interrelationships among the attribute vectors. Because this set of quantities determines completely the metric properties of the continuum, it is usually referred to as the *fundamental* or *metric tensor* (Einstein, 1952).

Direct Measurement

The alternative procedures, the direct pairwise estimation of separations among concepts taken two at a time independently of the attributes, is not subject to the foregoing difficulties. This procedure of pair comparisons is well known to psychometricians and dates from antiquity. It is, in fact, an important component of the method of Descartes (1964), who says "when we have more than two diverse things to compare with each other, our method consists in reviewing them successively and attending only to two of them at a time [p. 33]." The logic of the method of pair comparisons is very simple: for any n concepts it is only necessary to form the $n(n - 1)/2$ nonredundant pairs and estimate the magnitude of difference between each pair on some numerical scale. (These procedures assume the symmetry of the distance, that is, that $S_{ij} = S_{ji}$. These are circumstances under which this assumption is violated and alternative procedures becomes necessary. These will be discussed later.) In the case of direct measurement, therefore, each of the $n(n - 1)/2$ cells of the distance or separation matrix $S_{(AB)}$ is estimated directly, rather than being calculated from still other measures.

Scales of Measure

Regardless of whether experiences are compared indirectly attribute-by attribute or directly one against the other, the act of measurement in both cases requires assigning some numerical value to the judged differences. Particularly in the social sciences the number of procedures for assigning numbers to experiences is extremely large, and it is safe to say that there is no single person who could name them all. So great is the variety of procedures which different social scientists use for measurement that students of scaling, in an effort to include them all, have been led to define measurement as "the assignment of numbers to observations according to some rule [Suppes & Zinnes, 1963]."

To be sure, while this definition is broad enough to include virtually any numerical scheme, clearly for any stated purpose some rules will be better than others. Nor is there complete unanimity about this defini-tion, and, as Torgerson (1958, p. 31) notes, physical scientists use the term much more restrictively.

The basis for most measurement devices in social sciences lies in a classification scheme for scales of measure set down by S. S. Stevens, and accepted with unusual unanimity by social scientists of every per-suasion. Stevens' scheme itself rests on the existential assertion that there exists an array of stimuli (a set of objects to be measured). If a measurement device is capable of discriminating the stimuli from one another, but incapable or arraying them in their (preexisting) order, the scale is said to be nominal, in that it only names the stimuli. If the device cannot only discriminate the stimuli, but array them in their ("true") *order*, the scale is called ordinal. If, in addition, the device can also express the true magnitudes of the differences (or distances) among the stimuli, it is said to be *interval*. Finally, if the scale can also assess the true distance of each stimuli from some limen or zero point of an exist-ing attribute, the scale is said to be a ratio scale.

Stevens (1951) himself recognized a fundamental philosophical prob-lem underlying this scheme at once: Although in the case of psycho-physical measures, such as measures of perceived loudness, one could calibrate the scale against physical measures of the phenomenon, in the case of purely psychological measures, such as liking or prefer-ence, no such correspondence could ever be established empirically, since no physical measures of the same phenomenon could be made. Thus the determination of whether a psychological scale was an ordinal, interval, or ratio scale was logically impossible unless one were willing to make some distributional assumptions about the phenomenon which themselves could not be verified by measurement:

> The variability of a psychological measure is itself sometimes used to equalize the units of a scale. This process smacks of a kind of magic—a rope trick for climbing the hierarchy of scales. The rope in this case is the *assumption* that in the sample of individuals the trait in question has a canonical distribution (e.g., "normal"). Then it is a simple matter to adjust the units of the scale so that the assumed distribution is recovered when the individuals are measured. But this procedure is obviously no better than the gratuitous postulate behind it, and we are reminded of what Russell said about the larcenous aspects of postulation [pp. 27–28].

Stevens (1951) did not himself give up the hope of constructing "ratio scales" for psychological attributes, however. He says

> we postulate, among other things, that the subject knows what a given numerical ratio is and that he can make a valid judgment of the numerical relation between two values of a psychological attribute. . . . If a series of items have been found that

stand in a *known* ratio, each to its neighbor, it is a straight-forward matter to assign to the other items numerals exhibiting the appropriate ratios to the first numeral. If the assumption is valid, the result is a ratio scale [pp. 40–41; emphasis in original].

While Stevens went on to construct some of the most precise and useful scales of measure in the psychological literature, his reasoning in this instance is not correct, since it makes reference to hypothetical knowledge about the distribution of the phenomenon independent of any measurement device: The phrases "make a *valid* judgment of the numerical relation between two values of a psychological attribute . . . ," and "if a series of items *have been found* that stand in a *known* ratio . . . ," require us to assume that *there exists* a "true" distribution along an attribute independent of the respondent's perception of it, and the correctness or "validity" of the ratio depends on the correspondence of the respondent's *perception* to the "true" state of affairs.

Thus, although the form of scaling Stevens used in his own work seems to us to be the correct form, and even though the empirical success of his procedures (and equivalent procedures used by those following his methods, such as Hamblin, 1974) is indisputable, his logical defense of his method rested on establishing a correspondence of the scaled values with the psychological phenomena themselves. That the establishment of such a correspondence in the case of psychological phenomena is impossible, however, is deeply entrenched in virtually all scientists, and as a consequence Stevens' position is even today probably considered an extreme one by most social scientists.

This realization fit well with the historical tendency of the great majority of social scientists to regard human phenomena as fundamentally different—qualitatively different—from physical phenomena, and led to a virtual abandonment of efforts to adopt physical principles of measurement to the human sciences. Even today the view that the identical principles of measurement apply identically to physical and social phenomena would be considered both radical and naive. The primary argument against such a view would be the argument just leveled: that there is no direct access to the world of psychological experience independent of some scale of measure against which any scale could be tested. While it is possible to compare one set of measures of psychological phenomena to a set of measures made with another scale, it is never possible to compare the measured values with the "true" values. Thus scientists can never know which, if any, of the scales they employ is the "correct" measure.

This much of the argument can be granted readily. But there is a second part to the argument seldom made explicit in the scaling literature. If measures of cognitive and cultural processes are different from measures of physical processes because they may not be experienced independently of some scale or measuring device, we must assume that physical processes may be experienced independently of some scale or measuring device. But as argued in Chapter 1 of this book, the most radical and fundamental insight of modern, as opposed to classical or mechanical physical science, is that no physical process may be observed independently of some "observing system," which includes both a human observer and a scale of human invention. As Capra states, "the electron doesn't have any properties just as such; it doesn't exist independently of the observer (Daily Planet)." If this is true, then it follows that the identical principles of measurement apply identically to physical and social phenomena, not because social phenomena are more "observable" than we believed, but because physical phenomena are less "observable" than we believed. It is correct to say that social phenomena can only be measured conventionally, but it is incorrect not to realize that all measure, physical as well as social and psychological, is conventional. Just as the arbitrary choice of different scales of measure will result in different maps of social phenomena, the choice of different scales of measure results in different maps of physical processes. None of these choices are "correct," but some are much more useful than others. Stevens (1951) never completely comes to this position, however, and seems to believe there is some direct correspondence between physical phenomena and the scales that measure them:

> The difference, then, between an indicant and a measure is just this: the indicant is a presumed effect or correlate bearing an unknown (but usually monotonic) relation to some underlying phenomenon, whereas a measure is a scaled value of the phenomenon itself. Indicants have the advantage of convenience. Measures have the advantage of validity.
>
> This distinction between measures and indicants disappears, of course, as soon as we learn the quantitative relation between the indicant and the object of our interest, for then the indicant can be calibrated and used to measure the phenomenon at issue. We measure electric current by means of a calibrated indicant composed of a coil of wire suspended by a spring in a magnetic field. We measure psychological pitch with a frequency meter after we have established a scale relating pitch in mels to frequency in cycles per second. The more mature a science, the more it uses *calibrated* indicants [p. 48].

Thus even though Stevens recognizes the physical use of arbitrary measurements, he still seems to believe they are justified at some point in the chain by a correspondence between some measure and the "object of our interest." But if the idea of the correspondence between phenomenon and scale value must be abandoned as a justification for the choice of a scale, what rule may take its place?

First, since the concept of difference or separation among experiences lies at the foundation of our perceptions, it may be defined as a fundamental or primitive variable, such as distance or time. And like other fundamental variables, it may be measured as ratios of some arbitrary subset of itself (see Einstein, 1961). Aristotle, although virtually completely qualitative in his own work, nonetheless seemed to recognize that internal psychological processes (such as remembering) always involve quantitative images, and furthermore that these quantitative images are the result of ratio comparisons:

> So likewise when one exerts the intellect (e.g., on the subject of the first principles), although the object may not be quantitative, one envisages it as quantitative . . . [*Memory and Reminiscence*, Chapter 1, 450ª 11. 4-6 in McKeon, 1941].

> But the point of capital importance is that (for the purpose of recollection) one should cognize, determinately or indeterminately, the time-relation (of that which he wishes to recollect). There is—let it be taken as a fact—something by which one distinguishes a greater and a smaller time; and it is reasonable to think that one does this in a way analogous to that in which one discerns (spatial) magnitudes. For it is not by the mind's reaching out towards them, as some say a visual ray from the eye does (in seeing), that one thinks of large things at a distance in space (for even if they are not there, one may similarly think them); but one does so by a proportionate mutual movement. For there are in the mind the like figures and movements (i.e., "like" to those of objects and events). Therefore, when one thinks the greater objects, in what will his thinking those differ from his thinking the smaller? (In nothing) because all the internal though smaller are as it were proportional to the external. Now, as we may assume within a person something proportional to the forms (of distant magnitudes), so, too, we may doubtless assume also something else proportional to their distances. As, therefore, if one has (psychically) the movement in *AB*, *BE*, he constructs in thought (i.e. knows objectively) *CD*, since *AC* and CD bear equal ratios respectively (to *AB* and *BE* (so he who recollects also proceeds) [McKeon, 1941, Chapter 1].

> Why then does he construct *CD* rather than *FG?* Is it not because as *AC* is to *AB*, so is *H* to *I?* These movements therefore (sc. in *AB, BE, and* in *H* : *I*) he has simultaneously. But if he wishes to construct to thought *FG*, he has in mind *BE* in like manner as before (when constructing *CD*), but now, instead of (the movements of the ratio) *H* : *I*, he has in mind (those of the ratio) *J* : *K*; for *J* : *K* : : *FA* : *BA*. When, therefore, the "movement" corresponding to the object and that corresponding to its time concur, then one actually remembers [*Memory and Reminiscence*, Chapter 2, 452ᵇ 11. 6-24 in McKeon, 1941].

Although Aristotle is aware of the function of ratios or proportions in mental processes, he does not grasp the arbitrariness of the comparative standard, nor does he realize the fundamental usefulness or generalizability of the process for the construction of a science. This realization begins to emerge only at the birth of the scientific revolution. René Descartes (1964), for example, considers the ratio rule the sole basis of knowledge of the world: "For I recognize the order in which A and B stand, without considering anything except these two—the extreme terms of the relation. But I can recognize the ratio of the magnitude of two to that of three, only by considering some third thing, namely unity, which is the common measure of both [rule IV, p. 32]." Descartes (1964) recognizes the arbitrary nature of the unit as well: "The unit is that common element in which, as above remarked, all things compared with each other should equally participate. If this be not already settled in our problems, we can represent it by one of the magnitudes already presented to us, or by any other magnitude we like, and it will be the common measure of all the others [p. 32]." Thus Descartes suggests that the process of measurement of any continuum requires setting aside an arbitrary subsegment of the continuum and comparing all other segments to the original. He (1964) quite explicitly expects this to be done in a way completely analogous to the measurement of length or distance: "Though one thing can be said to be more or less white than another, or a sound sharper or flatter, and so on, it is yet impossible to determine exactly whether the greater exceeds the less in the proportion two to one, or three to one, etc., unless we treat the quantity as being in a certain way analogous to a body possessing figure (i.e., physical shape) [p. 29]." Moreover, Descartes (1964), contrary to general belief, explicitly expects this rule to be used to measure phenomena other than length—even psychological phenomena:

> Incidentally also we have to note that the three dimensions of body, length, breadth and depth, are only in name distinct from one another. For there is nothing to prevent us, in any solid body with which we are dealing, from taking any of the extensions it presents as the length, or any as its depth, and so on. And though these three dimensions have a real basis in every object qua extended, we have nevertheless no special concern with them more than with countless others, which are either mental creations or have some other ground in objects [pp. 31–32].

As we have already argued, the validity of this process does not flow from any correspondence between the magnitudes measured on the scale and the "actual" magnitudes which inhere in the phenomena. Although many investigators suggest that the validity of this process in the case of length or distance flows from the fact that an actual rod can in principle be laid down again and again between the end points of the length to be measured, in fact physical distances are seldom measured in this way, and Einstein has made it evident that this is impossible even in principle, since the question of the invariance of the length of the rod under transport is unanswerable on philosophical grounds. Moreover, regardless of the epistemological status of length or distance, a moment's reflection makes it evident that no such laying end to end can be achieved in the measurement of time, which is measured by the same rule. Indeed, no psychological or cultural belief can be thought in any way to be more abstract or immaterial than time, yet time is measured fundamentally with precision approaching 1×10^{-16} seconds, and plays a central role in every important physical theory. And yet there is no way that time could pass the most elementary tests in current psychometric practice to qualify as a "ratio" or "interval" scale. We may calibrate one clock against another, but never directly against the phenomenon "time," for time, like the electron, comes to exist only as a consequence of our measuring it.

Clearly the validity, or more precisely, the *utility* of this type of measure does not follow from any correspondence between measure and phenomena, but purely from the logical form of the scale itself. The most important element of the logical form of fundamental ratio measurement is that it is formally infinite, that is, it may take on any numerical value whatever. This means in principle that the scale is capable of representing any outcome of measurement perfectly as a formal device. This is in marked distinction, for example, to a 5- or 7-point scale, which can represent only five or seven possible outcomes of measurement procedures regardless of the fineness of discriminations yielded by the measurement operations.

A second advantage follows clearly from Descartes' discussion, since it has the virtue of expressing our measurements of all phenomena in a form which is identical to that which is most familiar to us—that is, physical distance or extension. This is not to say that such scaling guarantees phenomena other than distances will behave like distances, but it does guarantee that differences we observe between any phenomena and distances as a comparative standard will not be attributable to artifactual differences in the purely formal structure of the scale which represents them.

A third advantage—and an important one—is that the expression of social or psychological phenomena on scales identical in formal structure to the scales of physical science can allow us to recognize differences between the two classes of experience uncontaminated by purely formal differences in the scales which represent them. If we are to calibrate the scales against each other, we should take pains to see that purely formal differences do not complicate an already complicated process.

A fourth advantage is the relative simplicity of the scaling model. This is not to say such scaling is *easy*, for as Descartes (1964) says, "the discovery of an order is no light task, as may be seen throughout this treatise, which makes this practically its whole subject . . . [p. 32]." It is to say, however, that it is the *simplest* way to establish numerical estimates of magnitude. Again following Descartes (1964), "human ingenuity can devise nothing simpler for the expression of differences of relation [p. 33]."

Thus, although there are procedures which yield numerical values which are easier to perform than fundamental ratio comparisons, none of these should be considered measurement in a formal sense.

We began by defining perceptions as perceptions of differences or separations. Measurement consists in the calibration of experiences against each other. We define measurement as it is practiced by science as the comparison of perceived differences or separations as ratios to some arbitrary standard separation. Within this overall definition, fundamental measures are defined as separations expressed as ratios to subsets of themselves, and derived measures are defined as ratios of fundamental measures.

Following from those definitions, separations among concepts in the representational domain R can be measured as ratios of any arbitrary standard separation within the domain. The method we actually employ follows this pattern exactly: An arbitrary separation S between two of the neighborhoods or domains in R, as represented by words in the vernacular language, is designated as a standard separation, and respondents are asked to judge the separations among the $n(n - 1)/2$ pairs of neighborhoods as ratios to this standard.

CHAPTER 4

THE REFERENCE FRAME

The Concept of Reference Frame

The concept of reference frame is implicit in the notion of relativity of perception which underlies modern science. It follows from the idea that the definition of an object of perception is given by comparison of the object with other objects associated with it in experience. Thus an object may be large when compared to some other objects yet small when compared to another set of objects; a foreign official may be friendly when compared to representatives of some nations yet hostile when compared to others; an object may be moving when compared with one object yet at rest compared to another, and so on. In general, any set of objects taken collectively which serves as a standard of reference against which the identity and activity of some object or set of objects is to be gauged may be defined as a reference frame. Clearly the choice of a reference frame has important bearing on the outcome of any investigation, and choices of reference frames are of primary importance in science, since observers making different choices of reference frames will in general not agree on the outcomes of their observations unless the transformations from one frame to the other are known and applied. As Edwards (1933) says, "Without a reference system it is impossible to specify just where (a) body is or how it may be moving."

Three kinds of reference frame may be distinguished. The first of these may be called accidental (or perhaps "natural") reference frames.

These reference frames are distinguished from others in that they are not created or developed deliberately by an observer, but are rather constituted informally out of the surroundings of the object observed at the time of its observation. In physics, the most important such frame has been the surface of the earth, which provides a convenient and commonly understood background against which the motions of other objects may be calibrated (Halliday and Resnick, 1966, p. 3). There is little doubt that the universal availability of the earth's surface as a standard of reference for terrestrial observations has had a facilitating effect on the growth of objective agreement among observers that has been denied to social scientists for whom physical motions relative to the surface of the earth comprise a relatively minor portion of the phenomena of interest. Within the social sciences (and in daily social discourse), accidental reference frames are made up of the physical setting of the phenomena of interest as well as the cultural and psychological backgrounds the individual participants bring with them to the situation. Insofar as there is less agreement about the frame of reference among social scientists (and lay participants) in a social encounter, differential interpretations of the phenomena of interest are commonplace among multiple observers, and frequently attempts to reach agreement about the characteristics of a social phenomenon involve efforts to establish common understandings of the appropriate reference frame against which the phenomenon should be arrayed (Goffman, 1974).

A second type of reference frame may be called "contrived" or "laboratory" reference frames, and these differ from the accidental frames only in that they have been constructed deliberately by the observer to serve a reference function. In high-energy physics, for example, the sensing grid on a spark chamber or the set of photographic plates in a bubble chamber comprise contrived reference frames fixed to the laboratory apparatus against which relative motions of subatomic particles may be calibrated. (The tick marks on an ordinary meter stick also serve as a contrived reference frame, as, of course, does the meter stick itself.)

Use of contrived reference frames is commonplace in social science as well, and virtually every laboratory experiment in the social sciences involves a more or less self-conscious attempt to standardize the set of reference objects by means of which experimental subjects understand the experiment. Much of the debate between advocates of field versus experimental studies in the social sciences can be seen to revolve about an explicit recognition of the extent to which the reference frame provided in the laboratory will cause subjects' actions and judgments to differ from actions and judgments outside the laboratory frame (Aronson & Carlsmith, 1968).

Differences in the understanding or interpretation of observations that result solely from different reference frames against which observations are projected may be considered artifactual or spurious, and the desire to eliminate such spurious differences is a major motivation for the use of contrived or laboratory reference frames in research. In the special case—and only in the special case—where reference frames are established in an experiment by means of rules specific enough to allow the exact duplication of the reference frame in another laboratory, observations made by independent observers may be compared directly without further manipulations. In the event that reference frames differ from observer to observer, some transformation of results is required by the principle of objectivization. In the common situation of social science where the required transformation rules are not known or poorly understood, artifactual or spurious differences in outcomes cannot be eliminated, differences in outcome cannot be accounted for in a precise way, and the principle of objectivization cannot be completely realized. Since the understanding of the nature and function of accidental reference frames in social phenomena is not well developed, transformations from laboratory reference frames to "real life" reference frames are not often possible, and this, in turn, gives rise to the controversy over the "external validity" of laboratory experimentation.

The notion of transformations across alternative frames of reference gives rise to yet another kind of reference frame which is abstracted from accidental and contrived reference frames—the mathematical reference frame. A mathematical reference frame may be thought of as an abstract and symbolic description of the main features of either an accidental or contrived reference frame. Einstein (1961) provides a description of the use of mathematical reference frames in his discussion of the measurement of the locaton of a cloud above Trafalgar Square. First, Trafalgar Square itself is located by means of either an accidental or contrived reference frame of fixed reference points attached to the surface of the earth in the manner we have already described. Then, an hypothetical pole is erected that reaches the cloud. The location of the cloud is then given by the location of Trafalgar Square and the length of the pole. But, as Einstein (1961) says,

We speak of the height of the cloud even when the pole which reaches the cloud has not been erected. By means of optical observations of the cloud from different positions on the ground, and taking into account the properties of the propogation of light, we determine the length of the pole we should have required in order to reach the cloud.

From this consideration we see that it will be advantageous if, in the description of position, it should be possible by means of numerical measures to make ourselves independent of the existence of marked positions (possessing names) on the rigid body of reference. In the physics of measurement this is attained by the application of the Cartesian system of coordinates. . . . In practice, the rigid surface which constitute the body of reference are generally not available; furthermore, the magnitudes of the coordinates are not actually determined by constructions with rigid rods, but by indirect means [p. 7].

Among the advantages to be gained by overlaying the set of accidental or contrived reference points with a mathematical coordinate system are two which are of decisive importance. The first of these is that each point in the domain of investigation is assigned a unique name (in a cartesian coordinate system this name is given by the coordinates of the point) which itself not only identifies that point, but immediately expresses the relation of that point to all other points in the domain, regardless of whether that point is coincident with an accidental or contrived reference object or not. Without the mathematical reference frame, the location of any point or object must be given by giving the relations of that point to the other named reference objects, but in the mathematical coordinate system, all this information is conveyed by the name of the point alone. Essentially, the establishment of the mathematical reference frame constitutes a translation of vernacular experience into the powerful and sensitive language of mathematics, and the efficiency gained makes it possible to formulate and work through complicated arguments (transformations or operations) on the observations in minutes or seconds which could not be accomplished in the vernacular language by the most sensitive humans in a lifetime.

The second advantage of establishing a mathematical coordinate system on an accidental or contrived reference frame is that it makes possible the transformation of observations made in one reference frame into their counterparts in another reference frame in a general, abstract, and specifiable manner. Let us assume, for example, that two independent observers A and B each perform a series of observations (see Figure 4.1). Observer A makes the observations relative to a set of accidental reference objects $R(ai)$ and observer B makes the observations relative to a different set of reference objects $R(bi)$. We further assume that some of the members of $R(ai)$ and $R(bi)$ overlap. (If there is no overlap of reference points whatsoever, no comparison is possible.) An arbitrary mathematical coordinate system is then laid over the accidental frame of each observer. Once this has been done, each of the overlapping members of the sets $R(ai)$ and $R(bi)$ will have two distinct sets of coordinate values, one in the coordinate frame of observer A and the other in the coordinate frame of observer B. By empirically fitting the function which maps these values onto each other, the function which maps the coordinate

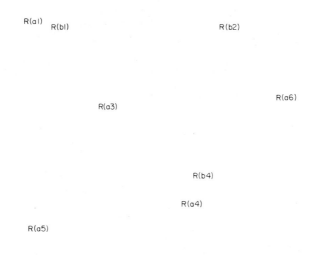

FIGURE 4.1   Reference frames $R(a_i)$ and $R(b_i)$ overlaid on each other.

system of observer A to that of observer B can be established. By means of this function, any observation made by observer A can be mapped onto the reference system of observer B and vice versa. To the extent to which empirical measurements show this function to be inaccurate for any single observation, we can say the observations of A and B disagree in a nonspurious way. Any differences between the observations of A and B that can be transformed away by this empirical function are artifactual or spurious differences relating solely to the use of different reference frames. In general scientific practice, only the former differences require explanation (J. D. Woelfel, 1980). The importance of this second function of the mathematical coordinate system is evident at once: If mathematical coordinate frames—however arbitrary—can be established over the reference frames of multiple observers, and if a sufficient set of common reference objects overlaps the reference frames, then mathematical functions which map the experiences of the observers onto each other can be found which will elimiate artifactual or spurious differences attributable to differential reference frameworks.

These remarks are not intended to imply that transformations across different reference frames are impossible without the aid of mathematics, or even that the process of transforming from one reference frame to another by mathematical means is fundamentally different from transforming from one frame to another in other ways. Such transformations are commonplace and occur in everyday vernacular discourse. In the simplest cases, any single individual may have available several alternative reference frames for the interpretation of any event, along with the implicit transformation rules across these frames. A typical case in point is humor, in which individuals apply different interpretations to identical words when they occur in or out of the context of a joke. In more difficult situations, two or more people may utilize different reference frames to interpret an event, and some third person (who is familiar with both reference frames) may be required to transform the experiences of one of the individuals into the frame of the others. This class of transformations includes counseling and other forms of therapeutic activities, as well as cross-cultural transformations. People who are able to transform experiences across reference frames from one culture to another are valuable individuals. The most difficult situations occur when there exists no person who is sufficiently familiar with the reference objects in two cultures or groups to provide transformations, in which case the reality of each group remains unintelligible to the other. These radical translation situations require that individuals from one of the cultures spend sufficient time interacting with the other to learn the set of reference objects in that culture and the transformations to their own set of reference objects, as is often the case in anthropological studies. In any event, the transformations always require that the relations of the set of reference objects in one framework to the set of reference objects in another framework be known; these relations then serve as the pattern for transforming other experiences by means of simile or metaphor.

Mathematizing these operations does not imply a radically different way of doing this. It simply refers to the process of abstracting the *form* of the transformations from the subject matter and recording it in a symbolic way, so that the comparative process may be routinized (and, most recently, computerized). What is gained in the process is speed, efficiency, precision, and consensus or objectivity.

Establishing Reference Frames for Meaning

A Physical Example

Since the process by which mathematical reference frames may be attached to meanings of any objects are similar to the procedures by which coordinate reference frames are affixed to physical distances, and since the mathematics are the same in any case, it will be worthwhile to work through a simple physical example to establish the procedures. Let us assume, for these purposes, that a stranger to the United States asks a native where Detroit is located. We can assume further that the stranger is not familiar with already established contrived reference frames such as north–south, or the longitude–latitude grid. (These are, in fact, fairly late abstractions from experience, and many cultures do not make use of them. On the island of Oahu in Hawaii, for example, directions are usually given in terms of four convenient landmarks: Diamond Head Crater, the region of Ewa, the mountains, and the sea.) If the stranger has visited some other U.S. cities, however, the native may choose these as a shared set of reference objects in terms of which Detroit's location may be calibrated. Let us assume these other cities are the 15 (in addition to Detroit) arrayed in Table 4.1. These 15 cities serve then as the set of accidental reference objects for the location of Detroit. (They are accidental in that they were not deliberately put in place to serve this function but "happen" to be there.)

The next step is to establish the interrelations among the elements of the reference set. If the stranger already knows the locations of these cities relative to each other, then of course this step could be skipped, but in any event they would have to have been learned at some time. These relations may be established by the pair-comparisons procedure described in the previous chapter. First, any arbitrary standard of distance is chosen. This could be the length of the stranger's arm, the distance between any two of the cities, or, for convenience in this example, the length of a standard meter. Each pair of cities is compared to this arbitrary standard and the distance between them expressed as a ratio multiple of the standard.

Once this has been done it only remains to express the relations of Detroit to each of the members of the reference set by the same pair-comparisons rule. The result of these operations is the matrix given in Table 4.1. This matrix contains complete information about the location of Detroit in reference to these other cities; there is, in fact, nothing more than can be said about the location of Detroit relative to these cities.[1]

Even so, it does not represent a visual map of the pattern among the cities. Although the geometry of the configuration of cities is given by the matrix, very few people could draw a map of the cities from this information. However, Young and Householder (1938) described a procedure for drawing maps from matrices of interpoint distances such as Table 4.1. The procedure requires establishing a coordinate system by expressing each point (city) as a position vector from any arbitrary point, then projecting each position vector onto all the others by form-

---

[1] Note that we assume each city's location is defined as a point, and that our distance function is symmetric, that is, the distance from A to B is identically equal to the distance from B to A.

TABLE 4.1

Separations in Space among 16 Selected U.S. Cities
(1 unit = 1 km)

City	Atlanta	Boston	Chicago	Cleveland	Dallas	Denver	Detroit	Los Angeles	Miami	New Orleans	New York	Phoenix	Pittsburgh	San Francisco	Seattle	Washington, D.C.
1 Atlanta	0															
2 Boston	1508	0														
3 Chicago	944	1369	0													
4 Cleveland	891	886	496	0												
5 Dallas	1160	2496	1292	1649	0											
6 Denver	1950	2846	1480	1974	1067	0										
7 Detroit	869	986	383	145	1607	1860	0									
8 Los Angeles	2310	4177	2807	3297	2005	1337	3191	0								
9 Miami	972	2019	1911	1749	1788	2777	1354	3764	0							
10 New Orleans	682	2186	1340	1487	713	1741	1511	2692	1076	0						
11 New York	1204	302	1147	652	2211	2624	1258	3944	1757	1884	0					
12 Phoenix	2562	3701	2338	2814	1427	943	2719	574	3189	2117	3451	0				
13 Pittsburgh	838	777	660	185	1721	2124	330	3437	1625	1478	510	2941	0			
14 San Francisco	3442	4343	2990	3485	2386	1524	3364	558	4174	3099	4137	1051	3643	0		
15 Seattle	3511	3979	2795	3260	2705	1643	3118	1543	4399	3381	3874	1792	3440	1091	0	
16 Washington, D.C.	874	632	961	492	1907	2404	637	3701	1485	1554	330	3191	309	3929	3849	0

60

ing the matrix of scalar products, which Young and Householder call B. In this coordinate system, the coordinates of the end point of each vector are given by its projection on all the remaining vectors, so that every entry of B,

$$b_{ij} = \rho_i \rho_j \cos \alpha_{ij}, \tag{4.1}$$

where ρ_i is the length of the ith vector from the origin, ρ_j the length of the jth vector from the origin, and α_{ij} the angle included between the ith and jth vectors.

Although the B matrix does represent a coordinate system within which the points are arrayed, it is not a particularly convenient or graphic coordinate system, since the coordinate axes and the position vectors representing the points are the same vectors. Only in the most special of cases would these coordinate axes be at right angles to each other as are regular cartesian coordinate axes. Finding the coordinates of the points on cartesian coordinates, as Young and Householder show, is easily done by transforming the B matrix to principle axes. Mathematically, the principle axes of the configuration are given by the eigenvectors associated with the B matrix. The transformation to principle axes is usually called factor analysis by social scientists.[2]

Most current users modify the Young and Householder procedure in a way introduced by Torgerson (1958). In the Young and Householder procedure, any one of the k points of the configuration could be taken arbitrarily as the origin of the coordinate system given in the B matrix. In the modified Torgerson procedure, the geometric center of the configuration is taken as the origin of the coordinate system. This modification is of no substantive importance, since the two procedures conform to within a translation of each other, but it is a very convenient choice in most instances because it assures that maps drawn from the resulting coordinates will be centered on the page. Torgerson refers to this "double-centered" matrix as the centroid scalar products matrix B^* with elements given by

$$b_{ij}^* = \frac{1}{2} \left(\frac{1}{k} \sum_i^k d_{ij}^2 + \frac{1}{k} \sum_j^k d_{ij}^2 - \frac{1}{k^2} \sum_i^k \sum_j^k d_{ij}^2 - d_{ij}^2 \right). \tag{4.2}$$

---

[2] Principle axes factor analysis is given by the unrotated solutions of a principle axis or Jacobi factor analysis. Social scientists would refer to the B matrix of Young and Householder as a type of covariance matrix. In a typical social science application, however, it would be not the covariance matrix that would be factored, but a correlation matrix derived from the covariance matrix. Most software available to social science users require minor modifications to factor covariance matrices, since eigenvalues less than zero are frequently encountered (Woelfel, Woelfel, & Woelfel, 1977). Results of a typical factor analysis of the intercities distances are given in Figure 4.2.

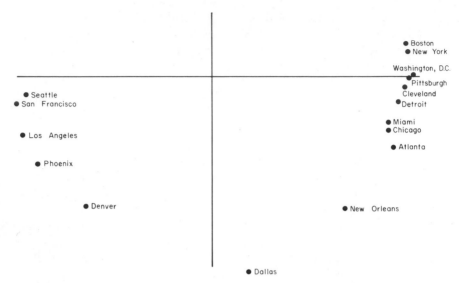

FIGURE 4.2   First two factors from factor analysis of matrix of distances among 16 selected U.S. cities.

In the Torgerson procedure, the eigenvectors of the B^* matrix constitute the set of cartesian coordinate axes onto which the points are projected. Since these are the principal axes of the configuration, they describe the overall shape of the configuration. The first eigenvector corresponding to the largest eigenvalue represents the principal direction of the configuration, that is, the direction in which it is longest. The second eigenvector will pass through the longest extent of the configuration perpendicular to the first eigenvector. The third eigenvector represents the largest span of the configuration perpendicular to the plane of the first two eigenvectors, and so on. Figure 4.3 illustrates the principal axes of an egg. Due to its symmetry relations, an egg has three eigenvectors whose lengths λ_1, λ_2, and λ_3 are of magnitude $\lambda_1 > \lambda_2 = \lambda_3$.

Coordinates of the cities projected on these reference axes are given in Table 4.2, and a plot of these coordinates is shown in Figure 4.4. The first principle axis of the configuration (column 1 of Table 4.2) is represented as the x axis in Figure 4.4. The second principle axis (column 2 of Table 4.2) is represented by the y axis of Figure 4.4. The third principle axis (column 3 of Table 4.2) is not represented in the diagram, but would be represented as a line from the origin perpendicular to the plane of the first two axes. The lengths of these axes are given by the square roots of their corresponding eigenvalues on Table 4.2 Each eigenvalue is equal to the sum of squares of the coordinates of its corresponding eigenvec-

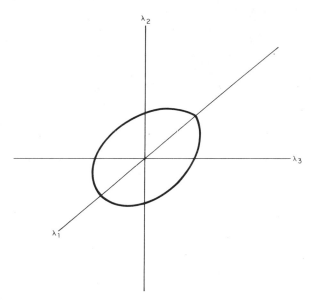

FIGURE 4.3   Principal axes of an egg.

tor, and all the eigenvectors are normalized so that they in turn sum to the trace of the B^* matrix. The trace of the B^* matrix is equal to the sum of its diagonal elements, and any diagonal element of the B^* matrix represents the projection of a position vector on itself, hence

$$b_{ii}^* = \rho_i\rho_i \cos \theta = \rho_i^2. \tag{4.3}$$

Thus each element of the diagonal of the B^* matrix represents the squared length of the position vector of a point, and the trace represents the total sum of squared lengths. (By a simple theorem it can be shown that the sum of squared lengths equals the total variance in this case. See Van de Geer, 1971, Chapter 3) By expressing each eigenvalue as a percentage of the trace, therefore, it is simple to describe each axis in terms of the amount of variance or squared distance in the map it accounts for, as shown in Table 4.2 The reader can easily derive other interesting features of this representation: The sum of squares of any row of the matrix in Table 4.2, for example, will equal the corresponding diagonal entry of the B^* matrix, and represents the squared distance of a point from the origin of the space. Similarly, since the map is centered at the middle of the points and since the axes are cartesian, the scalar product of any two columns of Table 4.2 will be zero.

Again since the coordinate system in Table 4.2 is cartesian, the elementary theorem of Pythagoras holds, and the interpoint distances

TABLE 4.2

Galileo Coordinates of 16 U.S. Cities in 4 Metric Multidimensional Space

City	1	2	3	4	5	6	7	8
1 ATLANT	-63?.91?	6??.010	815.981	-.414	-5.170	.792	.288	-.038
2 BOSTON	-1730.3??	-753.156	77.491	2.687	-158.295	-47.302	2.366	10.581
3 CHICAGO	-418.4??	-379.172	-42.774	12.183	55.957	40.906	-19.206	-9.949
4 CLEVEL	-909.630	-444.779	-14.112	16.803	24.190	15.869	21.132	-20.420
5 DALLAS	-320.2??	655.456	-270.314	-2.94	-27.149	49.706	31.212	6.333
6 DENVER	1043.610	-144.216	-167.956	.070	108.432	7.326	-2.883	25.412
7 DETROI	-760.197	-454.305	25.406	477.?02	-38.352	-.244	-.098	-.020
8 LOS AN	-2257.094	535.724	756.557	-20.022	7.144	-.621	-.005	-.027
9 MIAMI	-1574.307	1045.5??	-276.189	-14.019	-163.588	-46.508	-.221	-5.803
10 MINN	-389.977	917.677	-278.656	-400.019	-85.417	22.898	-10.940	7.877
11 NEW Y	-1747.715	-456.674	20.561	-14.333	39.222	-.116	.102	-.009
12 PHOEN	-1747.125	-500.269	-32.019	16.094	21.229	-6.547	-19.746	-11.732
13 PITTS	-1073.710	-336.951	-22.179	16.094	-.970	33.718	-12.399	-.101
14 SANF	2574.400	-156.346	-249.270	-12.012	139.889	-46.030	10.242	-5.387
15 SEATT	2277.691	-1227.691	-217.631	-63.563	-233.975	2.901	-.085	-.126
16 WASHI	-1390.267	-156.678	-211.256	66.195	316.853	-25.042	.239	2.838

EIGENVALUES (ROOTS) OF EIGENVECTOR MATRIX
73673336.000   6759578.562   1663453.500   489916.184   253572.936   13344.470   2571.950   1584.255

NUMBER OF ITERATIONS TO DERIVE THE ROOT
5   4   4   12   4   4   6   130

PERCENTAGE OF VARIANCE ACCOUNTED FOR BY INDIVIDUAL FACTORS
63.726   16.805   4.136   1.216   .630   .033   .006   .004

PERCENTAGE OF VARIANCE ACCOUNTED FOR BY INDIVIDUAL FACTORS IN THEIR OWN SPACES
76.574   15.770   3.952   1.141   .592   .031   .006   .004

SUM OF ROOTS   96209928.500
WARP FACTOR   1.305

NUMBER OF DIMENSIONS IN REAL SPACE   6

NUMBER OF DIMENSIONS IN IMAGINARY SPACE   0

FIGURE 4.4 First two principal axes of the configuration of 16 selected U.S. cities.

are related to the coordinates by the equation

$$S_{ij} = \left(\sum_{\mu=1}^{3} (R^{\mu}_{(i)} - R^{\mu}_{(j)})^2 \right)^{1/2}, \tag{4.4}$$

where $R^{\mu}_{(i)}$ is the coordinates of the ith point on the μth axis and $R^{\mu}_{(j)}$ is the coordinates of the jth point on the μth axis. If the distance between two points is given by means of the general equation (3.8),

$$S_{(AB)} = (g_{\mu\nu} S^{\mu}_{(AB)} S^{\nu}_{(AB)})^{1/2}, \tag{3.8}$$

then the components of the metric tensor are

$$G = \begin{pmatrix} 1 & 0 & 0 \\ 0 & 1 & 0 \\ 0 & 0 & 1 \end{pmatrix}$$

and the dummy indices range from 1 to 3.

A Cultural Example

The procedures for establishing a coordinate reference frame on a set of reference objects are identical whether the objects are physical or cultural, and the steps in the procedure can be abstracted from the example.

1.   The set of reference objects for the frame are identified. (These may be accidental or contrived according to the circumstances and goals of the analysis.)

2.   Any arbitrary pair of objects from within the set is chosen, and the separation between them is designated as a standard measure.

3.   The separations among all pairs of the remaining objects are estimated as ratios of this standard separation.

4.   The matrix of interpoint distances obtained from these steps is converted to a deviation matrix with origin at either an arbitrary point (Young and Householder method) or the centroid of all the points (Torgerson method).

5.   The deviation matrix is converted into a scalar products matrix by multiplying it through by its transpose. (Since the scalar products matrix is symmetric, it does not matter whether we pre- or postmultiply.)

6.   The resulting scalar products matrix is then transformed to principle axes and the result is the desired matrix R, within which each point A is represented as the end point of a position vector $R_{(1)}^{\mu}$ ($\mu = 1, 2, \ldots, r$) from the origin projected on a set of r orthonormal basis vectors e_i.

Steps 4–6 are usually referred to in the psychometric literature as metric multidimensional scaling. Although intended originally as a psychometric device, as we have seen the procedure is completely general and applies regardless of the domain from which the original set of objects is chosen.

To illustrate the generality of these procedures, we can show how each of these steps would be implemented to establish a cartesian coordinate frome for the set of basic human emotions. Emotions are an apt example, since they represent an aspect of human culture which many writers consider precisely that unquantifiable domain which distinguishes human phenomena from physical objects. Moreover, emotions are clearly nonphysical objects, at least as they are understood and experienced by people in everyday life and therefore apparently quite different from the set of intercity distances.

Identifying the Set of Reference Objects   As is the case with physical objects such as cities, we may choose either a set of accidental or contrived reference objects (or some mixture of the two) as a basis for locating any set of cultural objects on a cartesian reference frame. As we suggested earlier, accidental reference objects are those that some group uses as points of reference because they are conveniently available to serve such a function, without any formally specified rule. If the accidental reference objects are (as we defined them) that set of objects actually used by a group to define an object or set of objects, then determining an appropriate set of accidental reference objects is simply a matter of asking a sample of the members of the group to define the object in question. The *other* objects mentioned by those persons while defining the first will by definition constitute a set of accidental reference objects for the domain in question. In the present example, 22 persons from Asia, the United States, Australia, and New Zealand were asked to list what they believed to be the principle human emotions, as well as for a list of words they used to describe emotions. Of the total emotions listed by all 22 people, 16 were listed by at least 2 or more respondents, and these 16 constituted over 75% of the emotions mentioned and over 90% of the total number of mentions. Each of these 16 emotions was then taken as a member of the reference set. They constitute reference objects because people refer to them when they define the contents of the domain of emotion, and they are accidental since they were not deliberately chosen according to a well-specified rule.

To illustrate the use of contrived or laboratory reference points, six additional objects were added to the list. Much of the work of Osgood and his co-workers has been based on the assumption that there already exists for all meaning domains an accidental reference system with the desired cartesian characteristics. Osgood *et al.* (1957) argue that all experiences are represented in human thought by their projections on three attribute vectors defined by the line segments connecting the semantic opposites good–bad, active–passive, and potent–impotent; that these line segments intersect at a common origin, and that all three are mutually perpendicular, thus forming a three-dimensional cartesian coordinate system upon which are projected all other objects of cognition. To determine whether these vectors span the space of emotions in the manner hypothesized, these six words were included with the 16 emotions to form a list of 22 reference objects. While more sophisticated procedures for deriving the initial list of reference concepts will be discussed later, these simple steps will serve as an illustration of the way in which reference objects for a domain of cultural meaning can be established in principle.

Selecting the Criterion Pair   Establishing the criterion pair refers to the process by which the unit of measure is defined. According to the rule of fundamental measurement, the unit of measure is given by an arbitrarily selected interval in the domain of objects to be measured. In defining a unit of length, therefore, Einstein avails himself of the interval of distance between the end points of the measuring rod S; for the measure of temperature we may define the interval between the freezing and boiling points of water, or the triple points of various substances. As Descartes (1964) understood, the choice of a standard unit is philosophically arbitrary: "The unit is that common element in which, as above remarked, all things compared with each other should equally participate. If this be not already settled in our problems, we can represent it by one of the magnitudes already presented to us, or by any other magnitude we like, and it will be the common measure of all the others [p. 32]."

This is not to say, however, that it makes no practical difference which magnitude is chosen as the standard unit. In general, establishing the interval between any two points as a standard of measure establishes the invariance of that interval by definition. If any two intervals vary with regard to each other over time, therefore, choosing one as a standard of measure will attribute all changes to the other and vice versa. It does make a difference, then, which interval is chosen as a standard unit, but Descartes' recognition of the arbitrariness of choice follows from the fact that the decision cannot be made on the basis of observations alone. Different choices of standards will yield different realities, but there is no experiment by which the "truth" of one of these alternative realities could be determined. Since the development of a theory of cognitive process which fits our present human experience closely would require a much less substantial adjustment of our collective thinking than one which required a complete revision of existing ideas, it seems reasonable to choose a standard of measure which is relatively stable in the already established vernacular system. This will maximize the similarity between the new system and the old.

This specification is the same specification Einstein makes when he requires that the standard rod whose end points define the standard measure be a *rigid* rod. A rigid body is a body such that the distances among any set of points on the body remain invariant over time. But of course, invariant means that the measured values of these distances do not change relative to each other. If there are only two points on the rigid rod, then its rigidity is a function of the invariance of the interval relative to the measuring rod. In the measurement of cognitive and cultural processes, it is well to choose as a standard unit the distance between two points that most members of the culture would themselves consider to be relatively invariant—that would mean that users of the older vernacular measuring system will find the new procedure corresponds to their traditional outlook.

A second consideration in the choice of a standard measure arises when we consider the social character of the measurement process. If a

single investigator were establishing a standard of measure for idiosyncratic use not to be shared with others, it would be sufficient to choose a
criterion pair of points which seemed relatively invariant across time
within that individual's own experiences. But when a group of investigators establishes a standard measure to facilitate comparison of their
results, then it is appropriate to choose as a standard some distance
which seems relatively invariant to the group. This implies that all users
of the new standard will have some access to the standard. Thus it is
important to balance the desirability of a time-invariant standard
against the accessibility of the standard. As a minimum, the standard
should be accessible to all those who must use it. For these purposes,
multiple copies of many physical standards are often made and distributed. The ordinary meter stick, for example, is a facsimile of the standard meter, designed to make the standard accessible to a large number
of users. In some cases, of course, the need for time invariance and
precision may require the stipulation of a measure whose accessibility is
quite limited, and the basic standard measures of physical science today
are accessible only to scientists with the most advanced training and
equipment.

All these considerations come about because our efforts to introduce
standards of measure must fit within the set of standards already in use.
Even though existing standards may have been only informally chosen,
nonetheless they do exist, and our experience reflects those original
choices of standards. Changes of standards of measure always result in
some changes in the apparent structure of reality. Sometimes the
changes likely to result from new standards are perceived as unfortunate by those who will be affected by them and they are resisted. At
other times, the present structure of experience is seen to be undesira-
ble, and so affected groups argue for new standards. Many important
popular revolutions are fought in part over the demand for new standards of measure: The fourth item of the Magna Charta, for example, is
a demand for reform of standards of measure. At any rate, a standard
becomes a standard by agreement, and the *Mathematics Dictionary*
(James & James, 1976) defines *measure* as "comparison to some unit
recognized as a standard [p. 244]."

A minor but nevertheless important consideration independent of
these matters is the computational ease of applying the standard. If the
standard chosen is greatly larger or smaller than the objects to be compared to it, then those comparisons will involve somewhat more tedious
calculations than might be the case if the relative sizes of criterion and
objects to be measured were more similar. Particularly in the present

case, where nonscientists are expected to make use of the standard of measure, using a standard which requires calculating very large or very small ratios can lead to fatigue and computational errors.

More will be said about the basis for rational choice of standards later, but in the case of the present example, *love* and *hate* were chosen as the criterion pair, thus establishing the separation between love and hate as the standard measure. These were chosen because they are emotions which virtually all cultures recognize and symbolize in their respective languages. This means that this distance is likely to be accessible to most people. Second, love and hate are likely on the basis of informal experience to be relatively stable in the vernacular meaning system. Third, they are chosen from within the domain of emotions, and so ought to be relatively close to the other emotions—at least closer than concepts not implicated in the domain of emotion. This means that the standard rod does not need to be "transported" too great a distance before comparisons are made, and consequently the act of comparison ought to be relatively simple.

Since love and hate, again on the basis of informal experience, are likely to be among the most widely separated of emotions (many investigators might consider them bipolar), their separation was set at 100 units, so that the standard unit of measure should actually be considered 1/100 of the separation between love and hate. Of course there is no absolute basis for establishing the numerical measure (*or modulus*) for this separation, but this stipulation makes it unnecessary to estimate all separations in fractions of one unit, which would be a needlessly difficult task for lay observers. The effects of varying this number will be discussed in more detail in the following chapter.

Estimating the Separations   Once the criterion pair has been selected, the next step is to gather estimates of the separations among the remaining pairs of objects as ratios of the criterion pair from a sample of respondents drawn from the population of interest. Most literate populations are already familiar with the logic of ratio estimations, since they form the basis of all physical measurement and in fact instructions in the practice of ratio measurement form an important part of the mathematics curricula of most American elementary schools, sometimes as early as kindergarten (see Figure 4.5). The notions of ratio measurement are so pervasive, however, that children are able to make such estimates with surprising precision even before such formal instructions. In any event, even though general literate populations are usually able to perform ratio estimates, it is necessary at the beginning of the scaling task to explain unambiguously to the respondents that a ratio

FIGURE 4.5 Page of a kindergarten textbook.

rule is what is requested of them. This is particularly true of those who have some familiarity with normal psychometric devices which almost never utilize the ratio rule. Since most people are more familiar with ratio measurement than typical psychometric practice, however, very few people report difficulty understanding the instructions or performing the task. In those relatively rare cases where the instructions are not followed, interview data seem to indicate it is not for lack of ability to use the ratio rule, but from failure to understand that ratio judgments are requested. (Probably the most typical misunderstanding is the assumption that the numerical value assigned to the criterion separation is a boundary or limit establishing the highest possible score. Since the use of scales bounded at both ends is common practice in social measurement, this error particularly should be guarded against in the instructions.) Typical instructions for making the ratio judgments of separation are given in Appendix A.

If the point of the analysis is to establish coordinates of the emotions for any individual respondent, the results of this operation yield a set of distance matrices $S_1, S_2, \ldots, S_n$, where each matrix S_1 represents the set of pair-comparison judgments for each of the n individuals in the sample. Each of these may be centered, converted to scalar products, and transformed to principle axes to yield the set of cartesian spaces R_1, $R_2, \ldots, R_n$, each of which represents the configuration of emotions for a single individual. Each of these spaces will contain a relatively large uncertainty, however, since each of them will be based only on $k(k-1)/2$ nonindependent pairwise judgments made by a single individual, and each of them yields $r \times k$ coordinates where r is the number of dimensions or axes required to fit the configuration. Particularly when r approaches the value of k, the estimates will be uncertain. This point has caused some confusion in the literature, since some writers feel this is a consequence of the imprecision of the ratio judgment rule for individual cases relative to ordinary scaling practice (such as Likert-type and semantic differential-type scales). In fact, such evidence as exists seems to indicate that the ratio judgment procedures can be made more precise and reliable than Likert and semantic differential-type scales even for single case measures. (Quantitative evidence will be presented in the following chapter). Even though the ratio judgment procedures may be more precise than typical scales at any sample size, however, none of the measurement devices known to us—including the ratio judgment procedures—are capable of much precision for the individual case at this level of their development. As a consequence, psychologists and others whose interests require measurements of individual persons' cognitive structures have been led to explore procedures (such as nonmetric multidimensional scaling) which generate coordinates based only on gross aspects of the data (such as their order relations) and generic assumptions about the characteristics of cognitive structures (nonmetric scaling assumes all cognitive structures are real, euclidean, and of low dimensionality).

Once again the situation is quite analogous to high-energy physics: even though the properties of individuals can only be determined to within fairly wide uncertainties, properties of the aggregate of many individuals can be established with high precision. The procedures described here were in fact developed primarily to measure the properties of cultural aggregates, and in this context can develop surprising precision. As we shall see in Chapter 7, there is good reason to describe the cognitive structure of the culture as the structure of the mean of the individual members. A convenient way to accomplish this averaging is to average each pairwise distance estimate across all n respondents to create the average separation matrix $\bar{S}$ with elements

$$\bar{s}_{ij} = \sum_{p=1}^{n} s_{ijp}/n. \tag{4.5}$$

This mean distance matrix $\bar{S}$ is then converted to a centroid scalar products matrix by means of equation (4.2) and the principle axes of the centroid scalar products matrix are extracted as illustrated earlier. The result is the orthogonal cartesian coordinate system R in Table 4.3. While formally identical to the cartesian coordinate system on which the U. S. cities were projected earlier, the reference system for the emotions data differs empirically in two important respects. First, the space within which the emotions are arrayed is considerably higher in dimensionality than the space of the U.S. cities, which of course is basically three-dimensional. This is evidenced by the existence of 15 nonzero eigenvalues, each of which expresses the squared length of the eigenvector to which it corresponds. Secondly, 8 of the eigenroots are negative. Since the eigenroots are equal to the sum of the squares of the coordinates on each eigenvector, and since this sum is negative, the coordinates of the emotions on these eigenvectors are therefore imaginary. (This is so because the square of the imaginary number is negative, i.e., $i^2 = -1$.)

These imaginary coordinates arise because the interpoint distances among sets of points taken three at a time do not always obey the triangle inequality rule for metric spaces. A typical example is given by Fink, Serota, Woelfel, and Noell (1975). In an investigation of the ideological structure of college and university students, respondents reported mean distances between the concepts *the rich* and *big business* as 23 units, between *the rich* and *me* (i.e., the respondents' own position) as 313 units, and between *big business* and *me* as 237 units. The reader can verify quickly that these three points cannot be arrayed in a triangle on the plane that is consistent with these distances. Nor is it possible to conclude that this discrepancy is solely the result of random error of measure, since no transformation of these distances within their respective 95% confidence intervals completely eliminates the inconsistency. Rather it seems more appropriate to believe that these inconsistencies actually occur in human thought, and much research indicates

TABLE 4.3

Galileo Coordinates of Selected Emotions

Emotion	\multicolumn{8}{c}{Coordinate}							
	1	2	3	4	5	6	7	8
1 LOVE	51.610	-22.508	-22.925	31.748	26.270	7.460	-3.830	-11.411
2 HATE	-75.564	-36.872	49.933	23.319	16.106	-8.432	-5.560	.453
3 ANGER	-31.064	-37.336	.923	-1.169	11.667	4.605	-6.822	8.641
4 JOY	92.936	17.216	39.356	7.754	-.665	19.929	-14.764	-5.432
5 ENVY	-29.206	-15.475	-3.575	7.759	-6.685	27.232	2.105	-.035
6 FEAR	-31.077	-21.747	-20.310	6.660	-20.659	-32.463	22.905	15.322
7 JEALOUSY	-44.937	-26.130	-21.365	15.129	-10.851	15.768	-6.138	-17.452
8 HAPPINESS	34.463	19.495	.616	-.010	-.510	-8.001	30.023	5.015
9 SADNESS	-31.213	7.493	-25.577	-2.353	22.697	-8.299	-15.988	-11.013
10 ANXIETY	-14.043	-15.690	-6.377	21.531	-9.004	-15.307	-14.011	-4.702
11 EXCITEMENT	54.294	-43.030	13.550	-19.098	-28.463	-7.189	-1.693	10.351
12 INDIFFER	-30.527	84.142	38.510	-12.185	-1.486	-13.654	3.174	-17.075
13 DEPRESS	-52.421	15.443	-32.777	-.701	23.695	-4.398	10.584	-1.713
14 SELFISH	-35.170	2.330	16.095	-19.760	2.251	35.034	2.675	-5.635
15 GUILT	-46.267	-2.126	-8.133	-23.937	2.136	-12.071	9.340	-5.045
16 STRONG	41.451	-16.760	18.466	-37.584	41.956	.133	-3.025	21.581
17 BAD	-61.680	10.660	9.734	-37.335	-25.242	8.681	-12.319	25.367
18 ACTIVE	33.261	-44.905	22.848	21.320	-7.502	-10.504	17.521	-16.933
19 WEAK	-36.002	37.350	-4.438	-12.041	-29.467	-2.931	-1.510	-7.299
20 GOOD	73.039	17.059	-13.733	26.240	-.189	-29.328	-16.585	-7.735
21 PASSIVE	.267	73.222	-13.244		12.721	5.811	-2.540	22.863
22 YOURSELF	71.249	-.275	-45.517	-37.291	-14.695	22.057	2.607	2.255

EIGENVALUES (ROOTS) OF EIGENVECTOR MATRIX--
53955.944 24386.149 12719.904 10709.025 7390.673 6161.699 4097.677 3472.335

NUMBER OF ITERATIONS TO DERIVE THE ROOT--
5 6 313 35 22 9 13 53

PERCENTAGE OF DISTANCE ACCOUNTED FOR BY INDIVIDUAL VECTOR--
44.422 16.068 9.424 7.934 5.468 4.565 3.036 2.573

CUMULATIVE PERCENTAGES OF REAL DISTANCE ACCOUNTED FOR--
44.422 62.490 71.914 79.849 85.317 89.883 92.919 95.491

CUMULATIVE PERCENTAGES OF TOTAL (REAL AND IMAGINARY) DISTANCE ACCOUNTED FOR--
64.333 90.500 104.148 115.639 123.559 130.170 134.567 138.233

TRACE 83196.044

NUMBER OF DIMENSIONS IN REAL SPACE 14

EXCLUSION WORD IS 7777777777760000000

Coordinate

Emotion	9	10	11	12	13	14	15	16
1 LOVE	1.925	2.070	1.651	.977	-.817	-.077	-1.730	-5.455
2 HATE	-2.013	.779	-.805	-1.400	-1.012	.167	-7.219	1.363
3 ANGER	26.695	-5.853	4.422	2.078	-2.980	.003	13.694	-1.324
4 JOY	10.321	2.444	-2.245	-5.505	-.202	.132	-4.372	-10.414
5 ENVY	-15.214	12.703	-11.098	-13.758	.415	.012	3.337	1.037
6 FEAR	4.206	-2.107	-5.623	-.461	3.583	.058	3.647	-3.603
7 JEALOUSY	-17.392	-.007	2.769	14.782	-5.402	.071	1.051	2.274
8 HAPPINESS	-4.770	-2.841	1.374	.609	-1.254	.023	.046	9.532
9 SADNESS	1.661	1.043	-4.344	.387	13.930	.085	-3.012	7.357
10 ANXIETY	-10.952	-22.468	12.326	-12.180	-.800	-.021	-.728	-5.073
11 EXCITEME	-6.307	-3.131	3.537	3.213	2.001	-.045	-2.350	2.162
12 INDIFFER	-5.695	-5.815	2.652	.254	.034	.129	7.495	2.969
13 DEPRESS	3.216	-7.948	-12.031	-4.371	-7.902	-.110	-6.138	-4.797
14 SELFISH	5.127	-11.714	4.153	6.871	5.831	.054	1.645	-6.135
15 GUILT	4.016	24.095	21.866	-4.157	-1.030	-.027	-2.455	-2.737
16 STRONG	-7.569	-.025	2.476	1.824	-1.843	.053	1.300	15.937
17 BAD	-1.051	2.859	-4.119	4.787	.891	.033	-4.709	-4.770
18 ACTIVE	2.317	6.609	-7.616	-1.039	.442	-.076	-5.965	-4.741
19 WEAK	16.422	2.392	-3.275	-1.234	-3.776	.017	-.050	19.315
20 GOOD	-.107	4.789	-7.630	7.245	-1.560	.046	8.732	-8.311
21 PASSIVE	-6.056	4.797	2.601	2.891	.353	.044	-2.950	-11.102
22 YOURSELF	2.314	-3.681	2.834	-3.492	1.002	.152	-4.050	5.445

EIGENVALUES (-ROOTS) OF --EIGENVECTOR MATRIX--

| 2047.482 | 1661.334 | 1210.841 | 793.238 | 372.219 | .142 | -778.421 | -1336.817 |

NUMBER OF ITERATIONS TO DERIVE THE ROOT--

| 13 | 11 | 7 | 109 | 4 | 7 | 6 | 25 |

PERCENTAGE OF DISTANCE ACCOUNTED FOR BY INDIVIDUAL VECTOR--

| 1.517 | 1.231 | .497 | .588 | .276 | .000 | .577 | -.932 |

CUMULATIVE PERCENTAGE OF REAL DISTANCE ACCOUNTED FOR--

| 97.008 | 98.239 | 99.136 | 99.724 | 100.000 | 100.000 | 99.423 | 38.431 |

CUMULATIVE PERCENTAGE OF TOTAL (REAL AND IMAGINARY) DISTANCE ACCOUNTED FOR--

| 140.490 | 142.272 | 143.572 | 144.423 | 144.822 | 144.822 | 143.987 | 142.551 |

TRACE   4,136.044

NUMBER OF DIMENSIONS IN REAL SPACE 14

EXCLUSION WORLD IS 777777777776000000

WARP FACTOR   1.45

TABLE 4.3 (continued)

Emotion		Coordinate					
		17	18	19	20	21	22
1	LOVE	2.004	12.792	-16.894	46.056	-23.163	-19.340
2	HATE	.224	-.222	.517	7.146	2.002	70.682
3	ANGER	-17.611	-6.800	-8.684	-6.473	-2.156	5.663
4	JOY	.785	15.174	-.025	-20.010	43.859	-14.007
5	ENVY	-.135	-5.933	2.699	.433	-.649	-4.614
6	FEAR	7.275	20.565	-5.481	-11.224	12.834	-3.301
7	JEALOUSY	-5.236	6.122	-9.973	-21.609	25.013	-1.273
8	HAPPINESS	-11.290	-23.260	-14.899	12.650	37.959	7.526
9	SADNESS	-9.200	-7.254	-2.260	-7.459	19.157	-9.537
10	ANXIETY	10.765	-11.070	-13.936	-7.018	-11.476	-8.624
11	EXCITEMENT	-18.010	-3.324	37.204	5.224	-21.725	-21.255
12	INDIFFERENCE	-13.072	20.684	3.570	15.195	-16.595	-2.253
13	DEPRESSED	-8.523	-3.477	26.057	1.803	16.532	-21.783
14	SELFISH	19.355	-6.923	11.816	2.296	-.208	-1.501
15	GUILT	3.004	-2.301	12.072	2.691	14.215	-2.928
16	STRONG	16.046	11.996	3.506	-12.348	-.688	-23.948
17	BAD	2.700	-4.644	-16.499	36.743	15.954	-19.624
18	ACTIVE	-3.306	-7.536	-19.212	-14.004	-41.843	-17.349
19	WEAK	14.551	-6.603	-3.786	5.511	-16.117	-11.590
20	GOOD	20.290	-13.554	14.331	5.662	4.102	26.107
21	PASSIVE	-6.785	-7.772	-10.600	-29.401	-35.045	11.263
22	YOURSELF	-3.772	15.140	3.479	3.663	-11.760	6.630

EIGENVALUES (ROOTS) OF EIGENVECTOR MATRIX--

	17	18	19	20	21	22
	-2635.079	-3356.517	-4492.713	-6556.661	-9976.343	-12637.743

NUMBER OF ITERATIONS TO DERIVE THE ROOT--

	17	18	19	20	21	22
	9	11	25	28	7	1+

PERCENTAGE OF DISTANCE ACCOUNTED FOR BY INDIVIDUAL VECTOR--

	17	18	19	20	21	22
	-1.952	-2.487	-3.329	-4.358	-7.392	-9.353

CUMULATIVE PERCENTAGES OF REAL DISTANCE ACCOUNTED FOR--

	17	18	19	20	21	22
	96.479	93.992	90.663	85.305	78.414	69.050

CUMULATIVE PERCENTAGES OF TOTAL (REAL AND IMAGINARY) DISTANCE ACCOUNTED FOR--

	17	18	19	20	21	22
	139.723	136.121	131.300	124.265	113.560	100.000

TRACE 93196.044

NUMBER OF DIMENSIONS IN REAL SPACE 16

EXCLUSION WORD IS 7777777777 760000000

they are commonplace. Furthermore, while there are several theories of human cognition which suggest that human thought *tends toward* consistency (Heider, Festinger, etc.), there are probably no widely accepted theories which argue that human thought ought to *be* consistent at any point in time. Our own inclination is to regard these measured values as meaningful, and accept as a consequence that the space of human cognition is not euclidean or "metric" (cf. Blumenthal, 1970), but rather seems to exhibit the properties of a curved Riemann space. Figure 4.6 illustrates how the distances reported can be made consistent by assuming the space within which they are imbedded is itself a curved hyperplane.

Fortunately, such spaces are well known in modern cosmology, and the space-time continuum of Einstein and Minkowski constitutes just such a surface. Mathematically, the Riemannian space can be represented easily as a flat cartesian space with imaginary and real eigenvectors, as we have seen in Table 4.3. Conveniently, the general equations (3.8) and (3.10) apply directly to the computation of distance relations in the Riemann space if we relax the condition that the metric tensor [cf. equation (3.9)] be positive. To understand why this is so, we may review briefly the process by which distance among points is calculated given the coordinates of the points on orthogonal reference axes. First, the difference between the coordinates of any two points on any axis is calculated. This difference is then squared. The squares of the differences on all the axes are then summed, and the square root of the total is the distance between the two points. When the coordinates on any axes are imaginary, however, the square of their difference is negative; adding this negative component to the total is equivalent to substracting the absolute value of the squared difference from the total. It is convenient from the computational point of view, therefore, to treat all the coordinates as if they were real, but to substract the squared differences of the imaginary components from the total rather than adding. If we assume, then, that the coordinates of a reference system are real from

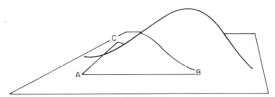

FIGURE 4.6   Three points on a Riemann plane. Triangle *ABC* need not obey the triangle inequalities rule since curvature of surface allows side *BC* to take on a value greater than *AB* + *AC*.

the first to the pth dimension and imaginary thereafter, we may treat each of the coordinates as if they were real, but define the metric tensor as

$$g_{\mu\nu} = \begin{cases} 0, & \mu \neq \nu, \\ 1, & \mu = \nu \leq \rho, \\ -1, & \mu = \nu > \rho. \end{cases} \tag{4.6}$$

While the noneuclidean character of the cognitive domain may be thought of as a minor inconvenience from a computational view, therefore, it is not an insuperable problem, since there already exists a well-developed mathematics for the representation of such spaces.[3]

The Meaning of the Eigenvectors   As we have suggested, the eigenvectors of the solution do not have absolute significance in and of themselves, but rather represent only the orthogonal axes of a cartesian coordinate system. Assuming that the eigenvectors have a meaning independent of the projections of the concepts on them is as meaningless as assuming that Einstein's imaginary rod stretched to the clouds represents increasing goodness as it reaches closer and closer to heaven. Social scientists have not always realized this, however, and, as we suggested in Chapter 3, many early factor analysts assumed that the orthogonal axes of the factor spaces they generated represented latent psychological traits or "factors" (which is the basis of the name *factor analysis*.) Even as late as 1957, as we have seen, Osgood *et al.* assumed that all human cognitions were projected on three and only three mutually orthogonal eigenvectors, which represented respectivelly, good–bad, active–passive, and strong–weak. Some psychologists no doubt believe

---

[3] This point deserves attention, because many psychometricians who write in the area of multidimensional scaling consider the presence of negative roots and imaginary eigenvectors as a pathology resulting from errors of measurement. Their common practice is to force all multidimensional scaling solutions into a euclidean space by means of a blind monotone transformation called nonmetric multidimensional scaling. We call the transformation "blind" because it is the result of an iterative process and the final transforming equation is in general not recoverable so that one does not know exactly how the data have been transformed, even after the fact. Moreover, the nonmetric transformation is usually many-to-one and hence has no inverse, so that the original data cannot be retrieved from the scaling solution without some loss. These losses are often very substantial and, in our opinion, have not been justified on theoretical grounds, since there is no widely known theory which predicts that the space of cognition, whether in individuals or cultural groups, ought to be euclidean. There are theories, however, which predict that it is not euclidean, including some of the most widely known and respected theories. A substantive interpretation of the imaginary eigenvectors is given in Chapter 7, along with a discussion of the theories (primarily balance theories) which suggest the space ought to be noneuclidean.

this today (although as we shall see, the evidence from the present emotions data do not support such a view).

With the advent of multidimensional scaling algorithms and the increasing mathematical understanding that accompanied these methods, attention began to be directed toward a more holistic consideration of the configuration of points projected on the eigenvectors. This has led in turn to an increasing understanding of the role of the eigenvectors as an intermediate mathematical device used to facilitate still further analyses. By far the most common use of these eigenvectors today is as a basis for plotting the configuration visually. As we saw with the example of the U.S. cities, this is done by representing each of the eigenvectors as an axis of a cartesian coordinate system on suitable graph paper. Figure 4.7 represents the first principle plane of the space of emotions. The horizontal axis represents the first eigenvector, and the vertical axis represents the second eigenvector. The resulting picture gives a rough visualization of the structure of the domain of emotions for this sample of respondents. Simple as it is, this picture is a great advance over the early practice of considering eigenvectors (or factors) one by one. We are able to see clearly, for example, that the line segment between the words *good* and *bad* appears to lie roughly parallel to the first eigenvector, as Osgood *et al.*, would suggest, but we can also see that it does not pass through the origin, contrary to Osgood's prediction. Moreover, it is also

FIGURE 4.7   First principal plane of the configuration of emotions and attributes for a sample of university students.

clear that neither good nor bad define the end points of the dimension, since *joy, happiness, hate, indifference,* and *excitement* all lie farther from the origin than *bad* does, and *joy, happiness, indifference,* and *hate* lie further from the origin than does *good.*

It is also clear from this picture that neither active–passive nor strong–weak lie along any of the principle axes of the space, nor is it likely that such deviations are within reasonable limits of error for this sample. Similarly, even this two-dimensional picture is sufficient to show clearly that the three line segments defined by connecting the terms good–bad, active–passive, and strong–weak do not cross at a common origin. (When more dimensions are examined, it becomes clear that they do not cross at all.)

It is also possible to see from the picture that *happiness* and *joy,* for example, are very different (far from) *hate;* that *active* and *excitement* are very different from *indifference* and *passive.* Nevertheless, as an examination of the relative sizes of the eigenvalues associated with these two eigenvectors shows, these two dimensions together only account for a part of the configuration (about 62% of the real part of the space) and so the picture is something of a distortion. Some of the distances will be shortened or lengthened more than others, but there is no a priori way to determine which distances are distorted the most short of examining the remaining (unplotted) eigenvectors.

FIGURE 4.8 Second principal plane of the configuration of emotions and attributes for a sample of university students.

This can be illustrated with the aid of Figure 4.8, where the vertical axis corresponds to the second dimension or eigenvector, as it does in Figure 4.7. The horizontal axis, however, represents the third eigenvector or dimension. If we think of the picture given in Figure 4.7 as the "front view" of the configuration, Figure 4.8 may be thought of as the "side view." (Since the configuration is multidimensional, it actually has more than 6 sides.) More precisely, it represents a 90-degree rotation around the vertical axis. We can see immediately that Figure 4.8 is not as "wide" as Figure 4.7; that is, there is not as much dispersion along the horizontal axis, which reflects the fact that the first eigenvalue (59,955.94) is larger than the third eigenvalue (12,719.98). Since the length of each eigenvector is given by the square root of the eigenvalue associated with it, we can see that the first eigenvector is $(59,955.94)^{1/2} = 244.86$ units long, which is about twice as long as the third, which is $(12,719.98)^{1/2} = 112.78$ units long. This means that the configuration in the first three dimensions is shaped something like a squashed football or egg, being wider than it is high, and higher than it is deep.

Viewing the configurations from the side shows then that some concepts which seem in the front view to be very close to each other are actually separated in the third dimension. *Happiness* and *joy*, for example, seem contiguous in Figiure 4.7, but are separated in Figure 4.8. *Depression* and *bad*, similarly, seem very close in the front view, but the side view shows them to be separated fairly widely.

While the visualizations, therefore, are very informative, and a large advance over analytic considerations of the eigenvectors one by one, they still do not tell the complete story, and, in our judgment, should never be the sole basis for judgments about the configuration or especially for later applied interventions into practical affairs. Moreover, it is important to understand that this objection is not specific to the scaling procedures described here, but applies with equal force to any system which can be devised, since there is no way that two eyes can view more than three dimensions simultaneously (see Figure 4.9).

The key word in this caution is "simultaneously," since it is possible to examine each pair of eigenvectors graphically and sequentially, that is, one pair after the next, as we have done here. The problem is, however, that the number of pairs of dimensions increases approximately as $\frac{1}{2}$ the square of the number of dimensions, so that, for example, 15-dimensional space will require 105 nonredundant pairwise plots. Although we would not rule out the possibility that later investigators may develop the ability to integrate these fragmentary pictures into a good understanding of the overall multidimensional configuration (see

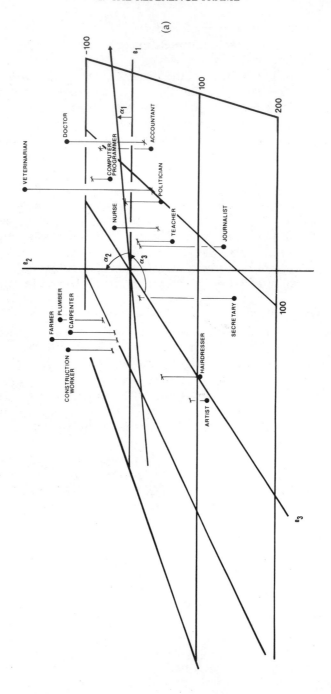

(a)

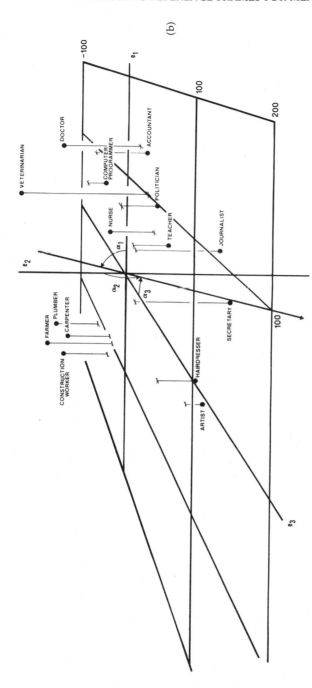

(b)

FIGURE 4.9 Three-dimensional projection of the neighborhood of 16 selected occupations for a sample of undergraduate university students. Axes e_1, e_2, and e_3 are the three first principal axes of the configuration. (a) The arrow (from lower left to upper right) represents the Treinan Socioeconomic Index values of the occupations. The angles α_1, α_2, α_3 which represent the orientation of this attribute relative to the three principal dimensions, respectively, are 26.2, 87.7, and 77.0. (b) The arrow (from upper right to lower left) represents the percentage of women in the occupations; for this attribute, the position angles are, respectively, 84.2, 121.0, and 63.6. (From Woelfel, Newton, Kincaid, & Holmes, 1979.)

Reichenbach, 1958), we have not been satisfied with our own ability to do so.

What we have preferred to do instead is to use the eigenstructure of the data as input to yet other mathematical operations which reveal certain aspects of the configuration that are theoretically and practically interesting in ways that do not involve the need for human intuition or the distortions of ignoring much of the available information. These "other mathematical operations" basically are equations which model psychological and cultural processes in the space, such as cross-cultural comparisons, conversations, and media and advertising campaigns. These equations, along with the derivations from the theories which suggest them, are presented in Chapters 6–9, along with worked examples.

There is no doubt that many social scientists in particular will see the movement from pictorial representations to mathematical representations as unfortunate, and, since the number of persons able to understand the mathematical language is much smaller than the number able to comprehend pictures, this is unfortunate. The problem is, however, that the amount of information contained in a typical noneuclidean multidimensional representation of a domain of concepts is too large to be conveyed easily in pictures or in the vernacular language. In fact, the equations are the theory, and the words surrounding them are not completely successful efforts to explain the mathematics.

CHAPTER 5

PRECISION OF MEASURE

Introduction

Other factors (such as cost and efficiency) equal, the quality of any measurement system can be seen to hinge mainly on two factors: precision and validity. Perhaps the most common didactic example used in teaching these notions to introductory social science students is that of a rifle in a fixed mount firing at a similarly fixed target. The rifle is likened to a measuring instrument, and each shot to a measurement made with the system. Precision and/or reliability is then likened to the tightness of the resulting shot group (i.e., the degree of dispersion around the mean location of a hit), and validity is referenced as the distance of the overall shot group from the center of the target. This example has some merit, since it does illustrate the prerequisite nature of precision for validity, since a measure clearly cannot be valid if it is not precise, but it can just as easily be precise but not valid, that is, off target.

There are very important problems with this analogy, however. First, clearly a rifle is not a measuring instrument, but in this example the target is the measuring device. It is, in addition, implicitly defined as a completely valid and reliable device as well. The validity of the target is assumed in the notion that the exact center of the target is in fact the "true" value of the variable in question, such that any deviation from the center is an unquestioned indication of the "invalidity" of the device. In this the example conforms exactly to the classical notion of convergent or concurrent validity, which suggests that an instrument is valid if its measured values conform or correlate exactly with those of a device already known to be valid. This leaves open, of course, the question of the grounds on which the original instrument is "known to be valid." As we suggested earlier, the notion of validity as the conformity of the outcomes of measurement to the "actual" or "true" values of a variable has no meaning. Since we have no access to the values of any variable independent of the act of measurement, at most we are able to observe the correlations between values obtained from one measurement system and those obtained by another measurement system. The only meaningful definition of validity, therefore, is the definition assigned to "construct" validity (American Psychological Association, 1966). As the APA suggests, a measure is valid when values obtained from its use are such as ought to be predicted by some established theory. If we find, for example, that a thermometer produces lower temperature estimates at the bottom of a refrigerator than at the top, we conclude that it is working as desired, since this outcome is predicted by the theory of gasses.

Any instrument or measurement system, then, is valid not when its results corresponds to "true" values, but rather when the pattern of measured values yielded by the system are nontrivially related to important theoretical or practical problems as defined by some human interest. Experience is constructed by the development of measurement instruments, and the validity of any measurement system must therefore be given ultimately by the utility of that system for human purposes, rather than by recourse to some "objective" correspondence of the outcomes to a "true" state of affairs. With that in mind, the validity of the system of measures presented in this book can only be judged in the context of the overall theoretical view of human cognitive process it yields and its utility for human purposes. For these reasons we shall defer any formal discussion of the validity of the present system in a traditional sense until the substantive theory and practical application of that theory are discussed.

In this chapter we shall examine the notion of precision as it applies to cognitive data in general, and to the measurement system suggested in this book in particular. Such a discussion is warranted because many social scientists are clearly convinced that the kind of precision which we claim can be achieved with these measures is impossible for these types of data in principle. Still others might claim that, even if possible, such precision is not required. In this chapter we shall try to show that precise measures of the type we have suggested are both necessary and possible in principle, and that levels of precision achieved with this measurement system in practice, although at a very early stage of development, already exceed those of typical practice by a wide margin. In the process, we shall try to show why contemporary practice has led capable investigators away from precise measures and maintained the use of imprecise category type scales for several decades even when superior instruments have been available.

Precision and Theory

For our purposes it will be convenient to define the precision of a measuring device as an inverse function of the size of the smallest interval it can reliably distinguish. In this definition, precision refers to discriminability, and reliability refers to repeatability. In this sense, precision and reliability are inversely related, since the cruder the distinction the instrument is called upon to make, the more confidently we can expect it to do so time after time. When we are referring to static measurements, therefore, precision refers to the smallness of the distinctions which can be made, and in dynamic measures, precision refers to the minuteness of events which can be discriminated from each other.

Viewed in this light, precision is important to theorists for two reasons. First, and most obviously, the more precision of measure available, the finer the class of events with which the theorist may deal, and the more precise the resulting engineering applications of theory. In this sense, improvements in precision of measure mean that the theorist may theorize about (and receive information about) events that were previously invisible, that is, undetectable by measurement.

Equally important is the scientifically well-developed idea of propogation of error (Gellert, Kustner, Hallwich, & Katner, 1977, p. 617). Although most social scientists learn early in their training that the standard error of the difference between two means is some function of the standard errors of each of the means and the sample sizes, very few have a quantitative grasp of the extent to which errors of original observations may multiply after several stages of manipulations of the raw scores have been carried out. Meyer (1975) gives a clear illustration of this for a very simple case. If, for example, one wishes to measure the difference in voltage between two dynodes, and did so first by measuring the voltage of each with a voltmeter capable of a precision of $\frac{1}{2}\%$, yielding values of $V_A = (2012 \pm 10)$ volts and $V_B = (1982 \pm 10)$ volts, then the voltage difference is $V_a - V_b = 28$ volts with an error of $(10^2 + 10^2)^{1/2} = 14$ volts, or 50%. Thus, even in this very simple case, measurement instruments capable of $\frac{1}{2}\%$ precision for direct readings yield fully 50% error when the difference between the two direct measures is taken.

This is vitally important, since all explanatory variables in theory are derived variables, that is, they are usually several stages of manipulation away from the primitive observed variables. If we examine a simple theory such as Newton's, for example, we may first measure the position of an object with a measurement system of relatively good precision, then measure it again at a later time with an equally good instrument. These are both direct measurements. We then find the distance the body moved by substracting the first from the second. This, of course, is a first-order derived variable.

With similarly precise measures, we may record the time of the first measure of position and the time of the second measure of position, which are also direct measures. We must then substract the first time from the second to determine the elapsed time, which is a first-order derived variable. To find the velocity of the moving body, we must then divide the distance moved (a first-order derived measure) by the elapsed time (a first-order derived measure). This new variable, velocity, is thus the ratio of two first-order derived variables, and may be considered a second-order derived variable, whose precision, by now, is diminished. The seriousness of the problem becomes clear when we realize that so far no explanatory variables whatsoever have been introduced into the theory; in order to do so, we must make yet additional measures of position and time to yield additional velocities. We substract these velocities from each other to yield changes in velocity as we add changes in time to changes in time to yield the total change in time. Acceleration is then derived as a ratio of these high-order derived variables change in velocity and change in time. These steps need to be repeated for another object before the relative accelerations of each may be expressed as yet another ratio, that is, the ratio of observed accelerations, which, depending on appropriate controls, may yield the explanatory variables mass and force. Clearly, if the direct measurements on which this structure of theory rests were not made with very high levels of precision, the values of the explanatory variables derived from the theory will be simply random numbers. It is clearly possible from this simple example to find reason why theory in the social sciences has languished, since measures of derived theoretical concepts are very seldom much more than random numbers in the human disciplines. It is not raw empiricism, then, or the neurotic desire of methodologists, but rather theory that demands great precision of measure. The more precise the direct measures, other factors equal, the higher the level of abstraction to which theories may rise, and the more powerful the conceptual system that can be developed.

Methods of Estimating Precision

In practice information about the precision and reliability of a measuring device is gained by making multiple repeated measures of the same set of variables and comparing the results of these multiple measures. The results of this procedure can be represented in several ways. Most common is the practice of presenting the mean value of such a series of measures along with the standard deviation if one is interested in the average precision of a single measure, or the standard error of measure if one is interested in the precision of the mean estimate. In a normal distribution, the standard deviation will represent the 68% confidence interval of the mean; that is, approximately 68% of all measures will fall within plus or minus one standard deviation of the mean. Other factors equal, the instrument which produced the smallest standard deviation or standard error is the most precise.

One of the "other factors" that must be equal, however, is the unit of measure or "least count" of the scale. If one of the devices measures, say, the size of a series of objects in meters, while the other measures in centimeters, obviously the scale which uses the larger unit will produce the (numerically) smaller standard deviation. Not so obvious, however, is the fact that the resulting standard deviations will not be simple multiples of the size of scale division or least count. It is not the case, for example, that the standard deviation of the scale using meters as the least count will be 100 times smaller than the scale which uses centimeters as a least count unless both measures are in fact perfectly error free. Nor is it the case that the functional relation between the two scales need be straightforward. If one is measuring the length of a room which is approximately 10 meters, for example, and one is prone to make errors on the order of magnitude of 1 or 2 centimeters, then we might expect about 50% of our measurements to yield values of 9 m and 50% to yield measures of 10 m. On the other hand, if the actual length of the room is closer to 9.5 m, then the same scale would be expected to yield values other than 9 m only in a very long series of measurements, since the likelihood of an error of 50 cm is so small. In the second case, the naive observer might be led to conclude he or she had no error of measure at all. The scale whose least count is 1 cm, however, will yield virtually the same error in both cases, which confounds the difficulties involved in comparing the precision of the scale whose least count is the meter and that whose least count is the centimeter.

This is not a new idea, but in fact is well known among engineers and scientists. As Wilson (1952) illustrates,

> Consider the case[1] where the least count is large compared withe source of error, say as large as 8. This might be the case in measuring with a millimeter rule the distance between two sharp lines on a glass plate. If the zero of the rule is set on one line and the position of the other read to the nearest millimeter, careful repetitions should always give the same value and all discussion of random errors becomes irrelevant because there are none. Even if it could be assumed that the normal law of error was operative, only one in about a hundred thousand observations would fall more than 4σ from the mean so that, unless the second line fell very nearly halfway between the two scale divisions, it is unlikely that a reasonable number of repetitions would give any different result. *Therefore averaging a large number of observations would not usually increase the accuracy.*

> (T)he process of rounding off has sacrificed considerable information. . . . Information concerning the limits of error is also lost. It can be shown mathematically that substantial gains in efficiency can be made by reducing the scale interval, or least count, to a fraction, perhaps one third or one fifth, of the standard deviation. In practice this means using sufficient magnification, or gain, and fine enough intervals so that *repeated* observations spread over perhaps ten to thirty intervals [pp. 251–252, emphasis added].

We might summarize the results of this argument by noting that the use of excessively course categories of scaling causes three serious problems.

1.   Precision is lost. (As Wilson later suggests, p. 252, on the order of one or so orders of magnitude is not unusual.)

2.   Information about the precision of the measure is lost. This is of real importance, since at the time when precision of measure is lost, information about how much precision remains is also lost.

3.   In many instances, the ability to gain additional precision by averaging multiple measurements is also lost.

The researcher who typically chooses a large least count—say a 5- or 7-point Likert-type or semantic differential-type scale—thus runs some interesting and important risks, since he or she suffers fairly serious losses of precision, and loses both the ability to know how imprecise the

---

[1] It is instructive to note that Wilson, a chemist, considers this an extreme case only for didactic purposes, but in social science it is commonplace for the least count to exceed the standard deviation by a factor of 8.

measure really is and the ability to improve that precision by standard procedures like averaging multiple measurements.

This is precisely the state of affairs in the human sciences, with only a few outstanding exceptions. Least counts usually range from about $\frac{1}{7}$ to $\frac{1}{2}$ the range of the variables measured, and statistics presented in defense of precision of measure in the best cases are underestimates of error and in the typical case are usually nearly worthless. This is particularly the case when, as is common, variables have been measured on nonstandard scales. In these cases, psychometricians have devised proportional reliability measures which are meant to be comparable across scales and across studies. This is a particularly acute problem for the human disciplines, since there are very few standards of measure and accordingly few scales which report their results in the same units. In such cases the problems are more serious than is the case when scales differ only in least count, because most often the transformations of scale units from scale to scale are completely unknown. This means that often one does not know which least count is smaller. It is easy to say (other factors equal) that a standard error of $\frac{1}{4}$ cm is smaller than a standard error of 50 mm, but it is not so obvious whether a standard error of .5 on a scale where 1 equals *strongly agree* and 5 equals *strongly disagree* is smaller than a standard error of .75 units on a scale where 1 equals *highly favorable* and 7 equals *highly unfavorable.*

The most common procedure used by social scientists to deal with this problem is to estimate the proportion of variance generated by the scale which is considered reliable. In practice this most often is accomplished by calculating the square of the correlation between two alternative sets of measures of the same data. This number may be interpreted directly as the proportion of reliable variance in the measure, and is often used as the sole measure of the precision of the measurement device. (The relative error, or ratio of the standard error to the mean, which is the proportional reliability measure more frequently used in physical science and engineering, is less frequently used in the human sciences.) Not only is this measure often used, but informal standards to which many social scientists subscribe usually designate $r = .9$ and $r^2 = .81$ arbitrarily as a "satisfactory" value, albeit one which is seldom achieved.

The problem with all such proportional measures of reliability is that without exception they tend to provide the highest values for the least precise scales. This is so because, while random error cannot be eliminated by increasing the size of the least count, evidence of such error is eliminated by this procedure. Thus scales whose least count is much too large for satisfactory scientific practice will usually yield the highest numerical estimates of proportional reliability. Put another way, one can always increase the ratio of reliable to unreliable variance by the simple expedient of reducing the total amount of variance detected by the scale. This is misleading, since, other factors equal, that scale is most precise which produces the most variance or discrimination among the objects scaled.

Not only do very imprecise measures appear satisfactory when proportional reliability measures are used exclusively, but in head-to-head comparisons, such measures will usually lead to selecting the worse scale over the better. Thus measures calculated to the nearest inch will produce lower proportional reliabilities than measures calculated to the nearest foot, other factors equal. This is of great importance in the present context, since the relatively crude Likert-type and semantic differential-type scales in common use will almost always produce higher estimates of proportional reliability than the much more precise scales advocated in this book due in part to their excessively large least count.

Three strategies suggest themselves for overcoming this problem. The first of these requires establishing as well as possible the functional relation between alternative scales so that the relative sizes of the smallest discriminable interval may be assessed. The second requires a determination of the absolute amount of reliable variance which can be generated by a scale. The third procedure requires transforming all scales to be compared into standard units[2] of measure—in this case, into the logical unit of information, bits—to determine the absolute amount of reliable information produced by the scaling operation. In the next section we shall apply these three procedures, along with other standard procedures drawn from both physical and social science methodology, to an assessment of the precision of the current social science measurement technology relative to typical applications of the ratio-type measures described earlier.

Precision of Ratio Judgments of Separation

There are two sets of measures whose precision is of greatest importance in the evaluation of the method of ratio judgments of separation. Of greatest importance are the pairwise dissimilarities judgments themselves, since these are the primitive variable from which the others are derived. Secondarily, the precision of the variables derived from the

---

[2] We do not refer here to standard or z scores, but to measures converted to a common metric.

pairwise separation judgments, particularly the coordinate values of their position in the mutidimensional Riemann space, needs to be evaluated. Since developments in this area have been rapid, however, estimates of the precision of current technology are likely to become dated rapidly, and so we shall be careful to discuss the factors on which precision of measures within the system might be expected to depend.

Prefiltering

It is important at the outset to understand that precision and sensitivity go hand in hand, and so the very precise scales discussed here are quite sensitive to ambient circumstances. In a typical conventional Likert-type scale, for example, the most massive disturbance from outside the system can have only limited effect on the mean value observed, since the range of variation permitted by the scale is so restricted. Since a typical Likert- or semantic differential-type scale is only formatted to 1 digit, no event conceivable could result in the accidental inclusion of a value more than twice the mean measured value if the mean lay somewhere near the middle of the scale. In a typical ratio judgment scale, however, which is formatted to 5 digits, accidental events can easily result in the erroneous recording of values many, perhaps even thousands, of times greater than the measured mean value of the variable.

Beyond any reasonable doubt, in our experience, the most common source of such catastrophic events is clerical error, particularly in keypunching. In a Likert-type scale, an error of keypunching might lead to placing a 9 where a 1 was intended by the respondent, an error of a factor 9. But in a typical ratio judgment of separation procedure, offshifting of a column can easily result in changing an intended value of one to a recorded value of 90,001 or an error of a factor of 90,000. Since a typical 100-case study can yield 1400 or more punched cards, such errors are fairly commonplace, even when great care has been exercised. Similarly, failure of a single individual to read the instructions for the questionnaire can lead to the inclusion of a great many values which are markedly different from the means of the variables.

While careful inspection of input data is essential in any case, the effects of such catastrophic errors can be reduced greatly by the simple expedient of setting a maximum value beyond which values are not allowed to enter analysis. Users have typically set maximum values at about 50 times the value of the criterion pair or standard of measure, so that, for a criterion pair of modulus 100, values greater than 5000 would be deleted from further computations. At 100 cases, such a strategy usually has no effect at all on most pair-comparison mean values, but occasionally will result in the reduction of percent relative error from as much as 70% to levels of about 10 to 20%. In practice, such a strategy results in a negligible loss in total information, since intentional judgments of dissimilarities more than 50 times the criterion pair almost never occur. In an extensive study of over 900 subjects, Gordon (1976) found that setting a maximum value of only five times the criterion pair led to the deletion of only about .12% of the reported values. Our own unsystematic observations have led us to suspect that beginning users often have the tendency to "overfilter" their data, but then tend to allow higher maximum values as their confidence in the scaling procedure grows with continued use. While some filtering is almost always called for, particularly in very small data sets, great caution should be used in the deletion of any values from any data sets, and users ought to be aware of physical practice in this domain, such as Chauvenet's criteria (Wilson 1952, pp. 256–258; Meyer, 1975, pp. 17–18). The most serious error which can typically result from careless filtering can lead to falsification of hypotheses on a purely artifactual basis. If we consider the case of a respondent in a panel design experiment, for example, who lists a pairwise difference as 6000, then, in a subsequent measurement, revises his or her estimate to 4000, we can see how a maximum value filter set at 5000 could lead an investigator to believe the mean value has increased when it has actually decreased, since the respondents initial value will be deleted when the second value will be included. While the typical social researcher might balk at the clerical burden, we strongly recommend that, in precise experiments, all raw values should be visually scrutinized insofar as this is possible.

Precision of Mean Separations

Gillham and Woelfel (1977) provided early evidence for the precision of the mean separation matrix in an experiment conducted in a sociology department of a large midwestern university. There, 29 graduate students filled out a Galileo™-type pair-comparison instrument which asked them to estimate the pairwise dissimilarities among 19 faculty members in the department. The standard of measure was the distance between two members of the senior faculty, and the modulus was set at 10. No maximum value filter was set. The administration was repeated 16 weeks later, and again 6 weeks following the second administration. Correlations among mean dissimilarities across contiguous time periods was .71. By assuming no actual change in the students' perceptions of the faculty (which Gillham and Woelfel argue is particularly unlikely under the circumstances prevailing in the department during the period over which measurements were made), this would indicate that about half the variance in the dissimilarities matrix was reliable.

As we have suggested, however, proportional reliability figures are quite misleading, and so it is appropriate to estimate the absolute information gained by the procedure relative to other possible procedures. Gillham and Woelfel measure several other variables in their study using 9-interval semantic differential-type scales, and their reliability coefficients calculated in the standard way range between .97 and .99, yielding proportions of reliable variance ranging from .94 to .98.

Although the ratio-scaled measures were formatted to 5 digits in this study, no number greater than 3 digits was observed, and so we conservatively estimate that only 3-digit numbers were possible in this study. We also assume that, if respondents had only been asked to place any arbitrary numbers in the same blanks, all numbers would be equally probable. Since there are 1000 three-digit numbers and 171 pair comparisons in the matrix, the maximum amount of information which could be conveyed by the matrix (in bits) is

$$H = (\ln 1000/\ln 2)171 = 1704 \text{ bits.}$$

On assuming the underlying dissimilarities were actually perfectly stable and that all deviations from a correlation of 1.0 are the result of unreliability of measure, then only half this information is reliable, which leaves a net sum of reliable information of $171(\ln(.5 \times 1000)/\ln 2) = 1533$ bits.

If we assume the semantic differential scales to be completely reliable, then the amount of information that could have been conveyed in the dissimilarities matrix using semantic differential scales would be

$$H = (\ln 10/\ln 2)171 = 568 \text{ bits.}$$

This means that, even if the ratio procedures were only 50% reliable, they could still generate $1533/568 = 2.70$ times as much reliable information as could the 10-point semantic differential scales, even if the semantic differential scales contained no random error whatever. This point is increasingly salient when one realizes that the Gillham and Woelfel study included only 29 cases, and so random error ought to be expected to be very high, while we have attributed no random component whatever to the semantic differential scales. An increase in the sample size, therefore, will yield increasing precision for the ratio judgments of separation, but would add none to the semantic differential scales.

This tendency was illustrated by Gordon (1976) who carried out an elaborate experiment using just under 1000 subjects in 9 independent treatment groups, in each group varying either the standard of measure or the modulus. With cell sizes in the dissimilarites matrices averaging just under 90 cases, Gordon found (1976): "(A)s the difference between the criterion pair was increased from 10 to 25, 50 and 100 units, the resulting (size of the) structural space was increased yet the interrelationships of the concepts to each other remained essentially the same. The extent of this similarity was truly exceptional with the treatment intercorrelations ranging from .933 to .988 [p. 70]." Gordon utilized a special procedure for setting maximum values, which ranged in the different treatments from 50 to 600. By always assuming the most conservative combinations, this means that the amount of reliable information produced at about 90 cases in the Gordon study ranged from a low of $\ln(50 \times .93^2)/\ln 2 = 5.43$ bits per cell to a high of $\ln(400 \times .93^2)/\ln 2 = 8.54$ bits per cell (assuming that the *lowest* reliability estimate Gordon made—.93—is the correct one). Since the maximum amount of information obtainable from a 10-point scale is 3.32 bits, this means that, in Gordon's study, the Galileo™-type procedures produced between $100(5.43/3.32) = 164\%$ and $100(8.54/3.32) = 257\%$ as much reliable information per cell as is possible with 10-point semantic differential-type scales, even if those semantic differential scales are assumed to be completely free of any random error at all.

Although informative, none of the previous studies were designed specifically to evaluate the relative performance of ratio judgments of separation scales and Likert-semantic differential-type scales. Danes and Woelfel (1975) describe a study in which such comparisons were explicitly made. In this study, 11 public figures were rated on three 7-interval semantic differential-type scales, good–bad, favorable–unfavorable, and positive–negative, by 50 undergraduate students at a large midwestern university. These 11 political figures, along with the end point descriptors of the semantic differential scales (i.e., good–bad, positive–negative, and favorable–unfavorable) were then included in a 17-concept paired-comparison instrument. Subjects were given the criterion pair good–moderate with modulus set at 50 and asked to relate all pairwise judgments to that standard. All 50 respondents filled out the paired-comparison instrument and rated the public figures on all three semantic differential scales. After a 5-week interval, all subjects again filled out both instruments. Test–retest correlation for the mean separations was .86, which, at 50 cases, lies between that found by Gillham and Woelfel and by Gordon. The correlations between the absolute values of the differences between each time 1 separation and its time 2 counterpart and the magnitude of the average of those separations was .60, which indicates that the larger values were somewhat less stable than the smaller values. (No maximum value filter is reported.)

The three semantic differential scales were averaged to produce a single evaluative measure of the public figures. This measure correlated with itself across the 5-week interval .99, which, by traditional standards in social science would be considered excellent. By contrast, the .86 figure given for the mean separations would be slightly below the arbitrary .90 cutoff figure considered satisfactory. The obvious conclusion—that the semantic differential scales are more precise than the ratio judgments of separation scales—which conventional practice would require, however, is completely wrong, as further analysis shows.

The mean separations matrix was entered into the Galileo™ version 3.0 computer program, and the correlation between the coordinates of the 11 public figures on the first dimension of the resulting Riemann space and their average evaluative scores from the semantic differential-type instrument was found to be .97. This indicates that the evaluative attribute lies at an angle of only 14 degrees from the first axis of the Riemann space and so for most purposes they may be taken as equivalent. Since this is the case, the first dimension of the space and the evaluative semantic differential instrument may be taken as alternative scales measuring the same attribute, and, since the same set of objects is arrayed on both scales, the relative sizes of the least count can be estimated. Danes and Woelfel estimate the slope between these scales as 17.16 by assuming that the value ±3 on the semantic differential scale was equivalent to the average absolute coordinate of the six evaluative descriptors on the first dimension of the space, which was 51.5. As Danes and Woelfel (1975) report,

Excluding the six evaluative descriptors, i.e., using only the eleven political figures yielded a variance of 241.58 for the transformed (semantic differential) evaluative measures and a variance of 678.75 for the evaluative coordinate (dimension) which indicated that for only the eleven political figures, the variance for the evaluative coordinate was almost three times as large as that for the (semantic differential) evaluative measures. A test for the significance of the difference in correlated variances ($r = .90$) yielded a t of 5.2 ($df - 9$) which was significant beyond the .05 level.

Using all the conceptions scaled, the variance for the 17 conceptions arrayed on the transformed (semantic differential) evaluative measures equalled 1146.565 while the variance for the identical conceptions on the evaluative coordinate equalled 1427.604. A test for the significance of the difference in correlated variances ($r = .97$) yielded a t of 7.76 ($df = 15$) which was significant beyond the .05 level. As noted above, the (semantic differential) stability coefficient equalled .99, thus the amount of stable variance in the semantic differential measure equalled (.98)(1146.565) or 1123.63. Further, the stability coefficient for the evaluative coordinate (dimension) equalled .97; thus the amount of stable variance for this scale equalled (.94)(1427.604) or 1341.95 which indicated there was almost 20% more stable variance in the evaluative coordinate [i.e., the first dimension—ed.] than in the (semantic differential) evaluative measure. In other words, the first coordinate (dimension) alone accounted for almost 20% more of the stable variance than did the (entire semantic differential) measure [pp. 10–11].

The authors go on to show that the first three dimensions of the 16-dimensional space account for about twice as much reliable variance as does the averaged semantic differential instrument totally. It should be pointed out as well that, like the previous examples, this analysis bends over backward to lend extra help to the traditional semantic differential-type format; at every stage the most conservative estimates of reliability are applied to the ratio judgments, while the most liberal standards are applied to the semantic differential scale. In the case of the regression estimates of the semantic differential scale, for example, no error due to the estimate is included, although the r^2 for this equation is .936, which means the reliable variances are overestimated for the semantic differential scale. Although several dozen more studies could be presented here, in none of them, by any combination of methodological slant we could devise, could the category scales be made to perform as precisely as the ratio judgment scales. The consistent pattern of all available evidence indicates that the mean separation matrix produced by the method of ratio judgments of separations contains quantitatively more precise and reliable information than can be produced by any other psychometric device yet tested, including the most commonly used instruments.

Two other issues ought to be considered before considering the precision of the coordinates derived from these mean dissimilarities. The first of these is the convenience with which change of scale operations can be accomplished using the procedures described here. Gordon, in the work mentioned, varied the pair of conetpts used as a standard across the nine treatment groups in his study, and the modulus assigned to these pairs, as we have noted. As we have already pointed out, he found the similarity of structure across these treatments "truly exceptional" (Gordon, 1976, p. 9). Since Gordon used two different standard pairs, and within each pair used four different moduli (10, 25, 50, and 100), we are able to make two separate measures of the linearity of change of scale resulting from change of modulus. This can be accomplished by fitting the function between the modulus and the trace of the solution. The trace represents the total variance in the matrix, and, if the change of scale is linear, should be related to the modulus as

$$T = ax^2,$$

where T is the trace of the scalar products derived from the dissimilarities matrix, a is a constant term, and x is the value of the modulus. Gordon used two criterion pairs, with four moduli in each, so that two separate tests of this hypothesis are possible. In the first case, using a pair of concepts that are widely separated in their domain, the linear equation

$$\sqrt{y} = a + bx$$

fit with a r^2 of .9994, and in the second case, using a pair of concepts not so widely separated in the same domain, the same equation fit with $r^2 = .9989$. Fitting a power curve to the same data yielded an exponent in the first case of 1.999 where a coefficient of 2 was expected and no increase in the r^2 value. In the second case, the exponent was 1.666, indicating a slight logarithmic rolling off of the scores at high values. This equation fit the data with $r^2 = .9995$.

These results are very useful, since they show that changing the modulus score produces a very nearly linear change in the values, with a slight logarithmic rolling off of high scores, a result which is consistent with previous work in magnitude estimation scales (Shinn, 1974). The reason the rolling off is noted in the second case and not in the first is most likely due to the considerably higher numerical values respondents must report when the ruler they use is small relative to the data, as it is in the second case. In sum, the picture drawn by these data is one of extremely well-behaved scales with properties virtually identical to scales typical of physical science and engineering practice.

The second point worth considering is that the extra precision and utility of these measures is not paid for by means of any appreciable increase in either respondent burden or nonresponse rate. As Gordon (1976) points out, most of the subjects were able to fill out the 78 pairs in an average time of 15 to 20 minutes.

Similarly, in an independent study, Gordon and DeLeo reported that subjects complete a 105 pair-comparison instrument in an average of less than 20 minutes (Gordon and DeLeo, 1976). These results are consistent with our own experience with the instruments, which seem to indicate that the response burden and completion rates for ratio judgments are about the same as more traditional instruments regardless of population from which the respondents are sampled. In a telephone survey of a simple random sample of residences from the telephone directory of a mid-sized eastern U.S. city, of those who agreed to be interviewed, 98% completed a 105 pair-comparison instrument about their perceptions of a medium sized state university in an average time of less than 15 minutes. This is consistent with the experience of Wallace (1979) who observed no difference in response rate between two otherwise identical instruments mailed to a sample of midwestern dairy farmers when one used ratio judgments to estimate the separations among 105 pairs of concepts related to dairy farming and the other used 5-interval Likert-type scales to estimate the same set of dissimilarities. Similarly, Kokinakis, using a 105 pair-comparison instrument dealing with the Women's movement, observed a mean administration time of 18 ± 7 minutes for a random sample of 100 telephone calls in a medium-sized midwestern U.S. city (Kokinakis, 1979). In general, we are aware of no evidence that the ratio judgment procedure substantially increases either the respondent burden, the costs of research, the completion time or the nonresponse rate when used in otherwise comparable studies. On the contrary, there appears to be substantial evidence that ratio judgments of separation used in a complete pair-comparison design produces more reliable information per respondent minute (or per experimenter dollar) than any other psychometric procedure. This is, of course, in correspondence with the fourth and fifth principals of Chapter 1, which require a maximally efficient coding system.

Precision of Coordinates

Since the coordinates of concepts are straightforward linear transformation of the measured dissimilarities, their precision is itself an analytic function of the precision of the raw measures. Nonetheless, the problem of how many reliable independent dimensions are required to array typical cognitive data has been of real substantive importance to psychologists (Barnett & Woelfel, 1979), and since the coordinate values provide the foundation for higher order calculations of derived theoretical variables, it is well worthwhile to present some evidence as to their precision here. Barnett (1972) presented the first direct evidence of this sort. He measured the perceived separations among a set of 16 environmental issues across a 2-week interval for some 300 undergraduate students at a large midwestern university, and took random subsamples of matched individuals of sizes 25, 50, 75, and 100 from the 2-point panel study. Canonical correlations among the coordinate values stabalized at about .9 at 75 cases, even though the 2-week interval was particularly turbulent, including the U.S. invasion of Cambodia and the Kent State killings.

The question of the stability of the dimensions of cognitive processes is confounded, however, by the jacobian transformation utilized to generate the coordinates. This procedure always identifies the principal axes of the configuration, and the orientation of these axes is dependent on the overall shape of the configuration at each time period. Changes in the dissimilarities relations of only one or several of the concepts scaled can result in shifts of all the coordinate values for purely artifactual reasons, therefore, and this artifactual variance must be transformed away by a "procrustean" rotation or rigid body rotation prior to precise estimation of their coorientation (Woelfel, Holmes, & Kincaid, 1979). Although such transformations have been discussed extensively in the psychometric literature, insofar as we know no operational scaling program could solve the procrustean problem for multidimensional Riemannian spaces in which some subset of the concepts were known to be stable while others were known to exhibit change until as late as early 1979. Barnett's early software (Galileo™ version 2.0) could rotate only up to six real dimensions to congruence, and even these rotations were subject to some minor error, most likely of the order of 10% or so.

In the study reported earlier, Danes and Woelfel computed the correlations and angles among the dimensions of the domain of 11 public figures and 6 evaluative descriptors. These figures, which were calculated from coordinates rotated to least-squares best fit with a later ver-

TABLE 5.1

Correlations (Cosines) and Angles among the Dimensions of the Domain of 11 Public Figures and 6 Evaluative Descriptors[a]

Dimension[b]	Angle (degrees)	Over time correlation	(Correlation)^2
1	14.0	.97	.94
2	35.9	.81	.65
3	30.7	.86	.74
4	45.6	.70	.49
5	40.5	.76	.57
6	50.2	.64	.40
7	67.7	.38	.14
8	71.3	.32	.10
9	68.3	.37	.14
10	63.9	.44	.19
11	55.9	.56	.31
12	87.7	.04	.02
13	90.8	−.014	.00
14	89.4	.011	.00
15	106.9	−.29	.08
16	94.2	−.074	.00

[a] Adapted from Danes and Woelfel (1975).
[b] The dimensions are rank ordered in terms of their absolute eigenroot value.

sion (Galileo™ version 3.0), still contain the troublesome error mentioned (which is due to the fact that such rotations are not commutative and hence depend on the order of pairwise rotations) but include rotations of all the axes, real as well as imaginary, and are presented in Table 5.1.

Even including this artifactual error component, the dimensions exhibit good stability—even the imaginary dimensions—sufficient to show unequivocally that this domain is both noneuclidean and multidimensional. Gillham and Woelfel (1977), in the study of university faculty described earlier, also report correlations among dimensions across the three time periods of their study. (See Table 5.2.) Although they present evidence regarding only the first three real dimensions of this domain, and although their early version software also includes the inaccuracy mentioned, they do introduce an alternative method of assessing the stability of the dimensions. Each of the three dimensions of the domain of perceptions of the faculty are used as independent variables in a pair of regression equations whose dependent variables are the semantic differential-type scales on which the political positions and degree of quantitativeness of research of these same faculty have been rated by the same sample members. The regression coefficients resulting may be seen as the projections of these attributes on the dimensions of the domain. Table 5.3 shows these coefficients to be very stable across the three time periods, showing at once that the dimensions themselves are quite stable, as are their orientations with regard to the attribute scales.

Gordon (1976) presents visual evidence of the stability of the first three real dimensions of his study (described earlier) in Figure 5.1. Figure 5.1 plots each of these conditions on common coordinates in order of increasing trace size. The relatively straight radial paths of the

TABLE 5.2

Correlations and Angles among the Dimensions of the Domain of 19 University Faculty for 3 Time Periods[a]

Dimension	$t_1 - t_2$		$t_2 - t_3$		$t_1 - t_3$	
	Correlation	Angle	Correlation	Angle	Correlation	Angle
1	.86	30.7°	.82	34.9°	.75	41.4°
2	.51	59.3°	.41	65.8°	.26	74.9°
3	.62	51.7°	.44	63.9°	.07	85.6°

[a] Adapted from Gillham and Woelfel (1977).

TABLE 5.3

Unstandardized Regression Coefficients from Multiple Regression of Qualitative Position upon Perceived Position

	Axis	t_1	t_2	t_3
Political judgments	1	−.16	−.20	−.13
	2	−.02	−.07	.02
	3	.07	−.11	−.05
	$R =$	.91	.93	.92
Quantitativeness judgments	1	.11	.19	.15
	2	.22	.16	.11
	3	−.27	−.28	−.06
	$R =$	.80	.79	.75

** $p < .01$, one tailed.

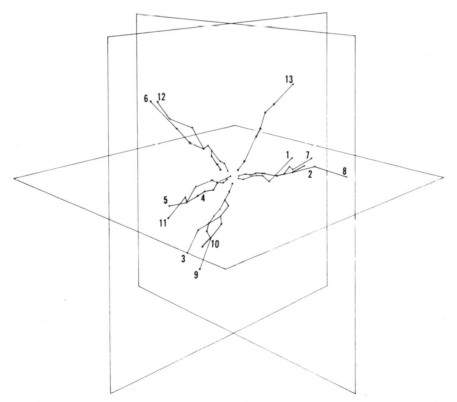

FIGURE 5.1 Three principal planes of a space of television shows and their formats for nine groups on common coordinates in order of size of trace (Gordon, 1976).

concepts conveys the accurate impression of a space which expands under change of scale while retaining its overall shape. (This is in spite of the fact that Gordon's early version Galileo™ software is prone to the same error already mentioned.) Later version Galileo™ computer programs (versions 4.5 and later) solve the problem of commutativity of rotation by carrying out near infinitesimal rotations (actually 1 degree) iteratively until the sum of squared discrepancies among identical concepts across datasets is minimized, and are capable at their default values of solutions accurate to $\frac{1}{2}$ degree. Woelfel *et al.* (1979), collected pairwise separations among 15 common occupation names from over 180 university students in two diverse states (Michigan and Hawaii) over a 2-year interval. Table 5.4 shows the correlations and angles between corresponding dimensions among three subsets of these data, Michigan 1976–1977, Michigan 1977–1978, and Hawaii 1977–1978, respectively. These rotations, carried out with Galileo™ version 5.1 computer program, show extremely close correspondences among the data sets, and show unambiguously that all data sets are highly multidimensional and reliably noneuclidean. These data strongly contradict the widespread and conventional psychometric practice of monotonically transforming data of this sort until only a few (usually three) real dimensions remain in the solution, since a very large body of precise and

TABLE 5.4

Dimension (Column Vector) Correlations between Time 1 (Michigan, 1977–1978) and Time 2 (Michigan, 1978–1979)

Dimension	t_1 Magnitude	t_2 Magnitude	Correlation	Angle
1	315.27	332.38	.992677	6.9
2	256.34	274.44	.989647	8.3
3	207.14	207.40	.978463	11.9
4	187.05	181.85	.974833	12.9
5	136.35	146.70	.904189	25.3
6	111.95	135.60	.940643	19.8
7	110.44	142.13	.941392	19.7
8	90.57	99.61	.719844	44.0
9	71.03	109.04	.962636	15.7
10	52.34	96.29	.917138	23.5
11	.00	12.32	—	—
12	.86i	.00	.394126	66.8
13	33.95i	21.36i	.470628	61.9
14	73.00i	74.71i	.732210	42.9
15	87.47i	90.78i	.833769	33.5

reliable information can be seen in the later dimensions, including the imaginary dimensions.

The stability of the dimensions of the space is only one way the precision of the coordinates can be illustrated. Equally interesting is the stability of the concepts themselves within the space. Since the position of each concept is represented by a vector of coordinates in the space, the positional stability of each concept across alternative measurements can be shown by the correlation between the rows representing the same concept across the different measurement events. Alternatively, since these correlations represent the cosines of the angles included between the position vectors of the concepts, these angles may be presented as a more intuitive indication of the precision of location of the concepts. Table 5.5 shows both correlations and angles between corresponding position vectors across alternative years and sites of the occupational study mentioned previously. As is evident, the general locations of the concepts are very precisely determined by these procedures. Moreover, the rotation system already described does not compel concepts to remain in the same spot if they have exhibited "true" motion over a measurement interval, as Table 5.6 illustrates. In the same experiment, four separate treatments were applied to the data. In the control situation, respondents read a fictitious press release announcing the

TABLE 5.5

Concept Position (Row) Vector Correlations between Time 1 (Michigan, 1977–1978) and Time 2 (Michigan, 1978–1979)

Concept		t_1 Magnitude	t_2 Magnitude	Correlation	Angle
1	Accountant	135.13	148.25	.974388	13.0
2	Teacher	79.96	118.13	1.015541	13.0
3	Hairdresser	173.73	162.77	.992251	7.1
4	Doctor	169.11	164.18	.982878	10.6
5	Secretary	121.93	136.29	.958856	16.5
6	Politician	137.54	150.39	.948095	18.5
7	Journalist	129.34	141.58	.979035	11.8
8	Carpenter	124.27	141.67	.983564	10.4
9	Farmer	144.29	163.10	.982833	10.6
10	Plumber	134.86	161.10	.994420	6.1
11	Artist	145.09	156.46	.982668	10.7
12	Construction	147.21	153.30	.999735	1.3
13	Veterinarian	148.16	170.42	.964460	15.3
14	Computer	133.28	142.02	.957581	16.7
15	Nurse	131.68	136.04	.908069	24.8

5. PRECISION OF MEASURE

TABLE 5.6

Distances Moved from Control Condition for 15 Occupations across 4 Conditions

Concept	03–07	03–11	07–11	03–07–11
01	33	37	28	50
02	$10i$	$22i$	17	$15i$
03^a	189^b	246^b	105	142^b
04	41	33	45	31
05	37	$27i$	29	11
06	40	38	46	39
07^a	111^b	136	103^b	49^b
08	39	$23i$	43	62
09	37	55	50	58
10	42	41	34	38
11^a	99	166^b	79^b	44^b
12	22	$7i$	7	36
13	19	35	43	49
14	29	$7i$	22	46
15	27	17	36	42
Mean motion x	36.54	36.77	38.85	39.75
Standard deviation	21.12	32.76	23.53	15.36

[a] Free concept.
[b] Manipulated concept.

publication of a "dictionary of occupational titles" which made no specific reference to any occupation. In the first experimental condition, a single sentence ("Did you know, for example, that the occupations hairdresser and artist are highly similar") was imbedded in the news-release. In the second condition, the sentence "Did you know, for example, that the occupations hairdresser and journalist, for example, are highly similar?" was included instead of the previous sentence. In the third treatment, the imbedded sentence said "Did you know, for example, that the occupations artist and journalist are highly similar," and in the final condition, the imbedded sentence said "Did you know, for example, that the occupations hairdresser, artist and journalist are highly similar?" While these are very subtle manipulations, as Table 5.6 shows, in nearly every case the manipulated concepts exhibit less stability than the occupations not mentioned. Table 5.6 shows the Riemann-ian distance each concept has moved from its position in the control condition. This distance is given by the square root of the sum of the squared differences between coordinates of the concept in the control and treatment condition. As Table 5.6 shows, although the treatments were very subtle, nonetheless there is ample precision of measure to identify and measure the motions of the manipulated concepts.

Summary

In a relativistic model such as the present one, evaluation of the quality of a scaling instrument in terms of its inherent correspondence to the phenomena which it is intended to measure is inappropriate, and other criteria need to be devised. While the foremost such criterion, that is, usefulness of the outcomes of scaling for some felt human interest, will be discussed later, initially this chapter has argued that, other factors equal, a scaling instrument is useful in proportion to the amount of reliable information it can provide per unit cost. The data examined in this chapter show that the ratio judgments of separation method suggested in Chapter 2 typically provide greater absolute magnitudes of precise and reliable information in typical applications without significant increases in cost or respondent burden.

CHAPTER 6

A CALCULUS
OF COGNITION

Introduction

As we have seen, the process of relativization requires that a standard of measure and a reference frame be established before relations among the elements of experience may be described, and procedures for the construction of both standards of measure and mathematical reference frames have been reviewed in Chapters 4 and 5. Once this work has been accomplished, comparisons of relations of elements within the reference frame are possible. In physical laboratory experiments in which laboratory coordinate frames are physically attached to measurement instruments, many repeated observations across time may easily be arrayed within the same reference frame, and comparison of observations becomes well defined. Similarly, when sufficiently precise rules for constructing such coordinate frames are available, other workers in other laboratories can create essentially identical reference frames, and so comparisons between the observations of different observers at different times are thereby simplified.

The state of knowledge in the social sciences, however, is not yet sufficiently advanced to make possible the construction of identical reference frames for different workers, or even to guarantee the identity of the reference frame used by a single observer with the reference frame generated by the same observer at a later time if any aspects of the experiment whatsoever have been changed. This is not due to any inherent characteristics of the measurement situation of physical and social scientists, but follows rather from the inadequate knowledge already accumulated about the stability of relationships among reference objects in the social sciences. If we recall that Einstein stipulates that the distance between two points on any rigid body may be taken as a standard unit, we can realize that insufficient data have yet been collected by social scientists to determine unambiguously which of the complexes of psychological or cultural objects ought to be considered rigid. In general, a body (or configuration of points) may be considered rigid if the distances among the points remain invariant. We can consider the relative invariance of interpoint distances in two general cases: cross observer invariance and over-time invariance. In order to serve as a proper yardstick, a standard ought to exhibit both forms of invariance to a high degree. As is the case with all measurements, though, invariance is a relative thing, and, as Edwards points out, there is no truly rigid body in all the universe (Edwards, 1933). Variability in the distance between points chosen as a standard measure may be thought of as *differences in scale*. Differences in scale generate artifactual differences in the measured values which result from the use of such scales.

A second problem which underlies much cognitive work is the problem of *differences in reference objects*. In a laboratory situation it is usually possible to maintain a set of arbitrary but conventional reference objects or to recreate a nearly identical set in an independent laboratory so that the set of reference objects may be held stable across observers and over time. But if one's work requires using accidental reference objects informally chosen by the population under study, one may sometimes find that different groups use different reference objects to describe the same phenomenon, or that the set of reference objects chosen changes over time.

A third difficulty refers specifically to the set of mathematical coordinates which are generated by the procedures described in Chapter 4. Since these axes are the principle axes of the configuration of points, the coordinates of all points will usually change even if only one of the points moves relative to the (rigid) set of remaining objects. This problem too can arise across groups or over time, and is closely related to the fact that the movement of a single point will usually change the location of the centroid of the set of points, thus changing the coordinates of all the points even though only one has moved relative to the others if the origin is forced through the centroid of the configuration, as it typically is. These problems of *orientation and origin* are basically problems of rotation and translation.

Of course there is no absolute way to resolve any of these three kinds of problems. But it is the case that choices of different solutions yields different constructions of "reality." The apparent hopelessness of the situation is quickly overcome, however, when we realize that any group of observers who adopt the *same* conventions for solving these problems will share an identical conception of experience to the extent to which the rules are clearly enough stated to be applied unambiguously by all members of the group. The set of stipulated solutions to these three problems may be thought of as *rules for making comparisons.* When applied to comparisons within a point in time, these rules establish what is technically called *statics,* and when applied to comparisons over time, they establish what is termed *kinematics* (the rule for describing motion and change).

Differences in Scale

As we saw in Chapter 4, a scale is established by designating the distance between two arbitrary points by some numerical value u, thus setting the size of the unit of the scale at 1. The procedure is usually accomplished in typical communication practice by means of instructions to respondents at the beginning of a questionnaire or interview. As is the case with any communication attempt, these instructions are sometimes misinterpreted by respondents. Two such misinterpretations are most common: First, there may be considerable variability among the sample members about the perceived dissimilarity between the criterion pair relative to the remaining dissimilarities in the set to be scaled. Second, due in part to the fact that many people have preconceived notions about what numbers should be considered "large" and "small," respondents may ignore the criterion number u suggested in the instructions and assign a different number to the criterion distance. In the first case, the result is equivalent to using several rulers of different lengths to measure any given distance, even though the rulers may be calibrated in the same numerical units; in the second case, the result is equivalent to using several rulers calibrated in different numerical units to measure any given distance. Typically, of course, both problems coexist in the same dataset. Both problems may be considered failures in objectivization (following Born, 1965) since they imply that different results will be obtained when different observers make measurements of the same experience.

If either or both of these problems occur randomly across sample members, and if the sample is large, it is easy to show that the mean scores will not be affected by either or both effects. Nonetheless it is the case that the standard errors of measure will be increased and the resulting loss in precision of measure can be costly if the effects are large. Furthermore, when these effects do not occur randomly, of course no increase in sample size will be sufficient to overcome the distortions introduced, and corrections must be made. It is always desirable, therefore, to assess the extent to which these effects may be present in the data so that adjustments can be made.

Choosing a rigid rod for a criterion pair requires information about the cross group and over-time invariance of the dissimilarities relation among the available criterion pairs. But as we have seen, selecting any pair of concepts and assigning a numerical value to their difference fixes the distance among them and attributes all variability among respondents to the remaining set of distances. Thus it is not possible to gain information about the separation between any pair of concepts once they have been chosen as a criterion pair. This means that after-the-fact adjustments are possible only if new information becomes available to the investigator. The most appropriate procedure, therefore, is to pretest several possible criterion pairs before the main study against yet another criterion pair (such as the "keep a 10-point scale in mind" procedure used by Gordon, 1976). Other factors equal, the pair of concepts which exhibits the smallest standard error is the pair which comes closest to being a "rigid rod" within the sample, and ought therefore to make a good criterion pair. As a result of the collective work of a body of scientists over time, sufficient information about the invariance of distances among concept pairs can be accumulated which makes such pretesting unnecessary. This is the situation which now prevails for most physical measurement: Long and collective investigations of the distances among physical "landmarks" has resulted in international agreement about suitable standards of measure for most physical domains. At least in part the absence of an equivalent body of information about the distances among psychological and cultural concepts lies at the root of difficulties in cross-cultural communication.

The second problem—the problem of attaching different numerical values to the same criterion distance—is more easily solved, and can be done after the fact. A simple procedure in use among communication workers is to include the criterion pair within the paired comparions list so that respondents are required to estimate the numerical value of the distance between the criterion pair. If any respondent writes a value other than the one assigned to this distance in the instructions, there is reason to suspect that he or she has misinterpreted or ignored the instructions and is therefore estimating the dissimilarities among the remaining set on a different scale. If we designate the numerical value assigned to the criterion pair by the respondent as u', and the numerical value assigned to the criterion pair by the investigator as u, then the scale has the unit u'/u instead of the expected unit. This is easily corrected, however, by multiplying every value estimated by the respondent (including the value of the criterion pair) by the ratio u/u'. This ratio is a scalar, and multiplication by a scalar represents change of scale. Once sufficient information about the relative distances among concepts used as criterion pairs in several different groups or cultures have been gathered, it becomes possible to readjust all such measures by exactly this procedure to yield well-behaved scales for cross-cultural measurements.

While these transformations are quite simple even in practice, they are important transformations and illustrate the decisive advantage of the cartesian (relative) measurement procedure presented here, since informed change of scale using traditional psychometric devices such as Likert-type and semantic differential scales is nearly impossible given the (unknown) reanchoring of these scales across stimuli. Even though the basic form of the traditional social-science scale has been in use since the 1930s, deliberate changes of scale are virtually absent from the literature in any area. (For a discussion of these points, see Hamblin, 1974, and Shinn, 1974.)

Controlling the Reference Objects

As we learned in Chapter 4, the reference frame can consist of any number of objects against which an object is judged. When measurements are made in more than one group or at more than one time, however, comparisons across groups or across time are not possible unless at least some of the reference objects are the same in all groups or in all time periods. But what does it mean to say that a set of objects is "the same" in two or more groups or time periods? Of course the fact that the set of objects are all designated by the same verbal symbol may be taken as initial evidence that the objects designated by those symbols are the same, but this is not a sufficient condition. For in fact the definition of any object or concept is given by its relationships with a set of other concepts according to the principle of relativization. This means, therefore, that a set of concepts is the same across two groups or across several time periods to the extent that the set of distances among those concepts remains invariant across the groups or times. Such relatively invariant structures or "rigid bodies" provide the basis for establishing cross-frame transformations, since they may be used as anchors for the coordinate system across groups or times. Basically the procedure to establish these transformations consists of finding the principle axes of the points of the rigid body within each group and then projecting the nonrigid or variable concepts onto these coordinates. In this way, the invariant substructures or rigid bodies are used as fixed constellations against which the changes in position of the free or variable concepts may be judged.

In field research, there is little choice but to search for such invariant substructures, and to the extent that many such substructures are identified and cataloged, our collective ability to determine cross-group and over-time transformations is enhanced. A classic example of such an empirical rigid body is the set of assumed bipolar adjectives good–bad, active–passive, and strong–weak. Osgood and his co-workers believed that these six generic concepts formed an invariant unit cross (like a child's jack) which formed the basis of the coordinate reference frame for all cognition. While there is insufficient empirical evidence to determine the extent to which these concepts remain invariant across time and across all subgroups, there is some evidence (as we noted in Chapter 4) that they do not form exactly a unit cross, and that there is fairly substantial variance in this structure across males and females, at least when measured in the context of human emotions. Figure 6.1 shows the difference in this substructure across males and females based on data taken from the emotions questionnaire described in Chapter 4. Note particularly that in neither the male nor the female group do these concepts form a unit cross, although their general configuration is close enough to this form to show how easily the correlational procedures used by Osgood and his followers could mistake them for such a figure. Note also that the overall structure of these six concepts is fairly different within the two samples, but again probably sufficiently similar that the correlational procedures might not detect the difference. However variable these six concepts may be, clearly the discovery of relatively invariant structures across cultural subgroups and time deserves high priority because of the crucial role they may play in the objectivization of cultural experiences across observers and over time.

Within the laboratory, however, the researcher can almost always define a stable or rigid subset of concepts by appropriate randomization procedures, since in the laboratory one frequently does not need to rely on preexisting or accidental reference objects. An example of the use of stable laboratory concepts will be discussed in the next section.

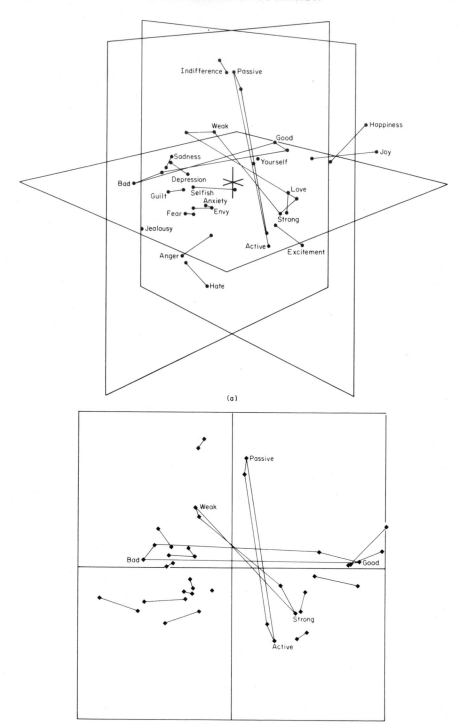

(a)

(b)

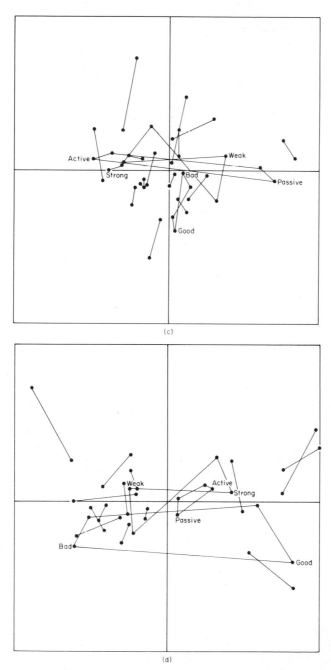

FIGURE 6.1 Cross sections of the space of emotions for male and female university students. Lettering designates male sample. (a) The first three dimensions of emotions and attributes for male and female university students. (b) The first principal plane of (a). (c) The second principal plane of (a). (d) The third principal plane of the same data.

Rotation and Translation

Once a stable subset of concepts has been discovered or established in the laboratory, it may be used as a basis for the transformation across multiple sets. As we said in Chapter 4, the basis for this process is the understanding that the stable subset of concepts will have two sets of coordinates; one in each of the two groups or times to be compared. The transformation which maps the coordinates of the stable set in one data set onto the coordinates of the same stable set in the second data set is the transformation which transforms away artifactual differences in the orientations of the two reference frames.

Since the set of primitive variables on which all other variables within this system of thought are based is the set of interpoint distances, it is appropriate to restrict ourselves to that set of transformations which will preserve these measured distances, which, of course, is the set of linear transformations. It can easily be shown that the set of distance-preserving or linear transformations includes only rotations and translations.

The set of rotations and translations required have as their intent the removal of spurious differences in the orientation of coordinate axes in multiple data sets. In this they must be distinguished from the set of "analytic" rotations (such as Varimax and Quartimax) familar to factor analysts. These "analytic" rotations have as their purpose arraying the concepts in a particular way with regard to the mathematical coordinates. What this way may be differs depending on the particular rotation scheme employed, but generally all aim at the production of what is usually called "simple structure" following Thurstone (1947). On the contrary, the "procrustes" rotations described here are indifferent as to how the configuration may be arrayed with regard to the mathematical coordinates, as long as the orientation of those concepts whose interpoint distance relations have not changed remains the same relative to the mathematical coordinates in all data sets. This problem has been carefully studied by psychometricians, and general solutions to the "orthogonal procrustes" problem have been presented independently by Cliff (1966) and Schönemann (1966). Mathematically, this problem may be described as the effort to find a linear transformation T such that

$$AT = B + e,$$

where A and B are any two coordinate matrices, and e represents an error term (usually defined as a least-squares error term) which is to be a minimum. Since the technical aspects of this procedure have been considered at great length in the psychometric literature, it will suffice here to point out that the transformation T can be seen as a series of pairwise rotations of axes, and the quantity to be maximized is generally taken as the trace of the scalar products matrix C, where $C = (AT) \cdot B$. The interested reader can easily prove that this procedure has the effect of minimizing the measured distance of each point in A from its counterpart in B. In effect, this transformation attempts insofar as possible to hold every point in the configuration as stable as possible across groups or over time. In the absence of some theoretical premise which provides a reason for assuming in advance that some of the concepts should be more or less likely than others to exhibit relative motion across groups or over time, this is an appropriate transformation. But when such information is available, modifications of the rotation procedure are required. In the case of a laboratory experiment, for example, in which some concepts have been manipulated while others have been controlled, it is obviously appropriate to assume that the relative motion observed ought to be attributed to the manipulated concepts rather than the control concepts. In this case it is appropriate to modify the rotation algorithm such that it attempts to minimize the relative motion of only the control concepts. This is simply a matter of rotating the coordinates until the trace of the scalar products of only the control concepts is set at a minimum. Figure 6.2 presents a worked example of such a procedure.

In the laboratory situation, the choice of a set of stable concepts is usually very straightforward, but in the case of nonlaboratory comparisons, whether cross group or cross time, there is no accepted rule, and the basis of the decision as to which concepts should be held stable must be made on theoretical grounds. In addition, the choice of an inappropriate rule can have devastating consequences for the development of further theory. A classic case in point is the historical debate over the Ptolemaic and the Copernican portrayal of the nature of celestial motion. Ptolemaic astronomy fixed the celestial coordinate system on the surface of the earth due solely to a philosophical belief that the earth should be taken as the center of the world, rigid and unmoving. Within this coordinate system (i.e., based on this rotation rule), celestial bodies described roughly circular paths around a fixed earth every 24 hours. The Copernican system, on the other hand, fixes the celestial coordinate system relative to the stars, and as a consequence of this rotation rule, the stars remain relatively fixed within the coordinate system and apparent motions are attributed to the movement of the earth and other bodies in the solar system. It is essential to understand that neither of these rotation rules is "correct," and the basis for preferring the latter to the former lies solely in the fact that a simpler theory of motion can be constructed for this coordinate system than for the other.

(a)   (b)

FIGURE 6.2 (a) Ordinary least-squares rotation with no free concepts. Space 1 (represented by triangles) was generated arbitrarily by assigning coordinates to the 5 numbered points. Space 2 (circles) is the same as space 1, but the coordinates of point 3 have been changed arbitrarily. Interpoint distances were regenerated from each of these sets of coordinates by equation (3.8). These two distance matrices were entered into a multidimensional scaling program (Galileo™ version 5.2 at SUNY at Albany) and rotated to common coordinates by an ordinary (unweighted) least-squares procrustes solution. Notice that concept 3 exhibits the largest motion, but that each of the other points exhibits motion as well. (b) Least-squares rotation with point 3 left free. Same data as (a) entered into Galileo™ version 5.2 with point 3 specified as free. In practice, the program does not include the free point's distance from itself across data sets in the total sum of squared distance between the spaces when checking goodness of fit. Translation to the centroid of all points except the free point(s) is performed prior to the rotation. Note that the program "correctly" finds that only point 3 has moved. (c) An ordinary least-squares unweighted rotation of 16 concepts at 4 points in time. Although concepts 10, 14, 15, and 16 have been manipulated between measurements, the concepts do not exhibit motions noticeably larger than the control concepts in this rotation. (d) Same data as (c), this time with concepts 10, 14, 15, and 16 specified as free concepts in the Galileo rotation. Notice particularly the dramatic movements of concepts 14 and 15 relative to the stable reference set.

Complex Coordinates

Although the mathematics of rotation is discussed carefully in the existing literature, none of the rotation schemes presented up until now are defined for Reimann spaces like those typical of communication practice. As we suggested earlier (Chapter 4), the coordinate reference frames underlying pair-comparison data taken by means of the ratio comparison rule usually have both real and imaginary coordinates. This does not pose any serious difficulty since, by definition, each coordinate axis of the reference frame is orthogonal to every other such axes. This means that, taken as a set, all the imaginary coordinate axes are independent of all the real axes. This makes it convenient to partition the coordinate system into its real and imaginary parts and to carry out the rotation scheme within each part, treating the imaginary components as if they were real. After rotation, the space may be "reassembled" by simply joining the (now rotated) real and imaginary components (Cushing, 1975, p. 262).

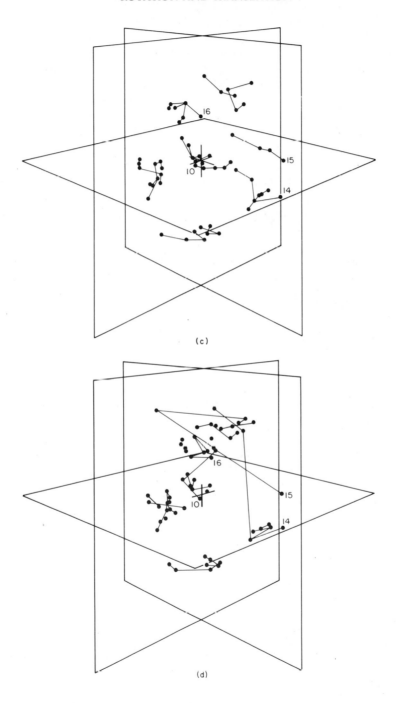

(c)

(d)

Equations of Motion

Once the rotation and translation rule has been fixed, the coordinate system constitutes a kinematic system within which motion and change take on precise definitions. Within this system, the meaning of any concept α is given by its position in the coordinate frame, and this, in turn, is defined in mathematical form as the position vector $R^{\mu}_{(\alpha)}$ shown in Figure 6.3. Change of meaning is given by any change in the length or orientation of the position vector. Figure 6.3 (adapted from Goldstein, 1950) illustrates the trajectory of the end point of a position vector over time. The vector $\Delta R^{\mu}_{(\alpha)}$ represents the average velocity vector across the interval of time Δt. The vector $\Delta R^{\mu}_{(\alpha)}$ represents the rate and direction with which the meaning of the concept (α) is changing, and is given mathematically by

$$\Delta R^{\mu}_{(\alpha)} = R^{\mu}_{(\alpha 1)} - R^{\mu}_{(\alpha 0)}, \tag{6.1}$$

and the average velocity $\bar{V}$ is given by

$$\bar{V} = \Delta R^{\mu}_{(\alpha)}/\Delta t. \tag{6.2}$$

Similarly, the instantaneous velocity of the attitude change is given by

$$V_{(t)} = dR^{\mu}_{(\alpha)}/dt, \tag{6.3}$$

and the instantaneous acceleration by the second derivative

$$a_{(t)} = dV/dt = d^2 R^{\mu}_{(\alpha)}/dt^2. \tag{6.4}$$

These partial differential equations take on a very convenient form, however, since the components of any concept across the reference axes

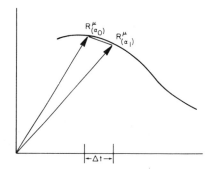

FIGURE 6.3 Illustration of the trajectory of the end point of the position vector $R^{\mu}_{(\alpha)}$ across an interval of time Δt (adapted from Goldstein, 1950).

are independent, such that their derivatives are additive, as

$$V_{(t)} = dR^{\mu}_{(\alpha)}/dt = dR^1_{(\alpha)}/dt + dR^2_{(\alpha)}/dt + \cdots + dR^r_{(\alpha)}/dt \qquad (6.5)$$

and

$$a_{(t)} = dV/dt = d^2R^{\mu}_{(\alpha)}/dt^2$$
$$= d^2R^1_{(\alpha)}/dt^2 + d^2R^2_{(\alpha)}/dt^2 + \cdots + d^2R^r_{(\alpha)}/dt^2. \qquad (6.6)$$

CHAPTER 7

KINEMATICS OF SELF

Introduction

The concept of self has played a central role in cognitive and social psychology in the twentieth century. In 1903, Cooley described the "looking glass self," a concept which has been a precursor of modern self-concept theory. The concept of the looking glass self captures two aspects of the self which form a basis for current concepts of self. The first of these is the self as actor or agency. This self, later designated the "I" by Mead (1934), represents the active component of the self. A second aspect of the self is the self as object. In Cooley's model, the self is viewed (through the reaction of the other) as an object of itself which may be defined as is any other object. The self as object Mead calls the "me." The self has an important duality in contemporary social psychological theory, since it can be at once the object of attention and the attender. Perhaps partly because of this, and despite its central role in social psychology, the concept of self still lacks precise definition as a scientific concept. Some, like Blumer, view this vagueness as necessary to the concept, whose character is supposed to be "volatile and evanescent" (Kuhn, 1964). Others, perhaps attending more toward the "me" than the "I," view the self as more structured. Although positions among theorists vary, in general self-concept theory has usually been associated with the more qualitative branches of sociology and psychology. The concept of self need not be defined only qualitatively, however, and in this chapter we shall try to show how the measurement procedures described so far can lend precise meaning to a concept of self.

Self as Object

The notion of the self as an object leads naturally to the idea of measurement of the meaning of the self as object by the procedures already described here. As an object, the self fits well within our earlier definitions, and should be defined relative to other concepts by means of a relative ratio rule. Any attribute (such as goodness, friendliness, grouchiness) or characteristic (such as my aunt, ready to fight, hungry) that may be applied in varying degrees to the self can be expressed as a distance from the self as object. Thus a person who is hungry is close to hunger; a hungrier person should be closer to hunger; a friendly person should be close to friendliness, and a republican should be closer to republican than to democrat. The idea that the self has a definition independent of its relation to other objects of experience, that is, that the self has an absolute meaning, is contrary to the principle of relativization that underlies modern science. Notwithstanding the centrality and fundamental importance of the concept of self as an object, it seems clear that its epistemological status as an object is no different from that of any other object. This suggests that it be defined in exactly the same way as any other object in the environment, and thus we may simply include some word or term designating the self among the list of objects included on a pair comparison with the same set of objects which form the basis for definitions of the other objects. Of course, this means that each concept—including the self—has only relative rather than absolute meaning, but this has been the epistemological basis of all that has gone before, and is consistent with the principle of relativization. Moreover, the fact that a definition of self may be determined by unambiguous and public rules means that independent observers following the same rules will arrive at the same definition, thus satisfying the principle of objectivization. And finally, by making the self the object of empirical measurement, this process satisfies the principle of empirical verification, since it makes observable what previously was shrouded in indeterminacy.

The Aggregate Self

While these procedures may suffice in principle to establish a definition and measurement procedure for the self, it is nevertheless true that the self of any person is clearly an individual level phenomenon. And it is also true that, at our current level of development, the level of precision of measure or "resolving power" of our measurement systems (regardless of type) is insufficient to locate the concept of self (or any other concept for that matter) within the domain of any single person with more than modest precision. This is not unlike the situation in contemporary high-energy physics, where aggregates of particles may be located with surpassing precision, but where the position and velocity of individual particles remain indeterminate. If we cannot measure the location of a single self precisely within a single cognitive system, however, existing measurement systems are quite adequate to the location of aggregate self concepts within aggregate domains of meaning. It may well be appropriate, for example, to consider groups of people to have collective self concepts which are some form of aggregate of the selves of the individual members. Such a view is certainly consistent with Cooley's notion of the "we" of the primary group, and seems equally consistent with Durkheim's notion of the collective consciousness. Insofar as we are discussing the self as object here, it might be preferable to name this collective self-concept *us* rather than *we* for the present, thus considering it the aggregate equivalent to Mead's *me*.

To illustrate how a measure of the meaning or location of the concept of "us" may be made, the term "yourself" was included in the emotions questionnaire described earlier, and each respondent was thus asked to estimate his or her distance from each of the emotions as well as from the six semantic differential descriptors provided. The result of this exercise are shown in Figure 7.1 and Table 7.1.

Figure 7.1 shows the first principle plane of the emotions data, with the locations of the concepts as described by females in the sample represented by small triangles, and the locations of the same concepts as described by the males in the sample represented by small circles. As we noted in Chapter 4, there is relatively good agreement between the two sexes on the overall locations of the emotions, even though the sample sizes are fairly small. In the right center of the plots, we find the concept "me," and once again the difference in the overall location of the me for males and females is not great. It is important to remember, however, that any graphical representation of these multidimensional, noneuclidean data sets will inevitably be only approximate, and in this case the first principle plane accounts for only about 58% of the real variance in both spaces. In general, the plots are good enough to provide a rough approximation of the structure, and, as can be seen, both males and females place themselves in the vicinity of the more socially desirable or pleasant emotions such as love, joy, happiness, and excite-

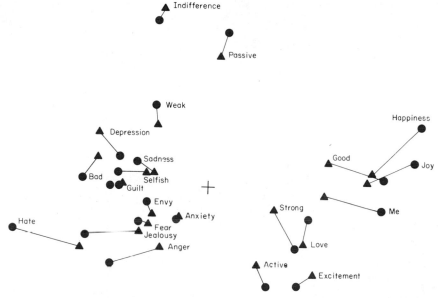

FIGURE 7.1 First principal plane of a set of emotions and attributes for male and female university students plotted on joint coordinates. Triangles represent female respondents; circles represent male respondents.

ment. The plots are not precise enough, however, to differentiate males from females accurately. Table 7.1 shows the measured distances from the self point of males and females to each of the remaining concepts. The first row shows the distance of the male self point from each of the remaining concepts, while the second row shows the equivalent distances for females, and the third row for the aggregate sample. Each of the rows may be read as if they were traditional undimensional scales, except that the numbers will always be reversed, so that a small number means the respondents are close to a concept, while a large number means they are far from it.[1]

Table 7.1 shows the women place themselves closer to hate, anger, envy, fear, jealousy, excitement, indifference, guilt, bad, weak, and passive (although not all these differences are statistically significant) and farther from joy and happiness than their male counterparts. Although generalizations from this merely illustrative data set to men and women in general are not appropriate, within this sample of college age

[1] Since these numbers are means scores, the appropriate test for the significance of difference of measured values is the Behrens–Fischer d, which is given by $d = (\bar{x} - \bar{y} - D)/[(s_1^2/n_1) + (s_2^2/n_2)]^{1/2}$ with degrees of freedom $\theta = \tan^{-1}[(s_1/s_2)(n_2/n_1)^{1/2}]$.

TABLE 7.1

Emotional Attitudes by Sex

		Love	Hate	Anger	Joy	Envy	Fear	Jealousy	Happiness	Sadness	Anxiety	Excitement	Indifference	Depression	Selfish	Guilt	Strong	Bad	Active	Weak	Good	Passive	N̄
Male	$\bar{X}$	25	239	146	26	121	135	142	28	97	81	52	161	108	118	131	38	128	33	131	50	133	33
	$\sigma_{\bar{x}}$	6	53	55	4	29	27	34	5	15	12	20	43	28	22	27	6	29	4	28	13	36	
Female	$\bar{X}$	24	160	85	38	85	103	84	41	90	78	39	142	99	109	105	45	105	41	97	45	93	46
	$\sigma_{\bar{x}}$	6	25	9	8	12	14	12	7	10	10	5	26	14	13	13	7	13	7	11	9	11	
Combined		25	193	110	33	100	116	109	36	93	80	45	150	103	113	116	43	114	37	111	48	110	79
		4	27	24	5	14	14	16	5	8	8	9	24	14	12	14	5	14	4	13	7	16	

126

students, the overall pattern is clearly one in which women's self-image is more negative than their male counterparts by a nontrivial amount.

Although these data can serve as an example of how the self-as-object may be defined both conceptually and quantitatively in terms of the distances among some self-point such as "me" or "myself" and a set of other objects, obviously there is more to the self than its interrelations with the set of principle emotions. It is much more appropriate to say that part of the definition of self at a single point in time is made up of the interrelations of self and emotions. First, even with regard to the emotions themselves, there are certainly more than 16 designatable emotions,[2] and so in this sense the description of self is incomplete. Secondly, the definition is incomplete insofar as the self is implicated in relationships with many objects other than emotions. One may consider oneself tall, busy, hungry, helpful, liberal, and so on. Rather the emotions ought better be considered a domain or neighborhood within which the self has a relative location and hence meaning. All of the other terms, such as tall and busy, themselves may be elements of other domains, such as the domain of physical space ("tall"), activity ("busy), physical needs ("hungry"), interpersonal relationships ("helpful"), and the political domain ("liberal"). Further, while each of these objects may have relatively well-defined relations (distances) with other objects within each domain, it may also be true that any given domain is so "far" from another given domain that an individual may not be aware in a precise way of the relationships of the objects in one domain to the objects in another. Thus, many respondents reported great difficulty relating the emotions to the three bipolar pairs good–bad, strong–weak, active–passive, while very few reported any difficulty relating the emotions (or themselves) to the other emotions.

This reasoning suggests that cognitive structure perhaps ought not be thought of as a single space, spanned by the three unit dimensions of Osgood, and within which lie all other concepts including the self as object, but rather it should perhaps be considered a set of domains or neighborhoods. Within any domain distant relations among the objects of the domain may well be relatively well defined, but distance relations between elements in one domain and elements in another may well be very poorly defined or even unknown. Furthermore, on a higher level of categorization, each domain may be considered an object, and we may inquire into the distance relations among the domains. These relations

[2] It may well be the case, however, as many scholars have argued, that all the subleties of emotion may themselves be compounded out of a small base set of emotions. The question of compounded meanings will be considered formally later in this chapter.

may be hierarchical or not, so that some domains may be subdomains of larger domains. Within the domain of the 1968 U.S. presidential election, for example, the concept "drugs" was identified as a campaign issue. The concept "drugs," however, is itself a domain, and a survey of drug users identifies subelements within this domain, such as marijuana, cocaine, and LSD. While the average voter is able to estimate the location of the drug domain relative to the other objects in the 1968 election domain to perhaps ±100% relative error, very few of those respondents could locate the elements of the drug domain relative to each other or to the larger set of objects in the election domain. On a more general level, those persons frequently described as "generalists" may be particularly well able to describe the locations of domains relative to each other, while "specialists" may well be more capable of precise estimates within the domain of their expertise while lacking a good knowledge of the location of that domain relative to other domains. Thus, this description of the self in terms of its relationships to the set of principle emotions is incomplete since the domain of emotions is only one of a much larger set of domains. Since the number of domains is large, however, and since the global relations among the domains is likely to be somewhat unclear to any individual, it is impractical to consider the self to be a single point within the macrocosm of domains, but rather is fruitful to identify a self point for each domain of meaning separately. The central processing capability of any human mind is certainly much smaller than its total storage capacity, and although an individual may remember a very large array of domains, only a very small number—perhaps only parts of a single domain—may be arrayed in consciousness during any small interval of time. The centrality of the concept of self is such, however, that an individual is likely to be able to estimate the relations among self and the objects of any of the domains of experience even though he or she may not be able to relate each of those domains to each of the others. In this sense the self is a unifying aspect of experience, since it is the one object that is always present in any situation. Because of the multiplicity of domains within which the self may be located, however, we may say that the self has multiple locations within the overall space, or perhaps simply describe each of these locations as one of a set of multiple selves.

This idea of multiple selves, or multiple locations of one self, is quite consistent with Mead's notion of the situational definition of self, and the sociological focus of analysis of self called role theory (Sarbin & Allen, 1968). Mead argues that the social self is defined in terms of its relationships to social objects. He further argues that each social situation includes only a subset of all possible social objects, and that there-

fore the individual will attend to a series of different social objects as he
or she moves from one situation to the next. This implies that the definition of self will shift from situation to situation as the set of social objects
in terms of which the self is defined themselves change. In the vocabulary presented here, we can define the same process by suggesting that
movement from one social situation to another calls out different domains of meaning in the individual consciousness, and that within each
of these domains of meaning the individual self has a location relative to
the objects in that domain. The location of the self within the domain
defines the perspective of the individual with regard to those objects,
and thus the definitions of both self and objects are situational. When
the situations into which the individual enters are radically different,
such that they call out domains that are widely separated from each
other in the cognitive space, the definition of self may be itself radically
different across those situations. If the different situations are far from
each other not only psychologically but also temporally—that is, if they
do not often occur in close temporal succession—it is even probable that
the individual may not recognize the extent to which he or she exhibits
a different self in these contexts. This would be the case particularly if
the sets of other persons whom the individual encounters in the different
situations do not overlap, so that there are no observers who can assess
the differences between the individual's selves in the different contexts.
Thus, for example, an individual may exhibit a liberal or radical self in
political situations, but may take on a conservative stance in the presence of his or her family without any sense of inconsistency. Furthermore, rapid changes in the social situation which an individual faces
(which are quite common, as when a new person enters a conversation
or a new topic is introduced) can result in calling up new domains of
meaning within which the self position is very different. These events
can happen quickly enough to seem discrete, and give the impression of
discrete and even whimsical changes in the self which are surprising not
only to observers of the situation but to the individual himself or herself.
In part, these rapid and apparently discrete shifts in the definition of self
within a situation clearly tend to give the self a mysterious and evanescent appearance, and it is not surprising that particularly sensitive and
perceptive observers of human interaction are led to believe that attempts to quantify and delineate the self are unwise and fruitless.

Multiple Selves

Within any domain of meaning, it is of course possible for individuals
to disagree both about the positions of the objects in the domain and

about the positions of themselves relative to those concepts. This is simply to say that individuals may differ in their beliefs about a set of social objects and about their attitudes toward them. This situation can be represented quite easily by superimposing the measured cognitive spaces of any two individuals (or two subcultural groups) and examining the differences that appear. In 1973, Saltiel (1978) asked a small sample of incoming freshman students at Montana State University to describe the differences between men and women. The 21 most frequently mentioned adjectives were recorded and, along with the words "male" and "female," were placed in a paired-comparison instrument of the type described here which was then administered to 120 incoming freshman students. Cognitive spaces for both males and females were constructed separately following the procedures described in Chapter 4 and then rotated to least-squares congruence as suggested earlier (Chapter 6). The first principle planes of each of these spaces were then plotted on the same set of coordinates and appear in Figure 7.2. As is shown in the figure, both men and women agree very substantially about the locations of the 21 adjectives on this plane, which is to be expected since both subsamples are primarily native English speakers and there is little reason to expect men and women to disagree about the meanings of these words in English. Very substantial disagreements are noted, however, in the locations of the words "male" and "female," indicating serious disagreement between the two subsamples over the way men and women ought to be described in terms of these words. Clearly, men see much greater differences between men and women than do women, who place the two words nearly twice as close together in the space. (It is also worth noting that the adjectives show a general increase in social desirability as they move toward the top of the page, and that women tend to place the term "female" higher and the term "male" lower, while for males this trend is reversed.)

If we assume for the purpose of this illustration[3] that the "me" of males is located near the word male as males describe it, and that the "me" of females is located in the vicinity of the term "female" as females locate it, we can see that the attitudes of males and females will be very substantially different, even though most of the beliefs of males and females about the domain are quite similar. This follows from our earlier definition of belief as any pairwise distance and attitude as the position vector from the self to any other concept. In this case the spatial model fits patterns of linguistic usage very closely, since we can say that, while males and females agree as to the overall structure of the domain,

---

[3] Saltiel did not include the term "me" in this research.

they take different attitudes toward it because their positions within the domain differ markedly. When men and women discuss the definitions of the sexes, each represents the situation as he or she sees it from his or her position. Again Mead's terminology fits the situation well, since learning the female's view requires a man to "take the attitude of" the women (Mead, 1934), while seeing the males' point of view requires a women to "take the attitude of" the men. Spatially, this meaning changing one's position in the space to look at the domain from the "point of view" of the other. Mathematically, these transformations consist entirely of the set of rotations and translations described in Chapter 4.

The spatial analogy also makes it clear that viewing the space eternally from only one perspective will result in a specialized and particular view which will find the ideas of others about the structure of the space erroneous or even incomprehensible, and such an individual would appear rigid, inflexible, and nonfunctional to others whose view was more global. One who was able through communication to view the domain from many perspectives, that is, to take the positions or at-

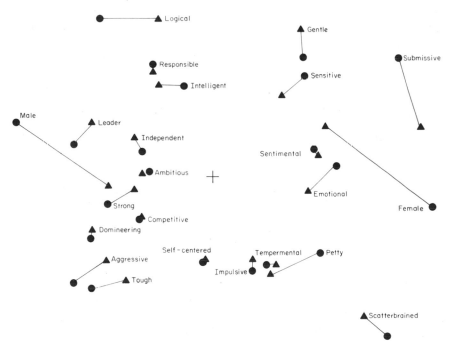

FIGURE 7.2 First principal plane of the space of the concepts male, female, and 21 descriptive adjectives as perceived by samples of male (circles) and female (triangles) university students.

titudes of multiple and disparate others, would be able to form a generalized view of the domain which would tend to converge on the generalized cultural view of the domain. This corresponds closely to Mead's notion of the "generalized other" which, of course, is synthesized from the viewpoints of multiple other persons. Such an idea is also very close to the understanding of Mannheim (1953) about the role social mobility plays in developing a "true" understanding of the structure of one's own society and culture if we understand "true" to mean the generalized view.

The advantage to be gained from this translation of Mead's thinking into the spatial analogy is twofold. First, the pictorial representation, while usually somewhat incomplete due to the need to project a noneuclidean multidimensional manifold onto a flat sheet of paper, nonetheless offers an approximate visualization which can lend insight into changes and transformations more difficult to conceive of in completely abstract terms. More importantly, however, the translation into the spatial model results in a formalized mathematical treatment of the processes under study. "Taking the attitude of the other" within this framework is always represented by a well-defined tensor, since every such change is always and only representable as a rotation and translation of coordinates. This makes it possible to speak precisely and quantitatively about operations previously defined only metaphorically and poetically without doing violence to the original intentions of such metaphors. And of course the notion of "cognitive space" is itself a metaphor, albeit one which lends itself to quantification.

The Subcultural "Us"

So far we have described cognitive structure as a set of domains or neighborhoods within a global space. Each domain is constituted of a set of objects whose mutual interpoint distances give the meanings of those objects within the domain. Within each domain lies a self-point, which gives the instantaneous definition of the self within the domain relative to the other objects in the domain. The perceived distance between any two points is called a belief, while the position vector from the self to any concept is defined as an attitude. Aggregate spaces representing the viewpoint of subcultures, groups, and cultures are constructed by superimposing the sets of individual spaces onto each other after suitable rotation and translation to Gaussian (least-squares) best fit on each other. These spaces can rapidly become congested with points as the number of individuals aggregated becomes large, and the computational burden of so many rotations and translations to congruence rapidly becomes uneconomical, so some approximation to this outcome which is simpler and cheaper is highly desireable. Moreover, since each individual space can be determined only fairly crudely given the current state of measurement knowledge, some form of statistical aggregation becomes desireable. One of the simplest and most fruitful such procedures is to average measured dissimilarities across the sample prior to extracting the eigenvectors and drawing the space. These procedures are commonly used in communication research and are quite robust even with relatively modest sample sizes. The result of such a procedure is a space in which each point represents the average location of a concept of self for the sample members. Although information is obviously lost in the averaging process, nonetheless the result is a space of real utility for practical decision making, since it represents the central tendency of the group scaled, or, as Durkheim says, "the average, then, represents a certain state of the group mind [Simpson, 1963, p. 27; see also Durkheim, 1966]." In most instances, and for most samples, averaging is the appropriate and desirable procedure, since it has the twofold effect of clarifying the central tendency of the group by eliminating individual variability, and secondly it averages out noise due to random error of measurement, which is high at our present state of development. In some instances, however, such averaging can produce somewhat misleading results, particularly when the sample of individuals drawn is not representative of a homogeneous cultural viewpoint. Such, in fact, is the case with the data from Saltiel presented earlier. Here analysis shows that two sharply different viewpoints are represented in the data: that of women and of men. The aggregate of all sample respondents (Figure 7.3) does not reveal the significant differences in viewpoint between males and females in the sample, as of course it could not. (Although evidence that something is wrong can be given by the relatively high standard errors—not given here—around the distances between the aggregate "me" and each of the other concepts, which shows either that respondents have a particularly hard time estimating their distances from the other concepts or that there is a wide difference in attitudes among the sample members.)

In this situation it is appropriate to segregate the sample prior to analysis, either due to an a priori notion that two or more subcultural views are present in the data as is the case with Saltiel's data, or as a result of a clustering algorithm such as Tucker's Three Mode Factor Analysis (Tucker and Messick, 1963). Once the subgroups have been distinguished, it is appropriate to aggregate within each group, construct the space for each group, rotate to least-squares congruence, and superimpose the spaces as we have done in Figures 7.1 and 7.2. The

FIGURE 7.3 First principal plane of the space of the concepts male, female, and 21 descriptive adjectives for an aggregate sample of 120 freshman university students.

position of each of the subcultures will then be represented in the space as a point, but it is more appropriate to refer to this point as "us" rather than "me." It is appropriate to use a plural pronoun, of course, because the point represents the average position of multiple selves, and it is appropriate to use the objective case since we are describing these selves as objects. Transformations from the viewpoint of one subculture or culture to another therefore can be carried out by means of rotations and translations, as was the case for individual viewpoints. Once again, the major advantage of this procedure is that every cross-cultural transformation can be represented precisely by a well-defined tensor.

Self as Process

As we noted at the beginning of this chapter, the self has two aspects, a passive aspect which is the object of attention, and an active aspect, which is the self as attendor. The active self, what Mead calls the "I," is the apparently spontaneous, instantaneous, and always changing consciousness which observes itself as a "me." The "I" can never be observed, since the act of observing it transforms it into the objective and historical "me." As Mead describes it, it is like the concept of "the present" or "now" which can never be observed because it slips into the past before it can be fixed. The "me" that is object to the "I" is composed of past "I's," as it were. The "I," then, can be described as the latest instantaneous point of the *process* of attending; that is, the process of being conscious. Like any point on a line, it has no real existance other than in the limit of the function at that point. This notion, coupled with the spatial analogy, leads directly to the idea of representing the self as the time path of the me; that is, the self can be thought of as a nonparametric curve in the cognitive space described by the succession of "I's" over time. This path may be thought of as locally continuous, although rapid changes in the domains present to consciousness and lapses of attention will appear as discontinuities in the curve. (We shall suggest later that such discontinuities should not be thought of as capricious or mysterious but will need to be accounted for by rapid flows of energy through the self system.) Viewed in this light, and consistent with Mead's understanding, we may define the "I" as the present point on the curve, and the "me" as the integral or "history" of the curve up to that point. Also consistent with our earlier analysis, the totality of the me will never be expected to be present either to the individual himself or herself or to any observer, but rather selected intervals of the curve will be called to attention consistent with those domains called to consciousness by relevant ambient circumstances in the present situation.

When two or more parties are present in a conversation, the spatial model depicts the interaction as two or more spaces populated with the same or similar concepts, superimposed on each other as described earlier. Within this joint space the selves of the participants will be represented as two or more curves developing over time. The conversation may be thought of as each of the individuals observing the relations among the other concepts (including the other selves and his or her own self) and transmitting information to the other person or persons about how the space appears from his or her own (changing) perspective. When the concepts or objects (other than the self) mentioned in the conversation do not line up directly atop one another in the joint space, that is, concepts $A, B, \ldots, N$ for person P, do not lie directly atop their counterparts $A', B', \ldots, N'$ for person P', to this extent each participant will misunderstand the communications of the other. Figure 7.4 illustrates such a situation graphically. When person P refers to the difference between A and B, he or she is referring to the distance AB, but person P' will understand the message to refer to the distance $A'B'$ and

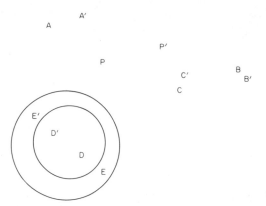

FIGURE 7.4 Hypothetical conversation space.

to this extent will misunderstand P's remark. Thus two individuals may disagree in two ways. First, they may disagree about the location of the concepts relative to all other concepts (which we might call differences in belief) and second, they can differ in their attitudes toward the concepts, which difference is represented in the diagram by a nonzero distance between the two self points P and P'. Conversations which result in increased agreement in belief will be represented by convergences among the concepts other than the self with their counterparts in the space, while conversations which result in increasing similarity of attitude will appear as spaces in which the self curves are convergent (Kincaid, 1980). Increasing disagreement in attitudes will show self curves which diverge.

Ultimately, information theory argues that the entropy of the system made up of the two interacting parties must increase, and this means that the potential (i.e., differences in locations of concepts) must be reduced as a result of communication. In the long run, and on the whole system level, information theory predicts that divergence is impossible. Local divergence within subsystems of the system are possible, however, and local reversals of entropy are commonplace. This process can be illustrated simply by Figure 7.4. Note the configuration of the points D, D', E, and E' in the lower left quadrant of Figure 7.4. If we assume that person P tells person P' that D is like (close to) concept E, person P' will interpret this remark to mean that D' is close to E'. This will result in a convergence of D' and E', which will result in a net motion of D' *away from* concept D, or a divergence within the inner subsystem consisting of D and D'. But the same message will result in a convergence of E' on the remaining concepts D', D, and E, so that in the larger system consisting of D, D', E, and E', the net entropy will increase.

Radical changes of topic, such as might be occasioned by a new person joining the conversation, would appear as discontinuities in both curves at approximately the same point in time as a new domain succeeds the old in consciousness and the individuals' selves reanchor on their self points within the new domain to begin new trajectories.

What has been said of individuals may be said as well for aggregates, only in this case the joint space in which the conversation or dialogue is to be mapped is a superimposition of two or more aggregated (averaged) spaces, and self curves will represent the trajectories of the we for each group, subculture, or culture. Converging self curves will represent increasing agreement in viewpoint among two or more such groups. As is the case of individual spaces as well as aggregated spaces, increasing global agreement concerning the whole constellation of beliefs will be given by a decreasing total difference between the locations of all the concepts other than the self in one of the spaces and their counterparts in each of the other spaces while convergence in attitudes will be given by convergent self curves. While the difficulty of measuring the locations and trajectories of points in individual spaces is quite severe, particularly due to the reactive effect of the measurements on the system measured, measurement of aggregate spaces for groups or cultures poses no particular problem as long as the populations of such aggregates are large relative to the samples drawn from them for measurement purposes. The reactive effects of measurement are thus usually negligible for all but small groups and individuals.

Relative Motion and Attribution: Rules for Anchoring Experiences

As we have seen, changes in attitudes for any individual that do not involve changes in beliefs about the objects other than the self can be represented by a change in position of the self concept relative to the other concepts. Such changes can be represented by a simple change of location of the me. This amounts to appropriately changing the origin of the coordinate system, which is a rigid motion (i.e., a combination of rotations and translations). But, as we saw earlier, all the motions within the cognitive domain are relative rather than absolute changes and as such remain inherently underidentified. This means that there is no absolute basis for establishing whether the self point moves through the space defined by the other concepts, or whether the self remains stationary while the other concepts move relative to the self, or whether some combination of these motions takes place. Mathematically, the former case involves a decision by the individual to fix his or her cognitive coordinates on the centroid of some set of relatively rigid objects, and within this coordinate system all motion (change of attitude) is attributed to movement of the self. Within this framework, change will be something which happens to the person, rather than something that the person does.

Although philosophically such choices are arbitrary, since all such systems are mathematically equivalent, in empirical cases, such anchoring rules are usually prescribed by the culture to which the individual belongs, and in fact different rules may be prescribed for different meaning domains. In those domains within which the individual has learned (or been taught) to believe his or her opinions are well developed, stable, and trustworthy, changes in attitude may well be attributed to changing relations among the objects of those attitudes. Such processes, for example, may describe the person who attributes a growing personal converatism to changes in external factors in the face of his or her own unchanging political position. Persons choosing the alternative rule, that is, anchoring their coordinate system on an external set of objects, would instead attribute their increased conservatism to a change in their own view over time. Whatever the mechanism by which such anchoring decisions (rotation rules) may be made, it is these decisions which determine whether an individual (or a culture, on the aggregate level) will believe he, she, or it controls its own destiny or is the passive recipient of external forces. Perhaps most important, individuals or cultures who use no systematic rule will find their experience chaotic and disorienting, as would an individual who was tumbling relative to the physical environment. Like the question of the Ptolemaic or Copernican rule for assigning motions to the elements of the solar system, there is no "correct" choice, although some choices will result in simpler patterns than others.

In addition to those changes in the cognitive space which can be accounted for by changes in the position of the self, that is, by the set of rotations and translations, there exist changes which cannot be accounted for by such transformations alone. These changes are made up of nonrigid motions among the concepts other than the self in the space. Such changes imply changes in both belief and attitudes, since it is impossible for concepts to move relative to each other without at least one of them moving relative to the self point as well. And since such changes cannot be accounted for by rotations and translations which relocate the self point relative to the other concepts, they cannot be attributed to changes soley in the individual's position or viewpoint, but must be attributed to changes in the relations among the concepts other than the self. In practical cases, most psychological and cultural changes likely involve both rigid and nonrigid motions, and the resulting patterns of change can become very complicated—more than complicated enough, in fact, to account for the apparent inexplicability of human thought processes even for the individual or culture which experiences them. The advantage of the spatial representation presented here, however, is again twofold. First, the spatial model allows an approximate visualization of the changes in such a way as to facilitate insight into the way such changes take place. Secondly, and more important, all such changes, both rigid and nonrigid, can be represented by tensors, which, in the case of rigid motions, take on a particularly simple form (McConnell, 1933, pp. 124–126). Thus every possible psychological or cultural process, regardless of complexity, has an exact mathematical representation, even though in empirical cases the measurement problem may be sufficiently severe to allow only approximate calculations.

The CTP: An Illustration

To illustrate how cognitive changes can be represented as time trajectories in a multidimensional space, 43 students at a small midwestern university were introduced to a (fictitious) concept called the "Cortical Thematic Pause," later abbreviated to the "CTP." They were told that they were to take part in an experiment on the diffusion of an innovation (the CTP), and that, although many of them may not have heard of the CTP, nonetheless their opinions about it would be useful even at this early stage in its diffusion. They were also told that the CTP was known to be harmless, took only a few moments to perform, and did not interfere with other ongoing activities. Moreover, they were told that the investigators had contacted researchers working on the CTP, and that they would be given any information received from these researchers when it arrived. Then each student was asked to complete a Galileo™-type paired-comparison instrument. Included on the instrument were the terms CTP, me, and 15 other concepts. Thirteen of these concepts were chosen to define the domain of meaning for the CTP. (Since the CTP does not exist, it has no "natural" meaning domain in the popular culture.) These other terms were sleeping, dreaming, daydreaming, intense concentration, marijuana high, good, depres-

TABLE 7.2

Mean Distances among Experimental Concepts as Message Sources

Concept pair	Time period			
	t_1	t_2	t_3	t_4
Pauling–reliable	66.79	61.60	64.67	61.38
	(7.822)	(10.36)	(11.658)	(12.097)
	42	42	43	42
Leáry–reliable	78.00	74.23	74.56	73.56
	(8.804)	(13.403)	(14.110)	(14.887)
	43	43	43	43
CTP–me	77.60	70.60	78.84	73.12
	(18.006)	(11.095)	(14.627)	(14.892)
	42	42	43	42
CTP–Pauling	90.19	53.929	53.63	57.05
	(9.661)	(10.592)	(9.837)	(10.361)
	42	42	43	42
CTP–Leary	91.88	81.548	51.81	55.86
	(4.994)	(15.107)	(9.486)	(10.056)
	42	42	42	42
Pauling–Leary	54.33	66.33	48.28	52.70
	(7.132)	(10.231)	(11.535)	(9.464)
	42	42	43	43
Pauling–me	80.36	99.52	81.16	79.76
	(7.13)	(10.23)	(11.54)	(9.46)
	42	42	43	42
Leary–me	83.35	101.98	83.72	82.56
	(7.74)	(11.70)	(12.21)	(9.93)
	43	43	43	43

sion, alcohol high, relaxation, alpha wave meditation, transcendental meditation, reliable, and the names of two persons who would later be cited as sources of messages about the CTP, Linus Pauling and Timothy Leary. These two names were selected on the basis of pretest information from a similar population which showed one of the two to be the most reliable (credible) source of information among those tested for this population, while the other was the least reliable information source of those tested.

Two days later the students were presented with a letter allegedly from the highly credible source (Pauling) which advocated frequent daily performance of the CTP, and then immediately filled out the instrument a second time. Four days later (unequal time intervals were required by the classroom schedule) the students received a second letter, this time from the less credible source (Leary), which was nearly

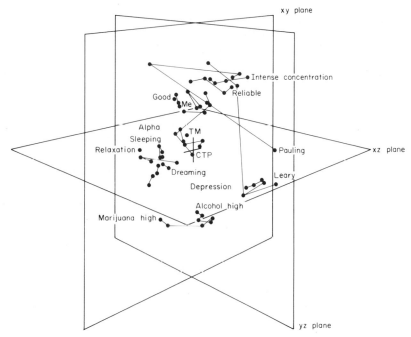

FIGURE 7.5   Three-dimensional view of concept motions over time.

identical in content to the first letter, and again they immediately filled out the instrument. Finally, 2 days later, the students filled out the questionnaire a fourth time. The subjects were then debriefed.

Results of this study are shown in Table 7.2 and in Figures 7.5–7.7. As Figure 7.5, the overall three-dimensional projections shows, there is an initial convergence of the CTP, the self (me) and Pauling (the credible source) after the letter from Pauling was read by the students, followed by convergence of Leary, Pauling, and the CTP following the message from Leary (the noncredible source[4]) but, as is usually the case with messages from noncredible sources, there is a divergence between the self and the CTP following his advocacy. Trajectories of the unmanipulated concepts (which were held stable by the least-square rotation algorithm) show small random patterns like Brownian motion.

An interesting and unanticipated finding is the apparent rigid substructure within the domain made up of three *person* concepts, Leary,

---

[4] Evidence that Leary is less reliable than Pauling for this sample is given in Table 7.2, which shows Leary 11.2 more units from the term "reliable," which pretesting shows to be the term those students use to mean "credible."

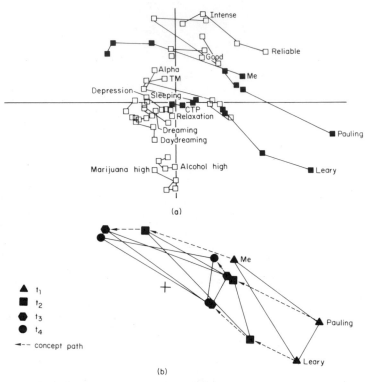

(a)

(b)

FIGURE 7.6   First principal plane of concept motions over time. Darkened squares represent manipulated concepts; lettering designates time 1. (a) The complete space. (b) The Leary–Pauling–me triangle at 4 points in time.

Pauling, and me. These three concepts form a triangle (Figures 7.6 and 7.7 show, respectively, the front and side views of the first three principle dimensions of the space) which remains relatively rigid during the period of the experiment, although the entire triangle shows a displacement to the left and upward on the first principle plane, with slight rigid twisting. When Pauling delivers the initial message, the net force is applied along a vector leftward and upward (Figures 7.6a and 7.6b) which displaces the triangle in the direction noted and distorts the triangle somewhat along the line of action of the force. When Leary delivers the second message, the force vector is applied in the same direction but its point of application is now at Leary's position rather than Pauling's, as was the original vector. This second force has the effect of returning the triangle to its original shape and displacing it

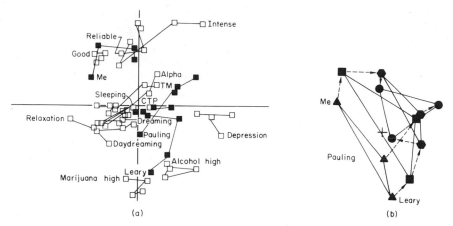

FIGURE 7.7   Side views of concept motions over time.

somewhat along the line of action of the force. The last measurement shows only a minor shifting of the triangle as a rigid body.

Of course a single set of observations from a single experiment does not provide a firm basis of inference, but in this specific case the pattern is suggestive of the possibility that, within this domain, the self is defined primarily in relation to the other persons in the domain, and the shifting location of these other persons resulting from the messages they delivered results in a similar relocation of the self in order to maintain the same approximate relations with those others. Such a result is not implausible and fits well with the notions of Festinger and others relative to the social comparison process (Festinger, 1957).

Moreover, if we assume that the individual readjusts his/her position to retain a relatively constant distance from the source, and that an existential ("is") message is more potent than an hortatory ("ought") message, then we might well expect to observe (as we do in this example) that the resulting motion of the self will be away from the position advocated. This is so because, in advocating a position, as source implies that it is his/her position; as he or she moves toward that point, the recipient of the message will then move away to retain a nearly constant distance from the source.

The trajectories of the twin terms "alpha wave mediation" and "transcendental mediation" shows these two concepts also seem to move as a rigid body relative to the other concepts, which means that their meanings relative to each other remain invariant while their relation to the other terms in the space change. Although this single experiment provides much too flimsy evidence for certainty, the confirmation of the existence of relatively rigid substructures within meaning domains would be of great importance to questions of induction and deduction within cognitive functioning. In any event, these findings provide interesting evidence for usefulness of time-ordered MDS spaces for the investigation of cognitive processes.

CHAPTER 8

DYNAMICS OF SELF

Introduction

Since the self has been defined here as the set of interrelationships among a set of objects as described by their interpoint distances in a cognitive space, the formation of the self (both individual and cultural) refers to those processes by which points come to be located in a specific way relative to each other in the space. Furthermore, since the self as defined here is clearly an information structure, changes in the relative locations of points in the space are always the result of information received from outside the self system, such as from observations of "objective" reality or messages received from other persons (significant others), and second, those changes which result from internal information processing in the absence of "new" information from outside the system. These latter changes are assumed to be the result of internal dynamics of the self-system such as have been proposed by consistency theorists such as Heider (1958), Newcomb (1953), and Festinger (1957).

External Forces

The model underlying this discussion is a relativistic model, since it takes as its starting point the assumption that no concept or object has meaning in and of itself, but rather takes on meaning only in relation to some other object or set of objects. This means that the smallest unit of meaning consists in the relation between two objects or elements. This of course is consistent with the fundamental psychological assumption underlying the model of perception presented here, namely, that the foundation of human perception is the ability to perceive discrepancy or difference between two or more stimuli. When only two elements of cognition are involved in a message, it follows that the only content which can exist is content about the extent to which the two cognitive elements or objects are similar or different. (To say that A is warmer than B, for example, makes reference to a third object, that is warmth.) The statement of the extent of similarity or difference between two cognitive elements, therefore, is the smallest meaningful utterance that can be made in this system, and such an attribution (such as "A is similar to B" or "A and B are different") is here referred to as a *simple message*. Furthermore, such messages are considered to be simple whenever they refer only to two cognitive elements, regardless of whether they are qualified (or better, quantified) by an adverb. Thus, "George is friendly," "Mary and George are very different," and "France and Germany are identical" are all simple messages. "Peter is heavier than I" is a compound message, since it refers to three concepts, and is thus a compound of three simple messages, that is, a message about Peter and heavy, a message about me and heavy, and a message about me and Peter. By the same token, "A rose is a rose is a rose" is no message at all, since it makes reference to only one concept. Simple messages occur very infrequently if, in fact, they occur at all, since any message which explicitly or implicity involves a source (such as "Mary says Frank is friendly") is itself a compound message. Nonetheless, insofar as compound messages can be understood as combinations of simple messages, it is useful to study the simple case as a foundation for understanding the more complicated situation presented by compound messages.

Simple Messages

The simplest of simple messages is the categorical assertion of identity,[1] which is a statement of the form "A is B." Assuming that A and B are objects separated by some distance in a space, this simplest assumption we might make about such an assertion is that it would produce a force toward the convergence of the two concepts along the line segment connecting them (Woelfel, Holmes, Cody, & Fink, 1976). Following from conventional physical practice, it is appropriate to represent this force as two vectors F_1 and F_2 along the line segment connecting the two concepts, equal in magnitude and opposite in sense, as shown in Figure 8.1 (Woelfel & Saltiel, 1978). The concept of force, it should be noted, has no

FIGURE 8.1   Hypothetical representation of forces generated by a simple message.

empirical standing in either physical or cognitive matters, but serves simply as a heuristic device to aid in the formalization and quantification of observations. Moreover, the "existence" of forces is never an empirical matter, but rather forces are inferred to account for motions of objects whose trajectories deviate from a course assumed on some grounds to be "natural" or normal (J. D. Woelfel, 1979, 1980; Woelfel & Werner, 1979). Hertz (1956) is explicit about the "make-believe" nature of forces in mechanics:

> Thus according to our fundamental law, whenever two bodies belong to the same system, the motion of one is determined by that of the other. The idea of force now comes in as follows. For assignable reasons we find it convenient to divide the determination of the one motion by the other into two steps. We thus say that the motion of the first body determines a force, and that this force then determines the motion of the second body.
>   Strictly speaking it [force] is a middle term conceived only between two motions [p. 28].

Although it is not possible at this state to estimate the magnitudes of these forces (which, of course, requires yet a third force to serve as a measuring rod), it seems appropriate to assume that the assertion of complete identity is as forceful a statement as can be made about the similarity of any two objects, since identity does not admit a quantification (i.e., it is not meaningful to say "A and B are very identical" or "A and B are somewhat identical"). We assume, therefore, that noncategorical statements of similarity should all exhibit less force toward convergence than a statement of categorical identity. Noncategorical statements of similarity, therefore, such as "A and B are similar" can be represented in the same way as are categorical statements of identity, although the magnitudes of the force vectors might be expected to be smaller. Very substantial evidence from Cliff (1959) and others indicates strongly that the magnitudes of these forces can be affected by adverbs, such as "very," "extremely," and "somewhat."

Given two and only two objects it is possible to estimate the relative force of different messages by the rates of convergence of those concepts

---

[1] We confine our discussion here to "existential" messages, for example, "A is B" rather than "horatory" messages, such as "A should be B." Evidence seems to indicate the latter are considerably less effective than the former (Woelfel et al., 1980).

subsequent to receipt of the messages.[2] Forces, like distance, have no absolute significance, but may be determined only up to an arbitrary multiplier. In parctice, the force generated by an arbitrary message is designated as one unit, and the force of any other message may be expressed as a ratio to this arbitrary standard force. Based on the assumption that the forces generated by a message are impulsive (instantaneous) forces, the relative magnitudes of two forces may be defined as the ratio of the distances traveled by the objects over an arbitrary interval of time, as

$$F_1/F_2 = s_1/s_2,$$

where F_1 is the force generated by message 1, F_2 the force generated by message 2, s_1 the distance traversed by the objects following the first message, and s_2 the distance traversed by the objects following the second message. Such procedures provide a simple and unambiguous way to assess the relative effects of messages of all sorts. When combined with appropriate experimental controls, for example, such as randomization of treatments, adequate sampling procedures, and large sample sizes, such procedures could establish quantitative values for the effects of different adverbs in a way potentially even more precise than that of Cliff.

Implicit in the discussion to this point has been the notion that only two concepts exist and define a one-dimensional continuum. Along a one-dimensional continuum, and in the absence of other points of reference, it is of course impossible to establish whether or not the objects *A* and *B* are *differentially* affected by the message. In order to answer questions of this sort, it is necessary to embed the objects in a field of additional concepts which form a frame of reference against which relative motion can be gauged. In his classic description of this situation, Mach (1942) describes two magnets placed in jar lids floating on water in a flat pan (see Figure 8.2). The pan of water serves as a reference frame within which the relative motions of the jar lids can be described. If we assume (as is standard physical practice) that the forces generated by the magnets can be described as vectors of equal magnitude and opposite sense along the line segment connecting the two lids, then differential effects of these forces on the lids can be observed as differential magnitudes of motions of the lids *relative to the pan*. Since the forces are by

---

[2] In order to simplify the current expositon, we shall assume that brief messages produce "impulsive," that is, instantaneous forces, rather than setting up a continuing field of force. If the latter turns out to be the case empirically, the equations described here need to be rewritten as differential equations and integrated with respect to time. Nevertheless, the principles involved remain the same.

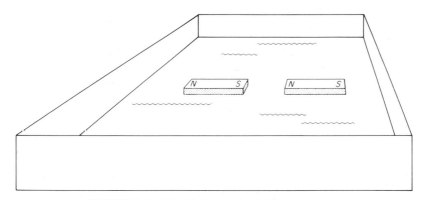

FIGURE 8.2.   Mach's floating magnet experiment.

definition equal and opposite, differential motions of the lids must be
ascribed to differential characteristics of the floating objects relative to
the reference frame. This characteristic is defined as *inertial mass*. Inertial
mass must not be thought of as an empirical entity, but rather as a
property of the interactions of the elements of the system and their
reference frame. Insofar as inertial mass is defined as a passive or resis-
tive concept, it may be measured empirically as the inverse of the ratio
of distances each jar lid travels relative to the reference system, that is,

$$m_A/m_B = s_B/s_A,$$

where m_A is the inertial mass of lid A and magnet A, m_B the inertial mass
of lid B and magnet B, s_A the distance traveled by lid A relative to the
reference frame, and s_B the distance traveled by lid B relative to the
reference frame.

Once again, as is true for all scientific concepts, these inertial masses
should not be thought of as properties of the jar lid–magnet systems
themselves, but rather relative properties within this reference system.
Choice of another reference frame may well result in different measured
values for the inertial masses of these same objects. Such measured
values, however, are valid within the chosen frame, and become very
useful when the reference frame is consensual and repeatable, that is,
the findings will have relevance and importance to all those who adopt
the same reference conventions. Similarly, the same findings can be
made useful to users of other reference frames as transformations across
reference frames are discovered and cataloged (see Chapter 4).

The concept of inertial mass is psychologically and sociologically useful, since it recognizes and quantifies the well-known but imprecise
notion that different psychological and cultural objects are more resis-

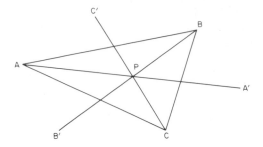

FIGURE 8.3 Hypothetical representation of a compound message.

tant to change than others within a given mind or culture.[3] It should be carefully noted, though, that the concept of inertial mass describes and quantifies such effects, but does not explain them.

Compound Messages

Compound messages, as the name implies, are those messages which are built up of multiple simple messages, such as "A is B and C." The assumption which justifies representing concepts as vectors in space, of course, is that concepts behave like vectors and thus may be described by the algebra of vectors. In this case, this assumption requires us to assume that messages will add (or more precisely, *average*) like vectors. The least complicated compound case is represented in Figure 8.3.

The strong form of the message, that is, the categorical assertion that *A is B* and *C*, implies that *B* and *C* are the same, and thus we should assume that this compound message is built of three simple messages: *A is B, A is C*, and *B is C*. If we assume further that the inertial masses of the three concepts *A, B,* and *C* are equal, and that the forces toward convergence generated by the messages are independent of the initial distances among the concepts,[4] then the resultant motions of each of the

---

[3] Plausible explanations for differential resistance to change among psychological and cultural objects have been offered by several communication scientists. Perhaps the most successful of these explanations suggest that those objects which have the largest information history, that is, which were composed out of the largest amounts of information are most massive or resistant to change (see Saltiel & Woelfel, 1975; Danes, Hunter, & Woelfel, 1978).

[4] The validity of this hypothesis has not been established empirically, but the algebra of the situation is not seriously complicated should it fail. We present the example based on the assumption for clarity of presentation, but differential forces by distance simply requires the insertion of scalars representing the magnitude of the forces in the equations. See Woelfel and Saltiel (1978) for a more detailed discussion of the implications of different forms of this hypothesis.

three concepts will lie along a vector from each respective concept passing through the midpoint of the line segment connecting the remaining two concepts. (The proof is elementary and is ommitted.) Thus concept A will move along the vector AA', concept B will move along the vector BB', and concept C will move along the vector CC'. Consistent with the expected vernacular meaning of these phrases, this algebra of vectors predicts that the three concepts will move toward a point of convergence at P, which is the center of mass of the system.

Since each of these points A, B, and C are usually represented in the model presented here as position vectors in the multidimensional space, the point P is given (from an elementary theorem of vector algebra) as

$$P = (A + B + C)/3,$$

where P also is represented as a position vector from the origin. We may then represent the three trajectories of the concepts A, B, and C as

$$P_A = A - P, \qquad P_B = B - P, \qquad P_C = C - p.$$

Finally, since the manifold is usually a Riemann manifold, it is convenient to represent each of the vectors as a tensor following the notation introduced earlier, which gives the position vectors of A, B, and C as $R_{(A)}^\mu$, $R_{(B)}^\mu$, and $R_{(C)}^\mu$ and the point P as $R_{(B)}^\mu$, so that

$$R_P^\mu = (R_{(A)}^\mu + R_{(B)}^\mu + R_{(C)}^\mu)/3, \tag{8.1}$$

and therefore the predicted trajectories of the concepts A, B, and C are given by

$$\Delta R_{(A)}^\mu = R_{(A)}^\mu - R_{(P)}^\mu, \qquad \Delta R_{(B)}^\mu = R_{(B)}^\mu - R_{(P)}^\mu, \qquad \Delta R_{(C)}^\mu = R_{(C)}^\mu - R_{(P)}^\mu. \tag{8.2}$$

Clearly, equation (8.1) can be generalized for any number of vectors n to give a general equation for any categorical message as

$$R_{(P)}^\mu = \sum_{I=1}^{n} R_{(i)}^\mu / n. \tag{8.3}$$

Equation (8.3) was derived based on the assumption that each of the concepts implicated in the message were of equal inertial mass, that is, that each resisted acceleration equally with each other. Based on that assumption, equation (8.3) predicts that each concept will converge on the center of volume of the distribution of the concepts, which is given by $R_{(P)}^\mu$ in (8.3). This is due to the fact that, in the equal mass condition, the center of volume and the center of mass are the same. In the event that the masses of the concepts are not the same, that is, given that they each resist acceleration differentially, the point of convergence, that is,

FIGURE 8.4   Representation of the message "A is similar to B and C."

the center of mass, will not correspond with the center of volume, and we require

$$R^{\mu}_{(P)} = \sum_{i}^{n} m_{(i)} R^{\mu}_{(i)} / \Sigma m_{(i)}, \tag{8.4}$$

where the scalar $m_{(i)}$ represents the inertial mass of the ith concept. Equation (8.4) can serve, therefore, as a general equation for any compound message of a categorical form such as "A is B and C," or similarly for any noncategorical message of the form "A and B and C are similar," regardless of how many concepts are implicated in the message. The condition for the applicability of (8.4) is simply that the message calls for a mutual convergence of all concepts on each other. Noncategorical compound messages which do not imply a complete mutual convergence of all concepts implicated in the message require a simple modification. Figure 8.4 illustrates the case of the message "A is similar to B and C." This message implies a convergence of A and B, as well as a convergence between A and C, but does not require a similar convergence between B and C.

In this case, we expect a convergence of A and B along the line segments AB, and a similar convergence of A and C along the line segment AC, but such convergence that actually occurs between B and C is solely the result of the fact that the vectors BA and CA are convergent.[5] In this case, the predicted trajectories are given by

$$P_B = B - A, \qquad P_C = C - A, \qquad P_A = A - P,$$

where $P = (B+C)/2$. Each of these equations can also be weighted for differential inertial masses of the concepts and generalized as before.

These equations are illustrative of the reason why we choose to con-

---

[5] Notice that in this situation the concepts B and C are not moving in the directions predicted in Figure 8.3. Precise empirical observation would be needed to differentiate between these two situations.

sider the space within which cognitive and cultural processes occur to be a continuum, that is, a space in which every point has a meaning, rather than only those points at which there are words. Equation (8.1), for example, predicts that the point given by the end point of the position vector $R_{(P)}$ has a meaning, even though there is no word coterminous with that point. The meaning of that point is given by (8.1), that is, the point in space designated by the end point of the vector is a combination of the meanings of the words A, B, and C. Similarly, equation (8.6) assumes that the point P has a meaning which is a combination of the concepts B and C. Thus every point in the continuum has meaning, although there can never be enough words in a discrete categorical language such that a single word is assigned unambiguously to each of the (infinity of) points in the continuum. These words should be considered "marker variables" in Cushman's sense (Cushman & Pierce, 1977), which designate regions of the space, and which may be used in combinations to designate regions at which no marker is located.

The notion that all messages may be compounded out of sets of pairwise messages does not discriminate the case where one person delivers multiple simple messages from the case where multiple persons each deliver a single simple message. This is consistent with strong empirical evidence that the beliefs and attitudes of individuals tend to cluster near the average beliefs and attitudes of their "significant others." Woelfel and Haller (1971), for example, showed that the level of aspiration (both educational and occupational) of high school youth is well predicted by the average level of attainment expected of them by their significant others. This finding was replicated independently by Mettlin (1970). J. C. Woelfel showed that the first few dimensions of the multidimensional array of political attitudes of elementary and high school youth correspond very closely to the first few dimensions of the same array averaged across their significant others (J. C. Woelfel, 1976). Saltiel showed that the coordinates of occupations in a multidimensional space which a sample of high school students chose to become were very well predicted by the average coordinates of the set of occupations their significant others expected of them (Saltiel, 1978). In general, the idea that persons' own attitudes and beliefs converge on the mean of the attitudes and beliefs of those with whom they communicate is well supported by data (Mettlin, 1973).

Messages and Language

Linguistically we may think of nouns, gerunds, pronouns, and adjectives as position vectors in the space whose meanings are given by their directions and magnitudes. Certain verbs, such as the verb *to have* or *to be,* may be thought of as operators on the space, in that their effect is to change the locations of nouns, pronouns, gerunds, and adjectives as we have just suggested. Adverbs, such as *very, somewhat,* and *extremely,* may be thought of as *quantifiers* of the operators. Thus, if one says "George is tall," both *George* and *tall* are defined as position vectors in the space, and the operator *is* has the effect of operating on the locations of *George* and *tall,* that is, it moves *George* and *tall* through the space. If the word *very* were added to the message, that is, "George is very tall," the adverb *very* has the effect of quantifying the action implied by the operator *is.*

Thus many words, such as nouns, gerunds, some adjectives, and pronouns, can be defined as vector quantities, while other words, such as verbs (particularly *is* and *have*) and adverbs, are defined not by their positions in the space, but rather by their effects on the space, and should be thought of as operators. The class of operators, however, may also be distinguished into subclasses. Some operators, such as the adjective "different" or the adverb "very," ought to be represented as scalar operators, since they imply magnitudes but not directions. Other adjectives, such as "longer" or "heavier," seem better represented as vector operators, since they imply direction in the space.

Certainly most words in vernacular language appear to lack the kind of precision of meaning that such a representation seems to imply, but it is important to distinguish between imprecise effects and imprecise linguistic expressions of definite effects. Figure 8.5 represents a hypothetical space in which the physical descriptions of a set of people are arrayed. Within the hypothetical domain established in Figure 8.5, the message "George is taller" is ambiguous; some recipients of the message may assume it to mean "taller than we now think he is," while others may assume it means George is taller than some un-

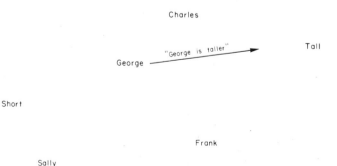

FIGURE 8.5   Hypothetical representation of the ambiguous message "George is taller."

specified referent, and, since the statement makes reference to only one object (George), for these people the message has no meaning, that is, it is not a message at all. Nevertheless, even though no English speaker could predict in advance the precise meaning of the message, differences in the structure of the domain before and after receipt of the message will show unambiguously the effect receipt of the message had on those who heard it. If no difference whatever is measureable, we are content to say the message had no meaning. Not all meaningful messages need to change the geometric structure of the space to change the dynamic characteristics of the space. Thus a message such as "George remains the same" should increase the inertia of the concept George. This would not change the position of George in the space, but would make George more stable in the space by increasing the mass (or momentum) of the concept, which is a change in the dynamic character of the space. Note that this message "George remains the same" is a two-concept message, since it implies "George (time 1)" and "George (time 2)". Whatever difference is found, however, is clearly the result of the message, and hence its meaning in the sense suggested here. The meaning of operators, then, is derived from their effect. That the same operator may have different measured effects in different groups and different domains should not be troublesome, since such a notion is entirely consistent with both the scientific principle of relativization, which suggests that no concept has absolute meaning, and with the contemporary understanding of communication theorists that words have no meaning independent of the people who use them and the context in which they are used.

Internal Forces

As we suggested earlier, changes of the structure of the cognitive or cultural space can be attributed to external forces, such as the receipt of messages, and to internal forces which describe the internal dynamics of the self or cultural system. In the previous section we described several ways in which external messages can be translated into the mathematics of the spatial manifold such that their direct effects might be measured. For simplicity of exposition, internal factors (with the single exception of the notion of inertial mass) were ignored. In practice, this simplification had the effect of requiring us to assume that all forces and effects could be considered instantaneously. Ultimately, any changes in a system in equilibrium must be attributed to external or exogonous factors, and the same is true of the self system and cultural systems. What we really mean by internal forces, then, are the delayed effects of external forces as they are mediated by the internal structure of either the self or the social system. On the individual level the internal dynamics of the self system may have their ultimate roots in the physiology of the brain, while the internal dynamics of cultural systems will be rooted as well in the internal communication structure of the societies which underly them. Too little is known about either of these underlying structures to make hypotheses of great precision as yet, but nonetheless it is useful to show how several existing theories of internal processes can be mapped by means of the models set forth here.

Learning and Forgetting

The fundamental psychological assumption on which these procedures rest is that perception is based on the discrimination of difference. In the absence of experience, all concepts are undifferentiable one from the other and the cognitive space is simply a dimensionless point. Initial perceptions resulting from incoming external stimuli may be thought of as energy inputs into the system which result in a separation of undifferentiated and simultaneous experience into a differentiated and sequenced reality. We assume, therefore, that energy in the form of information is required to differentiate the space and that structuring of the cognitive space represents fixed energy which can be released again by breaking down the structure. Leakage of energy from the system would be represented by a loss of information, which in turn is represented by a loss of distinctions among concepts—a shrinkage of the space.

The notion that forgetting implies a blurring or loss of distinction among objects once known to be different is not an uncommon one. Moreover, the increasing distinctions among concepts as a result of the reception of information corresponds in a formal sense to a local reversal of entropy within the self system, and the second law of thermodynamics unequivocally predicts that, in the absence of input information, the self system, like all other systems, would move in the direction of increasing entropy. Such a movement toward increasing entropy implies an increasing equivalence of outcomes, which is described in the spatial manifold by a shrinkage of the space. Although the empirical record is scanty, research on time-ordered measures without intervening treatments seems to show a reliable shrinkage of the space over time. In a previously unreported experiment, for example, Barnett and Woelfel read to a small sample of undergraduate students at a large midwestern university a set of descriptions of six hypothetical people to whom various characteristics had been ascribed at random and measured the sample's perceptions of these ficticious people over a period of several weeks. Later measurements showed a decrease in overall size of the space as measured by the trace of the space as the respondents forgot the initial descriptions.

The uniform shrinkage of a space such as the space of cognition can be described mathematically by positing a mutual gravitational force among each pair of objects in the space. In fact, saying that each object in the space mutually attracts each other object is simply a semantically different way of saying that the space, if left alone, will shrink, and the reader should recall that a gravitational force, like any force, does not refer to tangible entity, but rather to a formal property of observed processes expressed in a convenient way. It would be as accurate, for example, to say that each object is connected to each other by a massless elastic thread—no one really believes in the existence of such threads, but the mathematics which describe such a system are useful and the same as the gravitational model. It is also worth noting that gravity in physics is as bizarre a notion as any posited here, since physical gravity is described as a force transmitted instantaneously across any distance in the absence of any physical connection or medium whatsoever; it is precisely because of this absurdity that Descartes rejected Newton's theory and posited his own much more cumbersome model.

Should the notion of gravitational forces within the manifold prove useful, we should expect these internal forces to interact with the dynamics of external messages described in the previous section. If the gravitational model applies, for example, more force should be required to move an object away from a massive concept than toward it, and trajectories which lead objects along a tangent to a massive concept ought to be deflected along a vector toward the massive concept. In fact, such a model would predict that the tendency of the reader would be to classify the procedures described in this book as simply one of several equivalent multidimensional scaling procedures, and the amount of information (energy) which this book must convey in order to differentiate these present procedures from the more massive existing concept of multidimensional scaling methods should be expected to be quite substantial. Moreover, should the book provide sufficient information to distinguish these methods from existing multidimensional scaling algorithms in the mind of the reader, yet not prove sufficient to motivate continued intake of information about the system, we would expect the distinction to collapse over time, so that at some later time the reader might still recall that these are variants of multidimensional scaling procedures, but forget how—and perhaps even that—they differ.

Induction and Deduction

The notion of gravity is, in fact, implicit in the notion of induction and deduction. If we assume a two-stage hierarchy such that the elements a_i are members of the class A, and assume further that the meaning of A (i.e., its relative location in a space) is changed by the result of a message, then we may write (following Poole, 1977)

$$\Delta a_i = \alpha_i \, \Delta A, \qquad (8.7)$$

where Δa_i equals the change in location (meaning) of a_i and ΔA equals the change in location (meaning) of A, $0 \leq \sigma_i \geq 1$. If deduction is permitted, then the coefficients α_i will all be nonzero, that is, the location of a_i will be changed by a nonzero amount as a result of the movement of A. If the coefficients a_i are less than unity but nonzero, then we must posit a less than rigid connection between the two which may be represented mathematically as if it were a "force" connecting the A with the a_i in such a way that the set A constitutes an elastic body.

Similarly, if induction is permitted, and any a_i is impacted with a message, then A will transform as

$$\Delta A = B_i a_i. \qquad (8.8)$$

A nonzero value for the coefficients B_i indicates an inductive process, which once again implies a semirigid bond among the a_i.

Figure 8.6 illustrates this process. Each a_i represents a political candidate, and A represents the centroid of this domain or set of all such candidates. The strongest deductive hypothesis we might make asserts that a statement such as "all political candidates are criminals" would require that the set of a_i in A should move as a rigid body in the direction of the centroid of the set of criminals. Less powerful deductive models would suggest a more elastic situation, in which the a_i would be dragged along with some slippage toward the target, while the hypothesis of no deduction would suggest no movement of the a_i at all.

If, on the other hand, the message "candidate a_i is a criminal" is received, and if no connection whatsoever is assumed among the

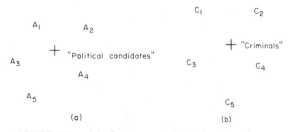

FIGURE 8.6   (a) Inductive and (b) deductive processes.

bodies, then the other a_i will not move at all, and the centroid of the set of the a_i will shift only by the amount given from the movement of one of the points in the distribution. This is the weakest form of deduction that can be posited within the spatial model. On the other hand, if stronger deductive processes occur, then each of the a_i will be "dragged" by the element that is moving, and the centroid will shift by a larger amount. Thus, both this inductive model and the previous deductive model are describable in terms of a gravitational model which implies a semirigid connection among the points.

Perhaps an even more fruitful model is to conceive of the spatial manifold as a relatively viscous medium and the set of points within the manifold as an elastic body. In this case, messages can be expressed as stress and strain tensors deforming the body. In this model, all relative motions can be accounted for in terms of the viscosity index of the space, the inertial masses of the objects and the elasticity indices for each pairwise connection. Extremely powerful messages may be thought of as generating forces in excess of the tensile strength of the bonds, which can result in shears in the manifold and radical discontinuities in mental processes which would result in disorientation and loss of function within the overstressed domains. Within these limits however, for relatively small forces, psychological and cultural processes within the domain might be expected to act as a system of damped linear oscillators, and therefore obey the differential equations

$$m_{(\alpha)}\ddot{R}^{\mu}_{(\alpha)} + C\dot{R}^{\mu}_{(\alpha)} + K^{\mu}R^{\mu}_{(\alpha)} = 0, \qquad (8.9)$$

where $m_{(\alpha)}$ is the mass of the μth concept, $\ddot{R}^{\mu}_{(\alpha)}$ the acceleration of the αth concept along the μth dimension, C the linear damping constant, $\dot{R}^{\mu}_{(\alpha)}$ the velocity of the αth concept along the μth dimension, and K^{μ} the restoring force per unit extension along the μth dimension. When outside forces (messages) are imposed on the system, we obtain

$$m_{(\alpha)}\ddot{R}^{\mu}_{(\alpha)} + C\dot{R}^{\mu}_{(\alpha)} + K^{\mu}R^{\mu}_{(\alpha)} = F^{\mu}_{(\alpha)}, \qquad (8.10)$$

where $F^{\mu}_{(\alpha)}$ are the μ components of the impressed force acting on the αth concept.

Inconsistency

Many theorists have posited additional internal psychological forces toward "consistency" or "balance." Although there are many forms of such theories (Heider, 1958; Newcomb, 1953; Festinger, 1957; Osgood et al., 1957), each of them shares with the others the notion that internal forces are generated whenever beliefs or attitudes are inconsistent with one another, and that these forces press toward consistency. Differences among these theories revolve mainly around definitions of elements of cognition and measurement schemes for determining inconsistency. Most such theories, however, are themselves consistent with Festinger's general contention that the magnitude of the forces (dissonance) is a function of the number of inconsistent elements, the importance of those elements, and the degree to which the elements are independent of each other (Festinger, 1957). With the exception of Osgood *et al.*, none of the inconsistency theories supplies a metric for measuring how inconsistent any single element may be from the pattern of the rest, although each theory implies such a metric.

The spatial model, however, provides an exact mathematical definition of inconsistency in the form of the triangle inequalities relation. As we noted in Chapter 4, any 3 points can be said to form a euclidean triangle if and only if the sum of any two of the distances among them does not exceed the third. For any set of k points, those points represent a euclidean configuration if and only if the triangle inequalities rule is not violated for any 3 of the points.

As we saw in Chapter 4, when the triangle inequalities rule is violated for any triple of points, the result is a Riemann manifold, which is represented by a coordinate system in which some of the dimensions are imaginary. In this case, as we have seen, the sum of the roots associated with the real dimensions will exceed the sum of all roots (since, of course, the roots associated with the imaginary dimensions will be negative), and therefore the ratio of the sum of the positive roots to the trace (the sum of all roots) provides a convenient measure of the degree to which the space is noneuclidean. This number, the warp factor, is an unambiguous measure of the global inconsistency of all concepts in a domain. No experiments have been performed explicitly to determine the relation of the warp factor to other variables of interest, but reductions in the warp factor have been noted during election campaigns as the election is approached (Barnett, Serota, & Taylor, 1976), and several investigators have suggested that the warp factor is related to the degree to which respondents are confused or ignorant of the domain being scaled, or to the extent to which objects or words are used ambiguously within a domain (Woelfel, Barnett, & Dinkelacker, 1978; Woelfel & Danes, 1980).

If internal inconsistency does produce forces toward consistency, persons or groups who exhibit high warp factors within specific domains ought then to exhibit behaviors leading to decreased warp over time.

These warps ought not to be thought of as pathological, however, any more than departures of dinner plates from perfect disks should be thought of as defects of the plates. Since the theory presented here assumes that all messages no matter how complicated are built out of pairwise simple messages, almost any message which resulted in the large scale movement of any pair of concepts ought to be expected to bring about inconsistencies or warps. Pressures toward consistency, should such exist, would then be expected to result in long-term adjustments of other concepts not implicated in the original messages.

CHAPTER 9

BEHAVIOR

Theory

When undergraduate students are asked whether attitude, belief, or behavior is the easiest concept to define, overwhelmingly they say behavior is the easiest. Actually providing such a definition, however, is another matter, and the discussion usually deteriorates rapidly into arguments as to whether "thinking" or "hiccupping" should be considered behavior. In fact, of course, the concept of behavior, like any concept, has only relative meaning, and behavior is given such meaning as it has by observers who define it relative to yet other concepts. Thus a person might be described by one observer as "sitting still," by another as "resting," and by a third as "doing nothing." Included among the list of observers should be the actor himself/herself, and, although it is usually but not always the case that we assign priority to the individual's own definition of his or her behavior, there is no fundamental epistemological reason to do so.

Within the system proposed here, however, and consistent with the principle of relativization, behavior (or behaviors) may be defined as (an) object(s) relative to other objects in a spatial array. Figure 9.1 shows the first principle plane of the domain of a set of ten behaviors ranging from mundane activities (walking, strolling, etc.) through specialized (practicing medicine) and rare behaviors (revolution), as they were perceived by a small sample of undergraduate students at a large midwest-

FIGURE 9.1 First principal plane of a set of 10 behaviors.

ern university in 1969. As we would expect, the least common occupation activity (revolution) is maximally dissimilar from the most common behaviors, while the specialized activity (practicing medicine) is also outside the cluster of common activities, but not so far out as revolution.

Clearly, any activity that can be represented by a symbol can be represented in such a space, from momentary nonvoluntary actions such as hicupping to whole careers of activity, such as practicing medicine or seeking the truth. Nor is it necessary to confine the objects in the domain to activities as such, but descriptors of behaviors (such as "pleasant" or "hard work") can also be included. In this way the meanings of any behavior for any group can be measured in the same way as the meanings of any object whatever are scaled.

Perhaps most important, however, is the fact that information from the domain of behaviors may be used to provide information about likely activities for individuals or groups by the simple expedient of including a self term in the manifold along with those behaviors. The assumption underlying such a procedure is simply that the likelihood that a person or group will engage in a behavior is an inverse function of the distance between that behavior and the self. (Although a self term was not included in the example just provided, measurements made a few days after those in Figure 9.1 showed that the concept "revolution" moved somewhat further away from the set of everyday occupations, while the concept "fighting" move much closer to the common activities. During the interval between measures, most of the students had participated in or observed massive demonstrations stemming from the Cambodia invasion and Kent State killings; during this period fighting was commonplace on the campus.)

Such research as exists seems to show a special relationship between the distance between an object and the self point and behavior relative to that object (Woelfel & Danes, 1980). Jones and Young (1972), for example, found graduate students were more likely to include on their graduate committees those faculty members closest to their self points on a multidimensional space, and similarly, Brophy (1976) found that the distance between pairs of faculty members at a large midwestern university was inversely proportional to an index of the total amount of communication between them during their tenure in the department. Danes and Woelfel (1975) showed that the correlation between the distance of political figures from the average self of a sample of undergraduate students correlated with the average evaluation of those figures $-.93$, such that the closer a political figure to the self, the more favorably he (the political figures used in the study were all male) was evaluated by the sample. In the realm of market research, several studies (Green & Carmone, 1972; Stefflre, 1972) found that products closest to the self in multidimensional scaling spaces show higher sales figures than those further from the self, and in fact a large proportion of commercial market research studies is based on this assumption. Similarly, Serota et al. (1977) showed not only that those political candidates closer to the aggregate self point received more votes, but that the proportion of the vote total each candidate received was inversely proportional to the distance from the self.

We do not assume, however, that the link between behavior toward an object and distance of the object from the self is due simply to an increase in the favorability of those concepts close to the self, since the relationship between distance from the self and favorability of the object is not perfect, and similarly the relationship between favorability toward an object and behavior toward the object is not perfect. Green, Maheshwari, and Rao (1969) for example, did not find any relationship between distance from self and favorability toward objects when dealing with products which ranged from low cost to beyond the economic reach of sample members. It is not the favorability toward an object which motivates behaviors toward it, in our view, nor is it the perceived benefits to be gained from a behavior which leads one to perform it but rather the "goodness of fit" between behavior and self as measured by the distance between self and behavior or self and object. Thus we assume that persons with chronic coughs would place coughing close to the self, but we would not expect this to mean that coughing was viewed favorably by the respondents.

The notion that behaviors close to the concept of self are more likely to be performed than those far from the self is particularly appropriate to a self-concept-based theory such as the present one. Perhaps the most common theory of human behavior in use by social scientists is the economic theory rooted in Aristotle's entelechy. Although wide variations exist, such theories assume that behavior is motivated by the hope of some reward or the fear of some punishment. These theories have the greatest difficulties with two classes of behavior. The first of these classes consists of those activities which clearly result in disadvantage to those who perform them, and seemingly with the complete knowledge of those same people. Thus alcoholism, for example, is a difficult theoretical problem, since alcoholics frequently report that they know and understand the negative consequences of their drinking and even often report little or no pleasure even during the drinking. It was precisely to deal with such cases that Freud was led to posit the unconscious mind, since he could then assume that some goal of the unconscious mind was served when the person could find no conscious goal to his or her activities.

The second class of behaviors troublesome to economic or goal-oriented theories consists of those activities performed without any explicit conscious recognition by the actor. Included in this class of behaviors are virtually all linguistic acts, such as the selection of appropriate words and phrases to express an idea, and virtually all of what are now thought of as nonverbal behaviors such as frowning or "preening" or crossing one's legs. Like the first class of behaviors, actors usually cannot verbalize any goal or purpose for the actions, but unlike the first class, most frequently the individual has no knowledge of performing the act at all.

These kinds of considerations have led several self-theorists to suggest that behaviors are not chosen on the basis of goals or advantages, but rather on the basis of their *learned appropriateness*. Such theories assume that individuals develop vocabularies of behaviors that they know how to perform, and that they also learn sets of circumstances under which each of the behaviors is appropriate. Thus, when a person identifies a situation which calls for a specific act within that person's vocabulary, that action is automatically called out and performed without any further calculation of satisfaction, cost, or reward (Mead, 1934; Lemert, 1951; Foote, 1951; Mills, 1940). In a different form, these same theories find a counterpart in what communication theorists often call the "rules perspective" within which persons are thought to learn socially prescribed rules concerning which behaviors are to be fitted into which situations. While motivation and reward may be involved (according to some theorists) in learning the rules or deciding to adhere to them, nonetheless in most specific situations behaviors appropriate under the learned rules are called out without the intervention of a cost–benefit decision at the time, in much the same way as a speaker follows linguistic and grammatical rules without specifically adjudging them during their use (Cushman & Pierce, 1977; Cushman & Tompkins, 1980).

An example of a specific theory modeled on these premises is the theory of the formation of deviant careers formulated by Lemert (1951). This theory suggests that children, being incompletely socialized into their culture, are liable in the course of their activities to perform many activities which are deviant from cultural norms either statistically (i.e., they are uncommon behaviors, such as, perhaps, exhibiting uncommon early interest in mathematics or spelling) or morally (i.e., they are behaviors that are culturally discouraged or prohibited, such as homosexual acts). These deviant actions are called *primary deviance* by Lemert, and are left unexplained.[1] Following from the notion of Cooley's looking glass self, however, children are frequently observed by others, particularly adults, in the performance of these acts, and the reaction of those others to the activity of the child provides a definition or *label* for the child. If the observer disregards or ignores the act, not much of consequence is to be expected. But if the observer identifies the act as a sign of a deviant role (e.g., if he or she should suggest that the act is the act of a smart person or a homosexual) then that reaction to the act serves as a role definition for the child. Repeated and consistent labels of such a type (you are a smart child, or you are a homosexual) can lead the child to accept the implied definition of self. Once having adopted the label, the child will then be expected to enact the behavior systematically as a part of the role he or she has adopted. Such behavior is called secondary deviance. Such secondary behavior differs from primary deviance in that it is not the spontaneous fitting of a behavior to a circumstance, but the systematic enactment of behavior consistent with a role that is appropriate to a person who defines himself/herself in a specific way. As a result of accepting the definition of self and the roles appropriate to such a definition, the child can be expected to learn other behaviors appropriate to the role and build a systematic repertoire of deviant behavior consistent with the role. It is important to note that the theory expects

---

[1] Lemert does not consider these actions inexplicable, but rather leaves them to be explained by others.

the child to adopt the deviant role not because it is pleasant or beneficial to do so, but because the consistent and systematic actions of others have led him or her to believe that the role definition is true.

Although Lemert's theory was originally intended to account for the formation of deviant careers, it is easily generalized to account for the formation of any career whatever, since a nondeviant career (such as teacher) may be construed as an object of the same epistemelogical status as a deviant career (such as burglar). Each career may be located in a multidimensional space by the procedures described in Chapter 4, along with a self point. In the case of an individual, the likelihood that he or she will adopt a given career may be assumed to be inversely proportional to the distance between self and that career, while, on a cultural level, the proportion of people who are engaged in any career ought to be inversely proportional to the distance between the aggregate self and that career.

Within this model, socialization of individuals into careers can be accounted for by the equations developed in Chapters 7 and 8, since each act of labeling by a "significant other" may be represented as a vector from the self-point of the individual to the career implicated in the label. Thus the statement "I think you will be a doctor when you grow up" can be represented as a vector from the self point of the child to the concept doctor. Multiple labels from either the same or multiple significant others might be expected to average as equation (8.4) implies resulting in a net force toward the average label or expectation of the set of all significant others (Woelfel, 1975).

Using a variant of the Occupational Aspiration Scale (OAS; Haller & Miller, 1971), Saltiel asked high school students in a consolidated rural school district to list the jobs that they (a) actually expected they might attain, (b) most wanted to attain, (c) after their schooling was over, and (d) when they were 30 years old. The resulting 34 most frequently designated occupations were then formed into a complete pair-comparison instrument according to the methods shown earlier. Because of the great length of this instrument, the final questionnaire was divided into three parts, and a third of the instrument was administered at random to each of the respondents, as well as to each of their significant others (who were identified earlier by means of a variant of the Wisconsin Significant Other Battery; Haller & Woelfel, 1969). Each of the significant others was also asked to respond to the identical variant of the OAS on which the students had listed their occupational choices, although appropriate pronoun changes were made to indicate that each significant other was expected to list his or her expectations for the student for whom he or she was a significant other.

The result of this work was a multidimensional space, averaged over all students and their significant others, within which are arrayed the 34 occupations. For each student in the sample, the coordinates of all the occupations listed in response to the modified OAS were averaged to produce the coordinates of the average occupational choice for that person. This set of averaged coordinates thus designates a point in the space which represents the average occupational choice for that student; we might reasonably expect that the occupation nearest this point would have the highest probability of being chosen by the student.

Similarly, the coordinates of the set of occupations that all significant others for a single individual expected of the student (as measured by the modified OAS) were averaged to yield the average occupational expectation of the set of others for each student. These averaged significant other coordinates, along with several variables such as sex, grade-point average, and number of extracurricular activities in which the student participated, were then used as independent variables in a linear regression equation to predict the coordinates of the student's average occupational choices. The resulting equations account for 84% of the variance in the coordinate of the average job choice on the first dimension. This first dimension correlates about .9 with the Duncan Socioeconomic Index (SEI) score for these occupations and may be taken as good measure of occupational prestige, and so the fact that this R^2 is about the same as that already identified in the status attainment literature for predictions of status aspirations seems very strong evidence for the validity of the procedure.

The same equation accounts for 93% of the variance in the average coordinate on the second dimension (which correlates highly with the proportion of women in each job) and averages about 60% of variance explained on the rest of the dimensions.

While the very high explained variance on each of the dimensions may itself be taken as a strong indication of the usefulness of these procedures and the applicability of the underlying theory, taken holistically these results are even more impressive. As Figure 9.2 illustrates, the predicted value from the regression equation defines a point on each dimension which is the predicted coordinate of the student's job choice on that dimension. The confidence interval around that predicted value defines a band within which the student's chosen job is likely to be located. Since each dimension is orthogonal to each other, these bands intersect to form a hyperrectangle (the shaded area in Figure 9.2) within which the actual job choice is likely to be located. The probability that the job choice actually lies within this region is given by the product of the confidence levels around each of the predicted values given by the regression equations.

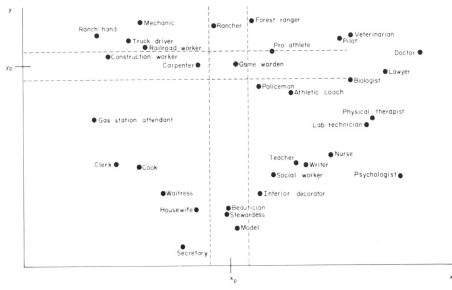

FIGURE 9.2 First principal plane of a set of occupations (following Saltiel, 1978). $x_p = \Sigma_i b_i x_i + e_x; y_p = \Sigma_j b_j y_j + e_j$.

Although the precision of Saltiel's predictions are remarkable compared to conventional practice in the area of occupational choice research, nonetheless the difficulties of a pioneering effort and the budget limitations of the Saltiel study lead us to believe that more elaborate efforts can lead to predictions of actual job choices with levels of precision in excess of the precision with which researchers can now predict only the status level of job aspirations. Much more important, of course, is the fact that the theory underlying Saltiel's investigation is completely general and can be applied to *any discrete choice situation whatsoever*. This means that the identical procedures used by Saltiel can be generalized to account for the selection of any discrete behavior from any set of potential behaviors, even when the behaviors are discrete, categorical acts. This reasoning applies as well whether the behavior is itself a relatively isolated act, such as going to a movie, or to a class of systematically related acts defined into a *role*, such as becoming a movie critic. By following the logic of deduction and induction discussed earlier (Chapter 7), the model will account for the inductive formation of roles as a consequence of adopting one by one many of the behaviors which constitute the role, or for the deductive formation of behaviors following from the adoption of a role.

In the former case, we assume the procedure operates much like the guidance counsellor who investigates the specific behaviors a child likes or performs frequently, and then attempts to identify a role (occupation) psychologically close to those behaviors. Thus the counsellor who finds that a student likes to draw and calculate might suggest he or she think of becoming an architect. In the latter case, an individual might adopt a general role such as wife or father as a result of a specific act (such as getting married or having a child). Adopting this role designation will of course result in a consistent shift in the type of responses the new role incumbent can expect from his or her significant others which will result in a relocation of the self into the region close to the role, and the behaviors included within the role will then be close to the new self point. The theory suggested by Lemert includes both inductive and deductive components, since the significant others for a child observe specific actions, (such as stealing another child's toy) induce a role (criminal) and then label the child with the role designation. This in turn leads the child who accepts the label to learn more about the behaviors included within the role, which is a deductive process.

Engineering: Behavioral Control

The fact that behaviors closest to the self point are performed relatively more frequently than those far from the self, along with the likelihood that concepts may be moved through the space by means of messages according to equations such as those derived in Chapters 7 and 8, gives rise to the possibility of deliberately changing the structure of individual and cultural spaces to produce precise behavioral change, particularly in groups or cultures. This can be accomplished either by moving specific objects or behaviors closer to (or further from) the self point, or, alternatively, moving the self point toward or away from specific behaviors or objects. Of course, this is done routinely in everyday discourse, and some of the illustrations we have used earlier are examples. Thus Lemert's theory can be seen as arguing that labeling has the effect of moving individual self points toward the position of deviant roles, and everyday advertising strategies may be assumed to intend to move specific products and services closer to the self points of markets and market segments. The equations developed earlier, however, provide ways to do this with much greater precision than has been possible heretofore.

The idea of using multidimensional scaling algorithms to aid in the development of persuasive messages is not a new one, and in fact multidimensional scaling procedures have made up an important segment of marketing research for about a decade. In a typical case, researchers will derive (by any of a variety of MDS routines) a configuration which includes the concepts to be manipulated (such as a product, service, or political candidate), a set of attributes or descriptors of those concepts, and some "ideal point" such as "the car I would buy" or "the ideal congressman," or a concept of self ("me"). Based on a careful examination of two-dimensional plots of the configuration, a message strategy is designed which attaches attributes to the manipulated concept such that, in the researcher's judgment, recipients of the message will judge the concept maximally close to the ideal point.

A typical example is provided by Barnett et al. (1976). Based on a telephone survey of a sample of voters in a congressional election, Barnett et al. identified five key issues in the campaign. These issues, along with the names of the candidates, their political parties, and the concept "me," were compiled into a complete pair-comparison questionnaire administered to 307 registered voters in the congressional district at three points in time prior to the election.

Based on a careful visual scrutiny of this plot (in several rotations), Barnett et al. suggested that the candidate attach the attributes "law and order" and "Democrat" to his name as a means of moving closer to the concept "me." Subsequent measures showed this strategy to be roughly successful; a reanalysis of these data by Serota et al. (1977) showed the candidate concept in fact moved at an angle of about 30 degrees from the resultant of the component vectors "Democrat" and "law and order," increased his vote total by doing so, and won the election decisively against a popular incumbent in a state where no other incumbent was defeated, even though his opponent outspent him on the campaign by a factor of 3.

Despite its apparent effectiveness, this procedure is flawed by its visual and intuitive character. In the experience of the present authors, visualizations of multidimensional configurations are frequently misleading, and in fact, the reanalysis of Serota et al. shows the message chosen in this case yielded a resultant vector about 44 degrees off from the theoretically optimal strategy. We now present a simple mathematical procedure for designing messages of this sort based on falsifiable elementary assumptions, along with unambiguous mathematical procedures for measuring the effectiveness of these messages.

We begin by defining the vector space $R^{\mu}_{(\alpha)}$, where each of the contravariant vectors $R^{\mu}_{(\alpha)}$ represents the projections of the αth concept on a set of covariant (basis) unit vectors e_{μ}. In practice, we expect the $R^{\mu}_{(\alpha)}$ to be the result of a multidimensional scaling analysis of a set of proximities data for k concepts, where r is the number of dimensions retained. Therefore, we allow α to range from 1 to k and μ from 1 to r.

We further designate the concept to be moved or manipulated (the "start" concept) as $R^\mu_{(s)}$ and the ideal point toward which it is to be moved as the "target" concept $R^\mu_{(t)}$. The goal thus becomes to move the start concept along the target vector $R^\mu_{(t)} - R^\mu_{(s)}$. For convenience, we first recenter the coordinate system with the start concept $R^\mu_{(s)}$ on the origin by the translation

$$R^\mu_{(\alpha)} = \bar{R}^\mu_{(\alpha)} - \bar{R}^\mu_{(s)}, \tag{9.1}$$

where $R^\mu_{(\alpha)}$ is the position vector of the αth concept after recentering, $\bar{R}^\mu_{(\alpha)}$ the original position vector of the αth concept, $\bar{R}^\mu_{(s)}$ the original position vector of the concept to be manipulated (the "start" concept), $\alpha = 1, 2, \ldots, k$, and $\mu = 1, 2, \ldots, r$; since $R_{(s)}$ (the magnitude or length of $R^\mu_{(s)}$) now is zero, the target vector is given by $R^\mu_{(t)}$, which is represented in Figure 9.3 as the "target vector."

As we suggested in Chapter 7, our understanding of the dynamics of these spaces is rudimentary, but we begin with the simple assumption that objects attributed to each other (in the form "x is y") will converge along the line segment connecting them. If one of the two concepts is very massive, that is, has a meaning that is highly resistant to change, then most of the motion to be expected can be attributed to the less stable of the two. In Figure 9.3, the sentence "the candidate is friendly" should therefore result in a motion of the candidate concept along the vector $R^\mu_{(p)}$, since it is reasonable to expect the meaning of the word "friendly" to be more stable than the definition of the candidate. This vector is labeled $R^\mu_{(p)}$ (predicted vector) in Figure 9.3. As yet, insufficient data are available to warrant predictions of the magnitude of this motion, but its direction is clearly given from our starting assumption.

Based on this assumption, determination of a single optimal issue may be simply accomplished. First, the angle $\theta_{(pt)}$ between any predicted vector $R^\mu_{(p)}$ and the target vector $R^\mu_{(t)}$ can be conveniently calculated as

$$\theta_{(pt)} = \cos^{-1}(g_{\mu\nu} R^\mu_{(p)} R^\nu_{(t)} / R_{(p)} R_{(t)}), \tag{9.2}$$

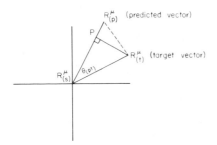

FIGURE 9.3   Hypothetical representation of a multidimensional scaling space.

where

$$R_{(p)} = \left| R_{(p)}^{\mu} \right| = (g_{\mu\nu} R_{(p)}^{\mu} R_{(p)}^{\nu})^{1/2}, \tag{9.3}$$
$$R_{(t)} = \left| R_{(t)}^{\mu} \right| = (g_{\mu\nu} R_{(t)}^{\mu} R_{(t)}^{\nu})^{1/2}, \tag{9.4}$$

and where the quantities $g_{\mu\nu}$ are given by the scalar products of the covariant basic vectors, that is,

$$g_{\mu\nu} = e_{\mu}^{j} e_{\nu}^{j}. \tag{9.5}$$

The $g_{\mu\nu}$ can be shown to be a covariant tensor of the second rank which defines the metric properties of the space and is therefore referred to as the fundamental or "metric" tensor. If the covariant basis vectors e_{μ} are real and orthogonal, then the $g_{\mu\nu}$ take on the familiar form

$$g_{\mu\nu} = \delta_{\nu}^{\mu} = \begin{cases} 1, & \text{if } \mu = \nu, \\ 0, & \text{if } \mu \neq \nu. \end{cases}$$

That concept whose position vector forms the smallest angle with the target vector will represent the concept which lies most nearly in the *direction* of the "me" or ideal point. The amount of change advocated by this message strategy is given straightforwardly by the length of the predicted vector $R_{(p)}$, which is given by equation (9.3).

Where the pth through rth roots are negative (corresponding to imaginary eigenvectors), the $g_{\mu\nu}$ are given by

$$g_{\mu\nu} = \begin{cases} 0, & \text{if } \mu \neq \nu, \\ 1, & \text{if } \mu = \nu < p, \\ -1, & \text{if } \mu = \nu \geq p. \end{cases} \tag{9.6}$$

Given these considerations, and equations (8.2)–(8.4), we can now solve any part of the triangle $R_{(s)}^{\mu}, R_{(t)}^{\mu}, R_{(p)}^{\mu}$ in Figure 9.3. If the message equating the start concept $R_{(s)}^{\mu}$ with the concept $R_{(p)}^{\mu}$ were completely successful, such that the concept represented by the end points of $R_{(s)}^{\mu}$ moved to the end point of $R_{(p)}^{\mu}$, then the distance between the start concept and target concept (after the message) would be given by the distance $\left| R_{(p)}^{\mu} - R_{(t)}^{\mu} \right|$.

Such an outcome is very unlikely in most cases, since we could at best assume the point represented by $R_{(s)}^{\mu}$ would move only part of the distance toward $R_{(p)}^{\mu}$. The point P in Figure 9.3 represents the orthogonal projection of $R_{(t)}^{\mu}$ on $R_{(p)}^{\mu}$ and gives the point of closest approach to $R_{(t)}^{\mu}$.

The length of this line segment is given by

$$\left| P R_{(t)}^{\mu} \right| = R_{(t)} \sin \theta_{(pt)}, \tag{9.7}$$

where $\theta_{(pt)}$ is as given in (9.2). Similarly, the distance along $R^{\mu}_{(p)}$ that the start concept must travel to reach P is given by

$$\left|PR^{\mu}_{(s)}\right| = \left|PR^{\mu}_{(t)}\right|/\tan \theta_{(pt)}. \tag{9.8}$$

The percentage of change advocated that must be achieved for this message to have its maximum effect is given simply by

$$\Delta \% \ max = 100\left|PR^{\mu}_{(s)}\right|/R_{(p)}. \tag{9.9}$$

These calculations, along with an empirically measured estimate of the proportion of advocated change actually to be expected, provide ample data on the basis of which the optimal single issue may be chosen.

Multiconcept messages are very easily (and similarly) determined on the basis of an additional assumption: messages average like vectors in the space. This is equivalent to the assumption that order effects (such as primacy–recency) are negligible over the life of the message campaign. Based on this assumption, the position vectors or any or more issues may simply be averaged to yield a resultant vector given (for two vectors) by

$$R^{\mu}_{(p)} = (R^{\mu}_{(\alpha)} + R^{\mu}_{(\beta)})/2. \tag{9.10}$$

This resultant vector is then taken as the predicted vector and the procedures just described are repeated.

Equation (9.10) can easily be generalized for n vector sums, as we have shown in equation (8.3), and weighted for inertial masses as in equation (8.4).

Evaluation of the degree of success of the message strategy is also simply a matter of determining the angles included between the predicted, target and observed vectors over the time interval Δt. In practice, however, it is difficult to hold the origin of the space at time $t + \Delta t$ precisely where it was at time t, and so it is convenient to choose yet a different origin. In our own work, we establish an origin at the centroid of the set of concepts not included or implicated in any message, and rotate the time t and time $t + \Delta t$ spaces to least-squares best fit among only those unmanipulated concepts. This procedure may be seen as an effort to use the unmanipulated concepts to determine a stable frame of reference against which the relative motions of the manipulated concepts may be gauged. Time 1 variables transformed into these stable coordinates will be represented by barred tensors (e.g., $R^{\mu}_{(s)(t1)} = \bar{R}^{\mu}_{(s)}$) and time 2 variables will be represented by hats (e.g., $R^{\mu}_{(s)(t2)} = \hat{R}^{\mu}_{(s)}$) as shown in Figure 9.4. Given these definitions we may define the predicted vector across the interval Δt as

$$R^{\mu}_{(p)} = \bar{R}^{\mu}_{(s)} - \bar{R}^{\mu}_{(p)}. \tag{9.11}$$

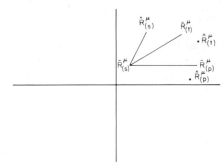

FIGURE 9.4. Multidimensional scaling space at time t and time $t + \Delta t$ represented on stable coordinates.

The target vector across Δt is defined as

$$R^{\mu}_{(t)} = \bar{R}^{\mu}_{(t)} - \bar{R}^{\mu}_{(s)}. \tag{9.12}$$

Similarly, the observed motion vector is given by

$$R^{\mu}_{(o)} = \hat{R}^{\mu}_{(s)} - \bar{R}^{\mu}_{(s)}. \tag{9.13}$$

Evaluation of the extent to which the start concept has moved as predicted is given simply by the angle between the predicted and observed vector, which is given by

$$\theta_{(po)} = \cos^{-1}(g_{\mu\nu} R^{\mu}_{(p)} R^{\nu}_{(o)} / R_{(p)} R_{(o)}). \tag{9.14}$$

Also of interest is the extent to which the start concept has moved in the direction of the target, which is given by

$$\theta_{(pt)} = \cos^{-1}(g_{\mu\nu} R^{\mu}_{(t)} R^{\nu}_{(o)} / R_{(t)} R_{(o)}). \tag{9.15}$$

Further Considerations

While these equations are sufficient to indicate the basic structure of the procedures, many valuable modifications can be derived easily by the interested reader. One such example is the unweighted summation of vectors in multiconcept messages given by equation (9.10), which assumes each concept to be equally effective. This assumption may be relaxed by providing weights $\beta_{(\alpha)}$ such that (9.10) is replaced by

$$R^{\mu}_{(p)} = \sum_{\alpha} \beta_{(\alpha)} R^{\mu}_{(\alpha)} \bigg/ \sum_{\alpha} \beta_{(\alpha)}, \tag{9.16}$$

where the $\beta_{(\alpha)}$ are estimated empirically by the regression equation

$$R_{(o)}^{\mu} = \sum_{\alpha} \beta_{(\alpha)} R_{(\alpha)}^{\mu} + e_{(o)}, \tag{9.17}$$

where $e_{(o)}$ is a least-squares error term.

The equations presented here, it may be noted, are all difference equations, reflecting the "before–after" or "treatment–control" designs typical of current practice. Clearly the emphasis on process implicit in this chapter suggests a much heavier emphasis on longitudinal or time series designs. When such data sets become available the transformation of these equations into differential form is straightforward, particularly when orthogonal MDS routines are chosen. Thus the infinitesimal displacement of the start vector $ds_{(s)}$ is given by

$$ds_{(s)} = (g_{\mu\nu} dR_{(s)}^{\mu} dR_{(s)}^{\nu})^{1/2}, \tag{9.18}$$

where the $dR_{(s)}^{\mu}$ represent coordinate differentials. Similarly, the instantaneous velocity of the start vector at time t is given by

$$V_t = ds_{(s)}/dt \tag{9.19}$$

and the instantaneous acceleration of the start concept at t is

$$a_t = d^2 s_{(s)}/dt^2. \tag{9.20}$$

Although our understanding of the dynamics of cognition is limited, such empirical evidence as exists seems to show that the equations are not too far off the mark. In a study designed specifically to evaluate these equations, Cody (1980) identified 96 traits used in prior studies to evaluate the credibility of sources of messages. A sample of 18 undergraduate students at a large midwestern university sorted these 96 traits into 11 categories ranging from "a quality a close friend of mine should not possess" to "a quality a close friend of mine should possess." The six traits which showed the lowest variability were included as concepts on a pair-comparison instrument. Also included were the names of three political figures, Hubert Humphrey, George McGovern, and Birch Bayh. The first of these were chosen because data from 54 additional undergraduates about 19 public figures showed them to be highly familiar to the sample, yet not currently the subject of much current incoming information. Birch Bayh was selected because he was moderately familiar and inactive in the information environment. To these concepts and public figures was added the concept "Ideal Credible Source." Thus, the six traits and their grammatical opposites, the three public figures, and the concept Ideal Credible Source made up a 16-concept pair-comparison questionnaire, which was then administered to 54 additional undergraduate students.

Based on the results of these administrations, all possible combinations of these words were taken one, two, three, and four at a time to find the combination which would move Birch Bayh closest to the Ideal Credible Source. The resultant of the concepts Humphrey, competent, just, and experienced correlated .932 with the target vector, an angle of 21 degrees, and this was the message selected. These concepts, along with synonyms selected from a thesaurus, were used to construct the following message.

Positive induction message:

Birch Bayh has demonstrated his skill and proficiency in public service time and time again. He is competent, demonstrably capable, and decidedly qualified to address the issues in America today. He is a seasoned veteran whose background and past experiences in public life have made him one of the most experienced men on the political scene today. Many analysts have commented on the similarities between Birch Bayh and Hubert Humphrey. Indeed, Birch Bayh may be viewed as *the* Humphrey legatee; an advocate of that which Humphrey represents and has represented since he entered politics. Their philosophies are similar. Their practice of politics is similar. Their experiences and personalities are similar. In addition, Birch Bayh deals fairly with issues. He is just, even-handed, and unbiased in his speeches.

An additional 45 undergraduates then read the message, which was attributed to a nonpartisan citizens' committee, along with a brief speech attributed to Bayh. On the assumption that the synonyms chose were indeed exact synonyms, and that the speech attributed to Bayh had little direct effect, the theory presented here predicts that the results of the message should be that Bayh would move directly along the resultant vector of the 4-concept message. In fact, the correlation between the predicted motion and the observed motion was .805, a departure of 36 degrees from the predicted trajectory.

In a second study, Cody (1980) attempted to move another public figure, Eliot Richardson, toward the Ideal Credible Source, this time choosing a 2-concept message. Data taken from 30 undergraduate students who had read the message showed the observed motion correlated .762 with the predicted trajectory, a deviation of 40 degrees.

Cody also attempted to determine the effects of negative messages, that is, messages which are negative in grammatical form. To do this, he utilized the identical messages already described, but changed each into negative form. Cody's working hypothesis was that this would have the result of moving the public figures away from the Ideal Credible Source. The results of this work have been somewhat ambiguous, however, since in one case the correlation between the predicted vector and the observed vector was good (Eliot Richardson moved along the predicted vector with a correlation of .757), but in the other it was poor (Birch Bayh moved along the predicted vector with a correlation of only .284). Cody suggests a plausible explanation for the poor fit of the negative model in the case of Birch Bayh. He reasons that the assumptions of the equations require that the concepts implicated in the message should be stable concepts, yet in the case of Bayh's message, Hubert Humphrey was included in the message yet himself exhibited considerable motion. Secondary analysis of the relative trajectories of Humphrey and Bayh seem to indicate the plausibility of this explanation, but until further research answers the question more conclusively negative messages probably ought to be treated with extra caution.

   Although the precision of control of the laboratory is hard to duplicate in the field, there is a growing body of consistent evidence that these procedures work well in actual situations. In 1976, a proposal to ban nonreturnable bottles and cans from the State of Michigan was put to a statewide ballot. Initial response of the electorate was quite favorable, with early polls showing approximately 70% of those who had formed an opinion favoring the proposition (Proposal A). Shortly after the proposal was put on the ballot, however, a massive industry sponsored campaign to defeat the proposal was initiated, including extensive radio, television, and newspaper advertising. This campaign was very effective, and within several weeks, polls showed a near even split among decided voters. About 6 weeks prior to the election, volunteer workers canvassed several dozen voters statewide by telephone to determine the concepts most closely associated with the election campaign. The most frequently mentioned concepts, along with the words

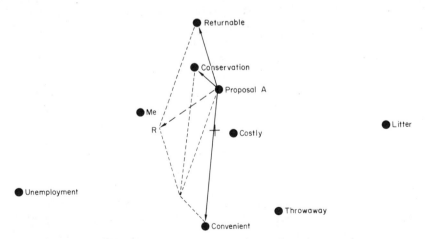

FIGURE 9.5   Best messages for a referendum.

"yourself" and "Proposal A" were included in a pair-comparison instrument of the type described here, and this instrument was administered to 30 voters statewide by telephone. The results of this work are shown in Figure 9.5. Calculations based on the equations described earlier in this chapter showed that the concepts 2 (returnables), 7 (convenient), and 8 (conservation of natural resources) combined to produce an effective message which would be expected to move Proposal A in the direction of the voters' position (concept 9), as shown by the resultant of those three vectors (marked R in Figure 9.5). The researchers recommended the volunteer committee utilize all its remaining resources to produce radio spot announcements which said, "Returnables: a convenient way to conserve natural resources. Vote Yes on Proposal A." When these spot announcements first appeared (3 weeks before the election), Proposal A was trailing in the polls about 48 to 52, but by the time of the election, Proposal A was adopted with nearly 70% of the vote. Although insufficient statistical controls exist to warrant any causal connections, nonetheless the dramatic change in the trend of the statistics coinciding with the advant of the campaign is suggestive, particularly since the opposition to the proposal outspent the proponents by a factor of 100.

CHAPTER 10

GROUPS, ORGANIZATIONS, AND CULTURES

Social Organization as a Thermodynamic System

The theory and equations presented in the last three chapters were written primarily to account for the processes internal to a single individual person or group upon the receipt of messages from the near surround. Nonetheless they have important implications for the structure of organizations built of multiple individual persons or groups. In this chapter, we shall attempt to draw some of the more important of those implications into the beginnings of a theory of social organization.

Network Structure

Each of the individual elements (persons, groups, organizations, or *nodes* as they are frequently called in network theory) are organized into networks which themselves have a systems character.[1] Each of these nodes may gather information (i.e., receive messages) from the near

[1] The terminology in this section is based on Schwartz (1977).

surround through *ports*. In the case of individuals, these ports consist of the sensory apparatus. In groups, each of the individual members may be thought of as a port, while in larger organizations, subgroups may be considered ports, and often in larger organizations specific subgroups are deliberately constituted to serve as ports for the purpose of gathering information for the organization from the near surround.

The information gathered from the near surround is distributed through the network of nodes by means of *links* or *channels*. Historically these channels have been interpersonal, consisting primarily of light and sound media within close physical proximity. Within the last several millennia, these channels were augmented by the physical distribution of paper and informed artifacts such as sculpture, pottery, and architecture, and most recently have been extended dramatically by means of the print and electronic media. Within any communication network, information is carried in *codes,* and a precondition for communication of any sort is shared code. The nature of the code determines the type and volume of information which can be carried through a given system, and much of this book has been devoted to a discussion of the relative advantages of different coding systems for the distribution of information relevant to human social organization. Within these networks, some of the nodes may serve special functions as *processors* of information. Processing consists essentially of decoding, transforming, and/or comparing information from multiple inputs, followed by encoding and retransmition of the result of such processing. In human communication networks, this processing function is always to some extent *distributed*, that is, processing of information is carried out to some extent by every node in the network. Different social organizations, in fact, differ to the extent that the processing function is centralized, and in virtually every actual human network, information processing is to some extent centralized into certain specialized processing nodes, such as senates and congresses, executives, opinion leaders, news bureaus, and governments. It is also common that human communication systems include other specialized nodes which may be called *concentrators* or *buffers* which provide such local processing as code translation and buffering or temporary storage of bursts of information (which might overload communication channels or central processors) for later transmission at manageable rates. (Secretaries and receptionists are examples of such a buffering function.) The earth serves as a buffer in the solar system, absorbing radiation on its day side and reradiating it on its night side.

Any communication network, regardless of whether constituted of material objects, machinery, or human beings, can be described in terms of nodes, ports, links, codes, concentrators, and processors, even though the networks themselves may be very different in character. Clearly, for example, networks may differ from each other at any point in time in their configuration or structure, which is determined solely by the nature, number, and relations of their component parts. Thus it is traditional to distinguish among star, loop, tree, mesh, line, and other types of networks, as well as centralized versus distributed processing networks, etc. Obviously, too, a network of human beings is different from a network of computers, which is different from a network of telephones or a network of molecules.

An equally important variable distinguishing communication networks is the extent to which their structures are time invariant. A completely time-invariant communication network is typified by a public address system in which each of the output speakers is permanently wired to the input port so that every input message is output through every speaker. A more variable network than this is the telephone network, which is reconfigured with each telephone call. A still more variable network structure is given by most modern computer communication networks in which the channels along which a message travels are determined by the content, size, and structure of the message and the status of the rest of the system at the moment of the transmission.

Since the structure of the first type of network never changes, we can refer to them as *unswitched* networks. Networks of the second type are called *line-switched* networks (following the analogy of the telephone network, even though in some networks no actual "lines" are involved). Networks of the third type are called *message-switched* or *packet-switched* networks. While artificial networks of each type may be identified, in human communication networks, pure types are seldom if ever found, and human organizations may be thought of as various combinations of the three types. The topological design of networks has important consequences for the characteristics of the organizations of which the networks are a part, such as their information-carrying capacity, reliability, error rates, speed of transmission, costs of operation, and retrieval times, but these topics have been treated carefully elsewhere and even quantified in important respects by scientists and engineers (cf. Schwartz, 1977), and so we will not deal with those aspects here. We shall be more concerned with the application of the principles developed earlier in this volume on the activities and processes taking place within systems of persons and groups within social organizations.

Thermodynamic Processes in Human Communication Systems

Coordination

In every case we know, physical processes of exchange obey the laws of thermodynamics to within the observational capabilities of science. On a global level, insofar as science can say, processes move toward increasing entropy, that is, available energy or information decreases for any system taken as a whole. And on a local level, reversals of this process can always be shown to come at the expense of the near surround of the system to within modern precision of measure, that is, gains in available energy for any subsystem equal losses in available energy from the near surround. The surface of the earth, for example, experiences net increases of energy locally, but these increases equal the amounts of energy due to the appropriate proportion of losses from the sun to within current error of measure. The solar system, taken as a system, experiences losses of available energy due to radiation.

All communication processes known to science involve physical interaction among the elements or nodes involved in the communication. Communication by sight involves the actual transfer of light in energy photons from object to object; verbal communication requires physical interaction of pressure waves in a conducting medium; broadcasting requires interactions of electromagnetic radiation between interacting parties; print media require the physical transportation of printed material between parties; and so on. An obvious necessary condition for the flow of information across nodes in any system, therefore, is that some "physical channel" exist between them.

Potential

The laws of thermodynamics, should they apply, would predict that the existence of a physical medium between nodes is necessary but not sufficient for communication. In addition to a physical medium, a difference of potential is also required. More precisely, the second law states that differences in potential will tend to vanish across the connection provided by the medium, and the process of reduction in potential is what we mean by communication. The elementary unit of communication is the single collision, where two elementary particles which differ in velocity contact each other in space and time and result in a transfer of momentum (communication) between the two particles. Most interesting communication systems involve multiple collisions, as is the case in the reception of light or sound waves over an interval of time, or when a fluid flows continuously through a pipe from higher to lower potential. The channel or link offers the opportunity for communication, while the difference in potential provides the motivation or force. The channel therefore provides the coordination in space and time between the communicating nodes; a channel may be said to exist when the nodes are coordinated in space and time. Differences in potential cannot vanish between nodes that are not coordinated in space and time, just as momentum is not transferred between particles that do not collide or otherwise interact (the collision being the elementary unit of coordination in space–time.)

In practical communication systems, therefore, it is necessary for communicating nodes to keep common measures of distance (space) and common clocks, so that their communication activities may be coordinated in space and time. Systems which keep common clocks can by synchronized in time. The comparison of processes requires either that each process be described against the same clock time, or that the transformations across the separate clocks on which each process has been measured are known. The more precisely clocks are synchronized, the more precisely may processes be compared and the more information may flow across a given potential in a finite interval of time. Indeed, increasing fineness of gradation of an interval of time increases the number of discrete communication events (collisions) which may be fit within the interval. This, from a communication point of view, is equivalent to increasing the total amount of time available to the communicating system.

In human systems, interpersonal communication channels exist in practice as a result of close physical proximity in time and space so that visual signals may be received by line of sight and sound waves greater in magnitude than ambient noise may be transmitted. McPhail (1974) has referred to the process of coordinating physical presence in common locations in space and time as the assembly process. Regular periodic assembly, such as is typified by scheduled meetings, may be seen as an example of line-switched networks, insofar as communication channels are opened across certain nodes at specific times whether messages are to be sent or not. If no differences in potential exist during such meetings, the nodes "have nothing to say to each other" and communication remains minimal.

Differences in potential may be domain specific, and refer to differences in the spatial structure of a domain across communicating nodes. Flow across the potential, following from the equations already presented, can be seen to reduce the potential, resulting in increased homogeneity across nodes within the domain of the communication. Mathematically, both the equations developed in the preceding three chapters and the laws of thermodynamics predict that all communicating nodes will converge on the mean of the structures of the individual nodes if communication is allowed to continue without limit; that is, if the channel remains open indefinitely. As we have seen, some research evidence available seems consistent with this hypothesis (Saltiel & Woelfel, 1975; J. C. Woelfel, 1976; Danes *et al.*, 1978; Woelfel & Haller, 1971). The mean of the structures of any domain within any system of communicating nodes, therefore, whether humans or otherwise, serves as an equilibrium value which a closed system will maintain and toward which each of the nodes in the system will tend.

Measuring Potential

No matter how interesting the concept of potential energy, it is of no practical use until it can be measured quantitatively. Fortunately, the concepts developed earlier provide a promising basis for such a quantification. First, it is important to understand that, in a relativistic system such as this one (and such as the physical theories which represent modern physical science), potential energy has no absolute significance, and only the concept of differences in potential is meaningful. Insofar as it is communication about cultural matters that interests us, *differences* in culture between nodes serve as the basic notion underlying potential energy. Insofar as the spatial array of concepts over time has been defined as the elemental description of cultural beliefs, differences in the structures of these spaces provide the primary quantities for the measurement of cultural potential energy between any two nodes. As we suggested earlier, conversations between individuals (or groups) can be described as mutual descriptions of the locations of concepts in the respective spaces of the communicating parties which result in forces for the mutual readjustment of those locations toward a common mean or equilibrium position. In the limiting case, two individuals or groups with identical spaces will experience no net forces toward readjustment, and the relative potential energy between them will be zero. As the nodes disagree increasingly about the location of objects in the spaces, the potential will increase, other factors equal. The total magnitude of the discrepancies among communicating nodes may be given directly by the trace of the scalar products matrix $\hat{S}$ in the expression

$$AT = B + E, \qquad (10.1)$$
$$\hat{S} = E \cdot E',$$

where A is the coordinate system representing the locations of the objects of interest for node A, B the coordinate matrix representing the locations of the objects of interest for node B, and T is a linear operator which minimizes the trace of $\hat{S}$.

The linear operator T represents the set of rotations and translations required to eliminate artifactual differences in the coordinate loadings between the two nodes described in Chapter 6. This is the matrix that transforms away differences in viewpoint and orientation. The trace of the scalar products $\hat{S}$ will therefore give the sum of squared distances between each object in A and its counterpart in B summed over all objects after artifactual differences have been removed. As such it should give a good estimate as to how different the two cultures are. (When there are no differences whatever, the trace of $\hat{S}$ will of course be zero.) The procedure has intuitive appeal because it is a fairly exact quantification of the reasonable premise that the potential of any group to change the opinions of another group is proportional to the extent to which the groups differ in opinion.

Even so, the notion of differences in belief or opinion is necessary but not sufficient for the understanding of relative potential energy between two nodes. As we suggested earlier, different cultural objects are differentially difficult to accelerate; that is, they have different inertial masses. If a given concept in the space of any communicating node has a small inertial mass, then the amount of energy required to move it to the equilibrium position will be small compared to the energy required to move a more massive concept through the same distance. Thus the ability of that same concept to do work on any other concept will be correspondingly small. In the physical analog, a 2-kilogram weight lifted a distance h will have twice the potential energy of a 1-kg weight lifted the same height. (Possibly more graphic is the notion that two 1-kg weights lifted to height h would have twice the potential energy of one such weight.) Thus the potential energy between any two nodes will be some function of both the overall difference or distance between the two cultural systems and the inertial masses of both systems. Since the potential energy is equal to the amount of work required to move the objects from the equilibrium position to their present position, and the work needed is directly proportional to both the mass of the object and the distance moved, then the work required is

$$w = ams, \tag{10.2}$$

where w is work, a is a constant representing the force applied, m the mass of the object moved, and s the distance from the equilibrium point.

When two objects are separated from each other, this expression becomes

$$w = am_1m_2s_{12},\qquad(10.3)$$

and the potential energy will be given by

$$U = -w,\qquad(10.4)$$

where U is potential energy. While these expressions are sufficient to define the concept of potential for a single pair of objects for a single pair of nodes, the actual situation for any pair of nodes involves multiple concepts, and so the total potential energy U will be proportional to the sum of the potentials for each pair of corresponding concepts, or

$$U = -w = \sum_{i=1}^{k} -a_{12i}m_{1i}m_{2i}S_{12i},\qquad(10.5)$$

where m_{1i} is the mass of the ith concept in node 1, m_{2i} the mass of the ith concept in node 2, and s_{12i} the distance between the ith concept in the first node and its counterpart in the second node.

The inclusion of inertial mass in the model not only influences the calculation of the potential energy function, but it changes the location of the equilibrium points as well, since the relative acceleration of the elements in the nodes will be an inverse function of their inertial masses. The point of convergence, that is, the equilibrium point, for communicating systems of different mass is given by

$$X_3 = (m_1X_1 + m_2X_2)/(m_1 + m_2),\qquad(10.6)$$

where X_3 is the equilibrium point, X_1 the position of the first node, m_1 the inertial mass of the first node, X_2 the position of the second node, and m_2 the inertial mass of the second node. On an aggregate level, the system composed of the two nodes may itself be thought of as a node at a different level of analysis with mean position X_3 and inertial mass m_3, where $m_3 = m_1 + m_2$. These equations can of course be generalized for any number of nodes and for any level of subsystem.

While it is true that the determinants of inertial mass are not well understood in the individual self-conception (notwithstanding the early experiments showing moderate linear correlations between inertial mass of concepts and their information history), on a system level this is not particularly crucial, since the number of persons in the system can serve as an obvious estimator of the overall system mass. Thus, for example, the total heat content of two bodies of liquid of equal temperature depends both upon their specific heat and their relative masses, but if the masses differ greatly enough (e.g., if we compare a lakeful of water to a glass of orange juice), the differences in specific heat become irrelevant and their relative heats are determined primarily by their different masses. We can say unambiguously, therefore, that the mass of the object "good," for example, in the state of New York is smaller that the mass of the concept "good" in the United States as a whole by a number which approximates the ratio of people in New York to people in the United States. Thus, even before a complete answer to the question of the determinants of inertial mass in the individual person is found, useful approximate calculations can be made for aggregate cultures.

Resistance

It is usual in empirical treatments of human networks to measure links between people or organizations as if they were dichotomous, that is, present or absent, but most analysts note that such links are of variable character. The notion of a link as coordination in space time makes clear the dependence of a link on numerical variables, such as distance and time, since nodes may be physically close over intervals of time, and probabilities of intersection depend on such distances while frequencies of coordination (collisions) depend on intersection probabilities. Rather than characterizing pairs of links as connected or unconnected, it is more realistic to consider the degree of linkage between nodes as a continuously variable quantity. In computer systems, for example, different nodes may be linked by lines of different capacities, and in human communication systems, different pairs of friends or acquaintances may be characterized by higher or lower rates of meeting or total duration in time of communication, while contiguous radiating bodies may differ in the area of surface in contact with each other. If we think of a single collision of particles as a unit of space–time coordination, then we may define the capacity of a link over an interval of time as the density of such units over the time interval. The rate at which two nodes will converge on the point of maximum entropy—that is, the rate at which they will grow similar or communicate—will be an inverse function of the resistance between them.

In most human communication systems, activities are periodic; that is, they occur at regularly spaced intervals in time. At the macro level, these periodicities usually refer to regularly spaced meetings, such as annual meetings of boards of directors, monthly faculty meetings, weekly bridge clubs, daily work attendance, or 4 a.m. feedings. Periodic activities of persons may occasionally coincide either deliberately or by accident, resulting in "collisions" of individuals or groups. More obviously, individuals or groups often deliberately plan periodic meetings for the specific purpose of "colliding" or interacting.

In the former case, coordination of activities is accidental, and results from the intersection of two or more periodic functions to yield a third periodic function; in the latter case, deliberate action has been taken to assure such coordination.

When two (or more) periodic functions are coordinated with each other completely, we say they are in phase or coupled. The rate of flow of information across any link, therefore, will be a function of the extent to which the periodic communication activities of each node are synchronized in space and time.

This gives rise to the likelihood that the domains of any two (or more) nodes may be expected to exhibit some oscillation (represented by periodicity in their eigenfunctions). Communications among such nodes can be expected to be inefficient when these oscillations are out of phase, and as well when they are out of phase with the periodicities of the links (i.e., their space time coordination may be out of phase with the eigenfunctions of their cognitive structures).

The inverses of the rates of communication among the links at any instant in time represents an $n \times n$ symmetric matrix, and the eigenvectors of the scalar products derived from this matrix will represent the axes of an r-dimensional multidimensional Riemann space. The eigenfunctions defined across a sequence of these spaces in time would provide a good representation of the processes within the communication network, and ought to be related to the eigenfunctions of the domain of cognitive or cultural beliefs for the same network. It is useful to consider a separate set of eigenfunctions for each domain, and the actual complexity of such functions may frequently be very great.

These concepts lead to the idea of cognitive and cultural domains which themselves show oscillatory movements resembling dialectical swings in opinion over time. These notions in turn lead us to consider the possibilities of system resonances and standing waves in the cultures which, while systematic and predictable occurrences given sufficient knowledge of the state of the system over time, would appear startling and perhaps even miraculous to naive participants in the culture. Under normal conditions, such oscillations might be expected to represent states of asymptotic equilibrium, but under other circumstances they could indeed produce the kind of unstable oscillations which rapidly move toward infinity, which would, of course, result in the disruption of the system long before taking on infinite values. Further work on wave-mechanical functions in cultural domains might result in greatly enhanced understanding of social systems.

In any event, whether or not this class of phenomena can ultimately be modeled by these equations, the apparently alternating flow of information through channels requires that we consider not only a resistance component for each link, but also an impedance component. Future research in the area can deal profitably with concepts such as transformers and impedance-matching. Although beyond the scope of this chapter, the concepts introduced so far of comparatively measured differences, potential, links, inertial mass, resistance and impedance, work, power, energy, and communication provide the basis for a fairly complete electric circuit analogy. Nodes in a circuit with a potential between them will communicate at a rate inversely proportional to the resistance or impedance between the nodes. Since impedances should be expected to differ at different frequencies, information will be tailored or modified in frequency by nodes whose impedance is frequency dependent. Buffers perform a capacitive function, delaying information in phase, with a power capacity which varies inversely with frequency. Libraries, for example, can carry information about events of very low frequency with high efficiency, while television systems can convey detailed information about high-frequency events. These two systems serve as bandpass filters in their communication systems. Some nodes, such as television systems, act as power amplifiers, by drawing energy from the near surround (in this case electrical energy) and using it to multiply the rate of flow of information through a social network.

Regardless of the eventual usefulness of the electric circuit analogy, these concepts establish the general characteristics of a communication system. In general, information will tend to flow through any system between nodes at a rate directly proportional to the potential or difference between these nodes, and inversely proportional to the inertial masses of those subsystems and to the impedances of the links. Left alone, any such system will tend toward the equilibrium value, which will be the weighted mean of the structures of the individual nodes, where the weighting values are given by the inertial masses of the subsystems. In mechanics, the equivalent statement is that objects in any system will gravitate toward the center of mass of the system.

Group Formation

The preceding mechanisms described apply to the processes to be expected in closed systems; that is, systems within which energy transfers between the system and its near surround are prohibited, and all energy flows take place solely among the subsystems of the main system. In such cases, thermodynamic processes such as those described earlier can be seen to lead to a homogenization of the total system (or, as Blau, 1974) would describe it, toward consolidation of parameters). In fact, of course, cultures do experience exchanges of energy or information with the environment. When these exchanges are negative (i.e., when energy is lost to the near surround), the rate at which the system moves toward entropy will be increased, while positive flows of energy from the near surround into the system will result in a decrease of the rate of movement toward entropy. While left to itself, therefore, a culture will inevitably move toward complete destructuring, and thus the ultimate source of structuring in a culture is inputs of information/ energy from the environment.

In practice, no system is "left alone," and information from the near surround will result in increases in potential between the receiving nodes and those nodes to which the receiving nodes are connected proximately. This will result in additional communication which will produce movement toward new equilibria. While one may, of course, anthropomorphize such a system by suggesting that it *intends* to seek such equilibria—that is, by assuming that each system has equilibrium as a goal—it is equally clear that communication processes may also be modeled without recourse to such teleological models by arguing that every system is constrained to move toward equilibrium by the laws of thermodynamics. Systems modeled on these assumptions are conservative in the sense that human cultures are often thought to be conservative; that is, they tend to minimize deviance from the system position. Since the mass of any domain in any subsystem of the system is the sum of the masses of the elements in the system, smaller subsystems will move proportionately further toward the position of the larger system than the opposite. In the case of an individual person in a group, for example, who receives information from the near surround which changes his/her position away from the group equilibrium point, both individual and group will move toward a new equilibrium point, with the individual being shifted toward the old group mean and the group mean being shifted toward the position of the individual. But the greater mass of the group will assure that the new equilibrium point will be closer to the old mean than the position of the individual, and so the individual's position will be shifted proportionately further. In this way the natural thermodynamic processes of group interaction will result in processes which tend to spread perturbations throughout a system rather than allowing them to accumulate in subsystems. Thus these processes will tend to erase radical or deviant activity by generating corrective or equilibrating forces proportional to the magnitude of the deviance.

In any actual culture, energy will not be expected to enter and leave a system uniformly through all ports, and so different subsystems of the culture will experience differential rates of exchange of information with the surround. Such differential exchanges will result in changes in the relative potential among subsets of the subsystems, which in turn will result in restructuring of the rates of flow of energy/information among the subsystems. Net influxes of available energy or information into a subsystem will result in an increase in its thermodynamic temperature. Subsystems of the culture with access to large pools of available energy relative to other subsystems will tend to radiate information to subsystems of lower potential. On the basis of these thermodynamic principles alone, therefore, we might be able to account for what scholars have called the "one-way flow" of information from technologically advanced nations to poorer, less well-developed nations.

Moreover, since the rate of convergence on the equilibrium point is proportional to the density of the links (or inversely proportional to the impedence in each link), relatively bounded subsystems will experience more rapid convergences on their own subsystem means than with the overall system. This can result in local reversals of entropy where relatively isolated subsystems can move toward local equilibrium in a direction away from the equilibrium point of the larger system, even though the net entropy over the whole system continues to increase. This describes well the process of polarization of groups in social settings often noted in human affairs.

The Formation of Stable Processes

The viability of a thermodynamic approach to the understanding of human organization has been given important support by recent developments in chemistry. Research by Prigogine and others has shown conditions under which nonequilibrium thermodynamic processes can give rise to ordered, structured processes.

It is important to emphasize that the structures that interest us include not only the probably rare equilibrium structure of a crystalline sort, but also the more frequent "dissipative structures" as Prigogine (1978) calls them. As Prigogine describes it, "When given boundary conditions prevent the system from reaching thermodynamic equilibrium (that is, zero S [entropy] production), the system settles down to the state of 'least dissipation' [p. 780]." Further from equilibrium, however, instabilities are often observed, which result in increased rates of production of entropy. These flows are themselves structured.[1] Again as

Prigogine says (1978), "Moreover, the state of flow, which appears beyond the instability, is a state of organization as compared to the state of rest [p. 780]." These patterns of flow represent regular processes characteristic of given cultures under given boundary conditions, and as such are part of the "patterned regularities" which comprise a culture. Under conditions specified by Prigogine (1978, p. 780), these processes become periodic, that is, "the chemical reaction leads to a coherent time behavior; it becomes a chemical clock [p. 780]."

Applications of the work of Prigogine and his associates to human cultural processes have not yet been made in the literature, but the demonstration that complex chemical processes of a highly structured sort can be expected as a result of random thermodynamic processes such as those described here should be considered encouraging toward similar applications to human cultures.

Furthermore, on a cognitive level, if the findings noted earlier (e.g., Saltiel & Woelfel, 1975; Danes *et al.*, 1978) which show the inertial masses of cultural concepts to be proportional to the amount of information out of which they are formed) prove general, then the model developed here also predicts that societies will preserve well-established older positions more forcefully than more recently and sketchily formed ideas. Thus certain core cultural beliefs will prove more highly resistant to changes due to new information than will less central beliefs. Moreover, since the local rate of change toward entropy in any link is proportional to the extent to which communicating nodes are coordinated in space and time, closely connected nodes will tend to become even more closely connected in proportion to their closeness, since increasing similarity implies increasing coordination in space–time. Links then are expected to grow stronger through use, according to this model. Since old links are therefore expected to be reused, the model has a learning capacity; that is, the system learns to communicate and remembers what it has learned. In fact, it is the concept of inertial mass which imparts the notion of memory into the system, and gives rise to the notion of intelligence.

Overall, it is clear that the maintenance or expansion of a cultural system is dependent on its continued access to net inputs of energy from the surround, and, on a long-range time scale, societies which develop capacities to extract energy from the environment will tend to have increased survival potential in a natural selection sense. On a biological level, for example, natural selection processes have led to the development of plants with the capability of extracting available energy from sunlight and converting it into structuring forces, as well as the development of animals capable of liberating energy from already existing plant structures and converting it to the task of maintaining and extending their own structures.

Societies also develop procedures, acts, or algorithms (such as building fires or petroleum distillation) by which energy can be extracted from the near surround either passively (such as by collecting wind, falling water, or solar radiation directly) or actively by catalytic or other chemical or atomic intervention by breaking down existing structures to liberate free energy. This energy can then be utilized to transmit information structures to other cultures, intergenerationally within the culture, or among subsystems in the culture to increase the overall level to which the culture is organized.

The energy accumulated in subsystems experiencing net influxes of information must be dissipated through links to other subsystems at lower potential or to the near surround. The capacities of these links relative to the potential differences plays a crucial role in the formation of groups, which may be described as sets of linked nodes whose cultural homogeneity is great relative to their surround. When net rates of energy input are experienced, subsystems whose internal channel capacities exceed capacities of links to the surround, ought to experience net increases in structuring, internal homogeneity and potential relative to the surround. Moreover, when energy drains from the group through several links at a rate lower than the net intake of information, energy in the form of structure should be expected to accumulate in the nodes between these links. Group structures ought to be expected to form and grow, therefore, along lines of communication. The key property in a node which accumulates energy and stores it in structure, then, is the property of "betweenness." Like all properties in this model, betweenness is a relative property. In this case it refers to the state of living between a source and a sink (which, of course, are also relative terms.) On a global level, life on earth is a consequence of the fact that the earth lies between the sun and outer space, thus experiencing a continuous flow of energy, a tiny fragment of which is captured and stored in the structures we refer to as life.

Culture and Intelligence

In spite of their importance to the human sciences, neither the concept culture or intelligence are well defined in a formal sense, although specific properties of each are widely recognized. On a general level, most writers would agree that culture is the pattern for a society, while disagreeing as to what constitutes such a pattern. On the most general level, the pattern of any society will consist of a set of relatively commonly defined symbols which represent important aspects of social life in the society. These symbols will represent a range of ideas from very stable and general notions, such as justice, good, evil, and basic emotions, to descriptions of common processes ranging from long-range activities, such as careers, to brief activities. Many of the patterns of culture in fact will be processes extended in time as is any behavior.

Information about how the society is organized, that is, information about how the society and its constituent parts act over time, constitutes what we mean by culture. As we suggested in Chapter 7, the totality of any culture is too large to be known by any subsystem within a society, and subsets of the total information pattern are stored primarily within local subsystems, including individual persons. Many important aspects of this information can be arrayed in the spatial form already described. Information is also stored in physical artifacts such as libraries and architecture.

It is the consensus of most writers that societies act to preserve their cultures, and in part the mechanisms by which this is done have been described in general by the learning properties derivable from the thermodynamic principles set down in this chapter. The Russian mathematician Liapunov (Shklovskii & Sagan, 1966, pp. 197–200) sees this maintenance of structure as the essential characteristic of life. According to Liapunov, living systems (which we take specifically to include human societies) control the flow of large amounts of energy and materials by means of much smaller flows of energy or material containing a large amount of information through definitely prescribed channels (Shklovskii & Sagan, 1966, p. 197). In the terminology presented here, Liapunov's view suggests that societies obtain information from their near surround through ports, which is processed, translated, buffered, and retransmitted through links throughout the system (either to central processors in highly centralized societies or to more distributed processors in less centralized societies, where it is compared with information already stored in memory). (In a human society, this memory is obviously highly distributed throughout the individual nodes and sub systems.) The differences between the incoming information and the stored information (the pattern for the society) provide the information set which guides the adaptive reaction of the society, which restructures itself and its near surround in an effort to retain the integrity of the system.

The use of small flows of matter and energy to control large flows of matter and energy is an integral component of human social life, which can be typified by a simple everyday statement such as "go to the store and bring home food." In this example, the minute energy flow embodied in the set of sound waves which constitute the message are used to control the physical transportation of a human body across space and time to distribute large amounts of matter (food, in this instance). On a larger scale, the transmission of blueprints and daily instructions to workers can result in the construction of a building or the excavation of raw materials. This process can result in the large-scale restructuring of the near surround after the image stored in the culture. In the same way, the transmission of information from older to younger generations tends toward the continuation of the pattern of organization of the culture across time.

The transmission of structure from one element to another by communication may serve well as a definition of purposive intelligence, even though the laws of thermodynamics may leave any element no option as to whether it will carry out such a function. We should also understand that culture is a process, that is, a time-dependent structure, and it is this time-dependent structure which society tries to maintain. Increasing abilities to control the reproduction of increasingly complex patterns over time and space may well be though of as increases in intelligence. Since the primary pattern which describes any culture is the pattern of activities of its subsystems, the ability to encode temporal processes and transmit information describing them throughout the system is clearly related to the intelligence of the system. The foundation of our thinking in this book has been that increasing fineness of discrimination of processes in time and space lie at the root of increasing the collective social intelligence and hence survival capacities of any society. Of greatest importance, therefore, is the collective capacity of a society to measure time and distance, since coordinated human activities require specification of coorientation of spatially distributed activities over time. A society which can measure time only to the nearest hour cannot describe any activities which take less than an hour to perform, and hence cannot provide instructions as to how multiple individuals should coordinate their behavior within hour-long time intervals.

Coordinated human activity requires the sequencing of multiple human acts in time, and from the earliest available records human societies have kept collective social time for the purpose of synchronizing human activities across persons. In the earliest times, macro-level activities such as hunting, planting, and harvesting have been synchronized against astronomical and other cyclical phenomena, such as the flooding of the Nile, and local behaviors have been coordinated against collective times such as those kept by means of ritual chanting, which provides a surprisingly accurate social clock against which individual behaviors may be calibrated and sequenced. Since prehistory, societies, particularly successful societies, have traditionally devoted very substantial proportions of their resources to the precise measurement of time.

The same argument applies to the measurement of distance and space, since human activity cannot be coordinated to smaller spatial tolerances than may be discriminated and encoded by the society; a society which can describe distances no smaller than a centimeter will be unable to distribute information about how to position material objects along intervals smaller than a centimeter. Clearly, the more precision with which societies may measure and communicate about processes in space and time, the more precisely can they compare their previous pattern to their present pattern, and consequently the more precisely can they specify and communicate about corrective strategies. In thermodynamic terms, increases in precision of coding reduce impedances among links.

Power

Increasing fineness of discrimination of difference, which results from improvements in measurement and coding systems, allows larger quantities of information to be carried in less space at a smaller energy cost. Moreover, increasing fineness of discrimination of time, as we have suggested, allows for more information to be transmitted per unit of time. Increasing density of communication links resulting from both increased use, improved coding systems and even technological improvements, further enhances the rate at which large quantities of information can be communicated for a given level of potential energy. Increasing control over the near surround also increases levels of available potential energy, thus further increasing the rate at which information can be transmitted and work can be done. The time rate of doing work is the classical definition of power. If potential energy represents the capacity for doing work, power represents the rate at which the energy is spent and the work done. Classical sociological definitions of power are usually quite different from this, and in fact are much closer to what we have called potential energy. Weber's (1947) classical notion of power as the ability of an agent to accomplish a goal against opposition forces, for example, is a virtually literal definition of potential energy as it is usually understood. On the contrary, in the view presented here, power has the same definition as its more common usage in physics. A powerful person or organization, following from this view, would be one who could produce relatively massive changes in some domain against large opposing forces rapidly.

In many cases it is appropriate to consider the deliberate application of power, as when a person or group makes deliberate efforts to alter some element of its near surround, but the concept of power as defined here has more widespread application. Whenever two nodes which differ in potential come into contact, each does work on the structure of the other, and the rate at which this work is done will represent power. In cases where the contact among the nodes is approximately periodic, the function which describes the potential difference, and the work done, will both be periodic. Moreover, due to the inertial properties of the structures, the wavefront of the structural change, that is, the work done, ought to lag behind the wavefront of the potential function, introducing a phase difference between these two functions. In this case, the power for such a system will be given to an approximation by

$$P = UI \cos \theta, \tag{10.9}$$

where P is power, U the potential energy, I the rate of flow, and θ the phase angle between the power and the rate of change.

The function for potential is given simply from the period of the meetings or communication acts of the nodes, while the function for the rate of flow is measured as the eigenfunctions of the cognitive domains of the nodes.

Phase differences reduce the rate at which work can be done, and result in collisions which dissipate power as heat. When a node is itself a system of internal nodes, the relative phase differences of the eigenfunctions of its internal nodes from each other and from the main wave function resulting from the macro-level communication with the other macro-level node impede the smooth transmission of power internally and generate internal heat in the system. Heat in this system, as in any thermodynamic model, is random motion of elements. Complex interactions of fundamental and harmonic frequencies of the eigenfunctions will result in random changes in the configurations or cognitive structures of the nodes relative to each other, and the structures will as a result be degraded into heat. In an earlier day, such phase differences in the eigenfunctions of the subsystem of a culture might well have been described as "inharmonious."

CHAPTER 11

PLANNED
SOCIAL INTERVENTION

Introduction

The procedures described so far in this book have been developed primarily with "pure" scientific goals in mind, out of felt inadequacies in theories, measurement, and analysis procedures available to the social scientist. But however exciting the process of science may be, and no matter how elegant the outcome, scientific theories rise or fall on their capacity to enable their users to survive in a competitive environment. As Brillouin (1964) has noted, science does not create information or knowledge, but rather extracts information[1] from the systems it observes, and while the total energy in the system remains constant under this operation (recall that the scientist is part of the total system of observed and observer), this information is gained at the expense of a general increase in the entropy of the system. Thus science consumes available energy, and this energy ultimately must be paid for.

Life itself may be seen as a local reversal of entropy, and, left alone, the energy bound into life will dissipate. In addition to the solar energy available in real time, energy stored in structures in the near surround

---

[1] We use the terms "information" and "energy" interchangeably here, although often information is used to refer to very low levels of energy (see Tribus & McIrvine, 1971).

may be liberated by a living organism, as food, oil and other organic structures are degraded to provide energy for human society. Energy stored in physical structures (such as rain and rivers) can also be liberated, and as always the decrease in the rate of increase in entropy for the sytem equals the increase in the same rate for the near surround. Living systems, therefore, go on living by extracting energy from the near surround. Liapunov (Shklovskii and Sagan, 1966) defines intelligence as a process which controls the flows of large quantities of energy and matter by small flows of matter and energy, and within this model we see science as increasing the efficiency with which human organizations can control the flow of information from the environment into the life sustaining and expanding process. An ultimate criterion for the success of a scientific theory, then, is the development of an efficient engineering application.

As has been the case so often in the history of science, the costs of gathering the information out of which the theory presented here has been made have been born almost exclusively by private enterprise, and in this chapter we will describe several of the studies performed by or for business, industry, agriculture and government using the theories and procedures described so far. Unlike the "pure" science reported so far, however, few of these studies are public, and so much detail must be omitted. Our purpose is therefore not to present the research for scientific scrutiny, but rather to give an idea of the range of situations to which the theory has already been applied.

Social Research as a Cybernetic Process

The notion of applied research is inherently bound up in the idea of an intelligent system seeking to maintain and expand its existence. Following Liapunov, we assume that this process requires the manipulation of large scale flows of matter and energy by means of small scale flows of matter and energy. Such intelligent organizations exist within a surrounding environment and interact with the surround by exchanges of matter and energy. The maintenance and expansion of the intelligent organization requires that the net flow be toward the organization from the surround. Ultimately, of course, the maintenance of such a flow indefinitely requires inputs of energy into the system from outside, and in our case most such energy enters our near surround from the sun. Although scientific progress has steadily increased our collective capacity to divert this constant flow of energy into the development and maintenance of intelligent structures (such as individuals, families, corporations, and nations), even today the net scarcity of such available energy and the multitude of organizations which compete for a share of the flow require increased levels of efficiency of control.

Again following Brillouin, we assume that this process requires the extraction of small amounts of information from the system, and, by means of theories, utilization of this information to predict and control future states of the system. A theory is efficient (and therefore useful) to the extent that it (a) minimizes the amount of information that must be extracted from the system, (b) maximizes the amount of information about the future state of the system that can be fixed based on such information, and (c) maximizes the range of control that can be exercised over the future state of the system, (d) while expending minimum energy. (This thinking is the basis of the fourth and fifth principles of science presented in Chapter 1.)

Commercial social science research, such as marketing research, political polling and the like, fits this paradigm quite exactly. In a typical study, an organization will draw a small amount of information from the public, a market or market segment, a political constituency, and so on, and based on this information and some theory (however informal) make some prediction of the future state of the system. Often this research is followed by an active intervention in the process, usually by means of advertising or some other information process. In every stage, one can see the sponsoring organization gathering information and directing information flows on a small scale (as in advertising) in the hope of redirecting energy flows (such as voting or spending behaviors) on a large scale.

The theories and procedures presented so far in this volume can be seen to increase the overall efficiency of this process in several ways. First, the theory specifies a minimum set of information which must be gathered from the system to predict its future states. It does this by arguing that the behavior of relevant subsystems (such as individuals, electorates, market segments) toward any object of interest may be largely specified by information about the dissimilarities among a (relatively small) set of reference objects in terms of which the relation of self and object of interest is defined.

Second, the comparative scales specified in this system, when realistically formatted to 3 digits, yield 9.97 bits of information per pair-comparison, which, for a 15-concept study (which is typical) yields 1046.85 bits of information per case. Typical 5-point Likert-type scales yield 2.32 bits of information per response, and coupled with 15 indirect measures typical of current marketing practice, yield approximately 34.8 bits per case. Thus, from the outset, the scaling methods suggested in this volume can yield in practice about 30 times[2] as much information per case as can methods now nearly universally applied in standard social science and marketing practice.

Casual consideration may lead one to believe that an inevitable increase in respondent burden might be a fault of these scales, but information theory leads us to understand that information and energy are different names for the same phenomenon. The withdrawal of information from a system necessarily costs energy, and increases in the amount of information withdrawn must yield commensurate increases in the price. Since the human brain can function for about a day on the food energy contained in half a peanut, however, the actual energy costs of withdrawing information from an individual mind are very small[3] and virtually negligible in comparison to the costs in physical energy required simply to sit erect while filling out a questionnaire. By far the larger part of the energy required for the administration of a questionnaire is consumed in transporting the questionnaire to the respondent and conducting the everyday communicative processes incidental to the actual extraction of the information.

Since this is the case, the largest part of the cost, both in dollars and in energy, of measuring beliefs and attitudes is independent of the actual instrumentation utilized based on current information technology. Thus, gains in the amount of information per case yielded by the scaling devices recommended here should be expected to yield considerable increases in economy.

Although little careful research has been directed specifically to the question of relative respondent burden, casual estimates made on university undergraduates find them reporting such scales require about 10% more effort to complete than 5-point Likert scales. Mean administration times for 15-concept direct-pair comparison measures of the type suggested in this volume run approximately 25 minutes in general populations, while very extensive instruments utilizing as many as 20 or more concepts average about 1 hour. Assuming conservatively that such

---

[2] Most users realize this when they first see their punched data decks. Using maximally efficient encoding (no blanks), a typical 15-item study, traditionally scaled, can be made to fit on 20 cards for 100 cases. Information gathered using the method we describe would require 400 cards for the same 100 cases.

[3] Actually, the amount of thermal energy is given by $E = k \ln 2H$, where $k = 1.38 \times 10^{-23}$ (Boltzmann's constant), H is information in bits, and E is energy in joules degree^{-1} Kelvin. Thus the amount of thermal energy required to generate the information in a single k concept pair comparison instrument formatted to 3 digits is only about 10^{-20} joules, or about the amount of energy in one slow neutron. By contrast, the basic metabolic process of sitting quietly for the 25 minutes required to fill out the questionnaire would consume about 1.5×10^2 joules.

procedures require double the administration time of ordinary Likert-type scales, this still represents a net gain of about 1500% per case, or over an order of magnitude more information per case holding costs constant. Since uncertainty of measure decreases only as the square root of the number of measurements made, utilizing conventional measurement procedures with increased sample sizes to achieve equal precision of measure is clearly not economical. Alternatively, the small losses in sample size (usually less than a few percent) that might be expected from the increased respondent burden resulting from use of the scales proposed here is vastly more than offset by increased precision per case. In economic terms, assuming double the administration time (which is far in excess of what actual experience with the procedures show), these procedures can produce about 15 times the information per dollar spent as can conventional practice.

A third way in which the theory increases efficiency results from its use of the metric algorithm for determining the coordinates of the objects in the continuum. This transformation is a completely reversible transformation in which no information is lost (except for negligible rounding errors which can be made as small as desired). As Brillouin (1964) points out, this mathematical transformation neither creates nor loses information and therefore leaves the total entropy of the system unaffected (except, of course, for the costs of computing). Analytic procedures now in common use, however, do suffer information losses which are sometimes quite substantial. Most serious are the losses suffered by the factor analysis algorithm (see Figure 4.2) which discards all information about vector lengths through standardization. This loss can range from none at all in the virtually impossible case where all objects of interest lie on the surface of a unit hypersphere to theoretically infinite losses when the vector lengths are infinitely variable, another impossible case. In practice, however, losses of the magnitude shown in the U.S. cities example are not atypical.

Less severe but nonetheless serious are the losses of information suffered by the nonmetric scaling algorithms, which may range from zero when the configuration of measured values is euclidean and of small dimensionality, but which can become large when triangle inequality violations are substantial. Warp factors of 1.5 and higher are observed occasionally in practice, and real dimensions often show variances of 5 to 10% of the total as far out as the fifth and sixth dimensions, so that in practice nonmetric programs might be conservatively estimated as losing about a third of the information gathered in the raw measures.

A fourth way efficiency is increased is through the observed correlation between behaviors and distance from the measured position of the self in the spatial representation. As Liapunov suggests, a necessary feature of any intelligent organization is memory, such that incoming information may be compared with past states of the organization. A theory, as Brillouin notes, establishes correlations among events or processes, such that when observations of one process or event correlated with another process or event are available, the second process or event may be fixed without further observations. In this sense, a theory "remembers" very large amounts of information and cuts down on the amount of storage required. In the present case, the observation that a particular behavior as measured in the coordinate frame is converging on the self in that frame suffices to show that, on the average, the frequency of performance of the behavior is or will be increasing. Similarly, this knowledge can serve as a goal state, such that deliberate attempts to move a concept or object toward the self point can be expected to result in increased behavior with respect to the object.

When the behavior involves voting for a candidate, buying a product, or other such activities, controlling the movement of the object or self serves as a "valve" or control process which results in many individuals separately inputting energy into the organization by voting for its candidate, buying its product, and so on. This meets Liapunov's definition of intelligence very closely, since the process clearly involves using small energy flows to influence much larger flows.

If the equations for controlling such movements within the manifold are correct, they represent a substantial increase in the efficiency of the overall process. In a typical 15-concept domain, and assuming that typical advertising practice is unlikely to use more than four concepts in any given advertising campaign, there are over 1000 possible messages that can be made of one, two, three, and four concepts. Most of these messages could no doubt be eliminated by everyday folk wisdom, and so the gain in efficiency is smaller than this. Realistically, the best of current practice might be taken as the best visual estimates made without the equations as illustrated by Serota *et al.* (1977; see also Chapter 9 of this volume), which were about 40 degrees off from the optimal strategy described by the equations in Chapter 8. We might estimate conservatively, then, that these equations might provide another 25% reduction in uncertainty over more intuitive methods.

While all the quantitative estimates made so far in this chapter are very crude, nonetheless we may conservatively estimate that the procedures described here, even though young and crude, yield as much as an order of magnitude more efficiency than the best of traditional social science practice. Even a much more modest gain than this would represent a dramatic advance in economy and utility for applied work. It is not surprising, then, that these methods have already begun to find wide applications in practical situations.

Advertising and Public Relations

Perhaps the most obvious applications of the methods described are in the development of advertising strategies for commercial products. Several such studies have been done for major automobile manufacturers, particularly prior to the introduction of new models. In a typical study, the auto company will designate a specific market segment as a target for the research. Ordinarily, a sample of respondents is bought from commercial research firms who, through continuous sampling of general populations, have identified persons who have recently bought or soon plan to buy a particular type of car. In one such study, samples of 25 persons who planned to buy a curent model of a specific car or two of its closest competitors were identified in each of two test market cities. These 50 persons were interviewed in depth and asked to discuss the cars they had considered. Of the several hundred attributes and characteristics of such cars the sample members mentioned, the most frequently mentioned attributes, along with the names of the car to be introduced, its current model year version, two of its closest competitors, and the term "me" were compiled into a complete pair-comparison instrument according to procedures discussed in Chapter 4. Approximately 300 additional sample members of the same type were then invited to a closed showing of the new car, its current model, and the two closest competitors in a large test market city. After viewing all four of the cars, the sample members filled out the questionnaire. As expected, sample members placed the car they planned to buy about one fourth the distance from the "me" as the other three cars. A computer program, Galileo™ (version 3.9) then solved the set of equations (9.2)–(9.10) based on these measured values to determine the set of attributes which should be associated with the car to move it as close as possible to the self point. Based on this solution, an advertising campaign was designed and implemented.

This study is fairly typical of perhaps the most common commercial use of these procedures. In a widely different context, for example, a study was performed for a nonprofit educational clearing house in a large eastern state. Descriptions of 65 of the educational products distributed by this firm were typed on file cards and a sample of education graduate students sorted the cards into piles. The resulting cooccurrence matrix was then clustered by a standard cluster analysis program, and the resulting three major clusters were named by another sample of

education graduate students. A small sample of educational administrators was then drawn from the state and interviewed by telephone
about these three types of educational innovations. The most frequently
used attributes, along with the names of the innovations and the term
"me," were compiled into a complete pair-comparisons instrument as
described earlier. This instrument was then administered to a one-third
random sample of all teachers and educational administrators in the
state. This sample was then subdivided into several classes of educators
(e.g., teachers, principles, counselors, school board superintendents),
and again optimal messages were generated by means of the Galileo™
computer program for each of the subsamples. A message that was
near-optimal for all groups was identified, and this message was included in a newsletter periodically distributed to the population. Executives of the corporation reported dramatic increases in demand for the
innovations following the administration of the newsletters, even
though intuitively generated appeals had been distributed via the same
medium for several years preceding.

Similar studies have found widely diverse applications, including use
by a large state university to attract qualified student applicants, by a
fast-food chain to attract customers in a highly competitive market, and
by a state dental association to promote dental health in a large western
state. In a study designed to illustrate the use of the techniques in
tourism, Korzenny, Ruiz, and Ben David (1978) interviewed 100 faculty
members and their spouses at a large midwestern university using the
procedures described here to find optimal ways to promote tourism in
Israel. The Korzenny *et al.* (1978) study is unusual in that it attempted to
move the concept "Israel" close to the concept "my vacation" rather than
to a specific self point.

Identical procedures have also found interesting applications in agriculture, and are being used in a continuing effort by a professional
dairy association (Dairy Herd Improvement Association, or DHIA) in a
large midwestern state to increase the utilization of a dairy herd testing
service (Wallace, 1979).

Small squares in Figure 11.1 show the first principal plane of the
configuration of the domain at the outset of the campaign. Notice particularly that the testing service (labeled "DHIA" in Figure 11.1) is
widely separated from the self point ("you" in Figure 11.1), probably in
part due to the fact that the DHIA test is so closely associated with
computers, which are in turn very far from the farmers' self point. (Information from the test is provided to the farmers on computer-printed
sheets.)

Appropriate messages (not discussed here) were calculated according

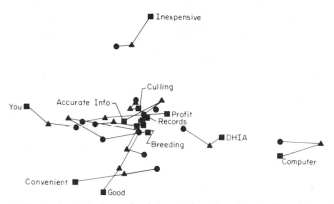

FIGURE 11.1   First principal plane of a dairy study at 3 points in time. ■, t_1; ▲, t_2; ●, t_3.

to the equations shown earlier, and diffused to the farmers primarily through an existing network of extension agents on a statewide basis. It is important to understand that this did not represent the beginning of a new effort, but rather the continuation of an ongoing campaign dating to 1903. The only changes are the changes in the content of the messages.

The triangles in Figure 11.1 represent the state of the configuration several months later. Note particularly the convergence of the concepts DHIA and you. The circles in Figure 11.1 show the same configuration several more months into the campaign. Note again the clear-cut convergence of the DHIA and you. While precise estimates of the rate of increase in actual use of the test are not available, shortly after these measurements deployment of further messages had to be curtailed because the testing facilities had become overtaxed by increased demand.

These same methods have obvious application to political problems, particularly elections, and have been used to define effective advertising strategies for political candidates (Barnett *et al.*, 1976; Serota, Cody, Barnett, & Taylor, 1978) and for referenda. We have already described the use of the procedures to aid in the passage of a statewide proposal to ban nonreturnable bottles and cans in Michigan (Chapter 9). Identical procedures have also been used to determine the acceptability of a millage increase necessary to establish an adult education center on the countywide level, and in pilot studies to determine effective strategies leading to the passage of the Equal Rights Amendment in a large midwestern state.

In a different type of study with important political ramifications, McPhail and Barnett (1977) identified concepts relating to television viewing for a sample of university students in a large Canadian city, and included them along with the call letters of major Canadian and American television stations serving the metropolitan area. They found that the distance of the stations from the self point correlated negatively with their share of the audience (i.e., the stations closest to the self point were most watched), and found further that those Canadians who watched most American television also placed themselves closer to the concept *The United States* and farther from the concept *Canada*. They interpreted these results to indicate the likelihood that exposure to foreign television acts as a force against nationalism, although they were careful to point out that simple correlational studies such as this one leave room for alternative interpretations.

Internal Adaptations

Although all the foregoing studies described are drawn from very diverse areas of application, they share a common feature. All of them gather information from the environment with the purpose of designing information structures which they intend to transmit back to the near surround in order to restructure it relative to the organization. Thus each of the studies described intend to restructure the information environment within which the sponsoring organization exists. A clear alternative, of course, might be to use the information gained from such a study to restructure the organization relative to its environment, and several such studies have been conducted. McPhail and Barnett, for example, also included several potential program formats within their pair-comparison list, and used the Galileo™ computer program to find the combination of programming strategies which would result in moving CBC-TV as close as possible to the self point. They discovered that the most effective change in program format appeared to be to increase the programming of music on CBC-TV. As a pilot study, the McPhail and Barnett analysis did not (as of this writing) follow up this lead by remeasuring to determine which types of music would be most effective in increasing the audience share of CBC-TV, but the study is sufficient to illustrate one way in which these procedures can be used to help an organization adapt its own structure to the near surround.

In a typical study, for example, a statewide association of mining companies interviewed a small sample drawn from educators, news-media, municipal leaders, and state legislators to learn the concepts they used to define their activities in a large midwestern state. Pair-comparison instruments were then administered to random samples of the first three of these groups to identify practices the association might adopt in order to forestall the necessity for stricter legislative regulation of the industry. Again the equations derived in Chapter 8 apply directly, since they can indicate which combination of practices, when associated with the industry, are likely to result in the movement of the industry toward the self point (or, alternatively, away from the concept of regulation). This alternative strategy, however, may be regarded as more self-serving, since it need not result in maximum public acceptability.

Many studies combine both internal and external reorganization as goals. A typical example is the ongoing study carried out for the college of agriculture of a large midwestern university. This organization coordinates the work of about 25,000 adult volunteers who serve as youth leaders in 4-H clubs throughout the state. Careful and extensive research has indicated that these volunteer clubs are very effective in youth development, both in rural and in urban areas. Although adult volunteers usually remain with the organization on a volunteer basis nearly all their lives in rural areas, the adult volunteers in the newer urban clubs show somewhat higher turnover rates. In a two-phased study, the organization interviews current volunteers to determine how the role of the volunteer might be modified to bring it closer to the self point of the urban volunteer in the hope of reducing volunteer turnover. In another phase, members of the general public are surveyed to find optimal appeals for those people most likely to fit well within the role of volunteer. Although the first phase requires changing the structure of the role itself and the second phase requires descriptive advertising of the role to members of the general public, both problems are solved by the same methods using the same equations.

These same procedures have begun to find wide application in the medical field. A newly organized health maintenance organization, for example, uses these procedures on a continuing basis primarily as an aid to evaluating the services it provides to the public, but secondarily to aid in acquainting the public with its services (Nels-Frumkin, 1978). This study is particularly interesting in that it involves a long-term longitudinal design, complete with a matched alternative site (i.e., a parallel survey is also being conducted in a similar neighbor city which has no health maintenance organization, and which is just outside the reach of the media of the city where the health maintenance organization is located).

A similar study of larger (statewide) scope was also undertaken by a large health insurance carrier. This study included not only members of the general public, but also samples of decision makers in industry and labor who jointly determine employee health care benefits. Again this survey had the twin purposes of finding ways to modify the services offered to make them maximally acceptable to these groups and to find maximally effective ways to describe those services within those groups.

Again within the medical field, a large metropolitan medical center used these methods to survey doctors within their area to find maximally efficient ways to modify the services offered to physicians and their patients.

Each of these studies described in this chapter represents work actually carried out, in most cases commercially. Studies which are sold commercially, of course, tend to be conservatively designed, since investigators are not usually likely to risk large sums of money on studies that have not been performed at least once before. Although it is much too early to consider these studies "traditional," nonetheless they have been done sufficiently often to be reliable and trustworthy. There is little risk that a research firm which has some experience with these methods will go far astray in executing a similar design. But these same studies for these reasons do not by any means exhaust the potential promise of the procedures described in this work.

CHAPTER 12

ETHICS

Introduction

Science often poses new problems for students of ethics in two senses, first because new scientific theories frequently challenge the world view on which ethical systems rest, and secondly because advancements in science often lead to the development of new behavioral possibilities which must be fit into existing ethical schemes. The theory developed in this volume is typical. First, the present theory is relativistic both in its founding epistemology and in its applied methods, and the development of a relativistic framework for the description of human behavior poses serious challenges to ethical systems of an absolute sort. No concept has absolute significance in a relativistic model, including the concept of the good. Moreover, the present theory defines the structure of experience in terms of measurement acts within an arbitrary but conventional framework, and the act of measurement inherently involves some uncertainty. Bronowski (1974) has made this conflict between relative and absolute systems of knowledge dramatic in his contrast between the development of the uncertainty principle in modern physics with the simultaneous but fundamentally opposite rise of fascism in Europe in the 1920s and 1930s. The truth of science, according to Bronowski, depends on observations (measurements) and hence is inherently uncertain and subject to revision in the light of further observation. Ethical systems based on such knowledge are typified by restraint, as Bronowski illustrates with a discussion of Leo Szillard's campaign among the atomic scientists to stage demonstrations of atomic bombs prior to their use on the Japanese people. On the contrary, the truth of absolute systems does not depend on observation. As such it is independent of verification and can be taken as certain. Ethical systems of such a type, Bronowski suggests, are typified by unrestrained actions which often outrage collective humanity, such as Hitler's attempted extermination of the Jews.

In the second sense, too, the present theory seems to provide realistic possibilities for substantially more effective procedures for measuring and controlling human cultural processes, and this leads to the question of how these new behavioral possibilities relate to ethical systems.

Philosophical speculation about the ethics of human behavior is relatively recent in human history, usually being credited to Socrates in the West, although Socrates' thought should be understood as a response to an already extant body of ethical thought due to the sophists. Moreover, much of the work of the Eastern philosopher Lao Tsu, which antedates this period, was ethical in character, as were the koan-like pronouncements of Heraclitus (J. D. Woelfel, 1977).

The sophists' ethical thought was relativistic in nature, and the basis of this relativism was human. The sophist Protagoras, for example, said "man is the measure of all things." Individual sophists differed among themselves, but in general taught a wide variety of skills, and measured the good relative to the domain of the skill. One could speak of a good doctor, a good archer, or even a good liar, without implying that each case of the good need to be related to the others. The activities of the sophists were often practical, and the good frequently pragmatic.

Socrates, on the other hand, was committed to the notion of the City State as an organic unity, and perceived that the maintenance of such a social structure was inconsistent with an individual relativistic code of conduct, but rather required the centralized direction of a unified absolute moral code. Socrates introduced the notion of the good for which the other goods existed, such that the good carpenter, the good plumber, and the good arrow all were called good insofar as they approximated an ulterior good. Plato in turn elevated the idea of the ulterior good to the level of the ideal good, the pattern for each instance of the good. In the Platonic system, the good is absolute and independent of human observation or measurement. Plato's good is itself a compound object, consisting of a harmonious balance of truth, justice, and beauty.

Like Socrates, Aristotle also posits an ulterior good for which other goods are sought, and this good he calls happiness, while acknowledging that others disagree among themselves about the meaning of happiness. Like Plato, Aristotle's good is also composite, a balance or equilibrium, but unlike Plato, Aristotle's good is explicitly a mean or average, and even more unlike Plato, the source of knowledge about the mean is observations which Aristotle is careful to point out are inherently approximate.

Even at the time of Plato and Aristotle, ethical theorists agreed in general that absolute ethical systems (such as Plato's) could not rest on an observational base, and that ethical systems which rested on an empirical base could be only relative.

Defining the Good

Since the good (or any other concept) has only relative significance in a theory such as the present one, any definition offered consistent with the theory must be itself relative. This leads immediately to the possibility of representing the good as a social object whose definition is given by its relationship to each of the other social objects distinguished by a person or culture by means of the procedures already described. We should understand as well that the relativistic base of the theory also denies any direct access to the good independent of human experience, and so this definition really is a definition of the human experience of the good, or the good as it is collectively defined by humans.

Within this framework, the good may be seen to be relative in several senses. First and most fundamentally, the good is relative in that it is given its meaning by its relation to other concepts. Thus the good is defined both in theory and in practice by the set of interpoint distances among the concept of the good and some set of other concepts, and is consequently relative to the meanings of these other concepts (which in turn are also dependent on their interpoint relations with still other concepts). In this sense the good can be seen as an attribute, which other objects and acts exhibit in inverse proportion to their distance from the good.

Frequently theorists consider, rather than the good, a good–bad continuum or polarity. Such a notion is described as a line segment in a multidimensional space, and the possibility and likelihood of motion in other dimensions requires that distances from good and from bad be measured independently, as Cody, Marlier, and Woelfel (1976) and Danes and Woelfel (1975) have demonstrated. Each object symbolized by the culture may be paired with any other to create a polarity, so that the good, for example, might be considered in contrast to the bad, but it

TABLE 12.1

Mean Measured Distances from 15 Selected Concepts to the Concept "Good" for 4 Time Periods ($N = 43$)[a,b]

Time concept	01 Sleeping	02 Dreaming	03 Daydreaming	04 Intense concentration	05 Marijuana high	06 Good	07 Depression	08 Alcohol high	09 Relaxation	10 CTP	11 Alpha wave meditation	12 Transcendental meditation	13 Reliable	14 Timothy Leary	15 Linus Pauling	16 Me	$\sum_{\alpha=1}^{15} R_{(\alpha)}$
t_1	54.1 (6.0)	53.9 (4.7)	52.2 (4.5)	49.9 (5.9)	59.8 (5.9)	—	85.3 (4.3)	65.9 (6.1)	31.7 (4.4)	53.3 (5.5)	46.4 (3.8)	43.3 (3.9)	44.0 (13.8)	92.7 (25.3)	83.7 (26.3)	35.8 (3.4)	857 (4.7)
t_2	50.9 (11.8)	48.5 (11.4)	55.5 (11.2)	55.7 (11.3)	72.7 (12.4)	—	79.3 (4.5)	89.1 (22.2)	40.5 (11.7)	56.2 (6.5)	52.5 (5.5)	46.4 (5.4)	35.7 (11.4)	76.8 (11.3)	65.6 (11.6)	47.4 (11.2)	872.8 (4.0)
t_3	46.5 (11.4)	52.4 (11.5)	58.5 (11.3)	58.4 (11.7)	80.6 (12.1)	—	85.6 (10.6)	73.3 (10.9)	35.8 (4.4)	61.0 (11.5)	60.5 (6.4)	56.9 (6.3)	34.3 (3.8)	76.5 (11.3)	68.0 (11.6)	39.9 (11.1)	888.2 (4.1)
t_4	47.4 (11.5)	55.0 (75.74)	57.8 (11.0)	55.5 (11.3)	74.6 (11.8)	—	85.7 (11.3)	72.0 (11.7)	43.7 (11.4)	65.7 (12.1)	57.1 (6.3)	55.0 (6.3)	41.5 (11.4)	71.8 (11.4)	63.6 (11.6)	32.0 (2.7)	878.3 (3.6)

[a] Numbers in parentheses are standard errors of measure.
[b] $R_{(\alpha)}$ is the length of the (α)th vector. Origin is at the Good.

might also be contrasted with evil. Or, it might be considered alone, rather than an a part of a pair of words, as was the case in the experiment described earlier (Chapter 7). In this experiment the word "good" was included among the set of paired comparisons (see Figures 7.5 and 7.6a). Table 12.1 shows the results of such measurements for 43 university students at 4 points in time. Prior to the second and third measurements, the students read letters allegedly from Pauling and then Leary recommending the daily practice of the CTP (see Chapter 7), but no direct manipulations of the "goodness" of any of the concepts was attempted. Although there is a movement toward the good on the part of the two message sources (Leary and Pauling) after the first measurement period, their measured positions with regard to the good show relatively high error in the first period and the changes probably cannot be taken as reliable. Overall, the distances from each concept to the good seem precise and relatively stable even with such small sample sizes.

The overall goodness of the domain itself shows a roughly declining trend across the life of the experiment, however. A summation of the distances of each concept from the good across concepts within each time period can serve as a useful measure of the overall goodness of the domain as perceived by the respondents. Figure 12.1 shows that the total distance of all concepts from the good increases after each treatment, then shows some decline at the last period. The percentage change is actually very small, however, although the scale presented in

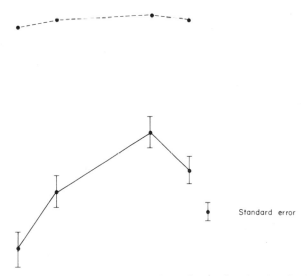

FIGURE 12.1 Total distance of 15 concepts from the good at 4 points in time. ——, Magnified scale; ---, absolute scale.

Figure 12.1 exaggerates these changes. The absolute scale (measured from zero) at the top of Figure 12.1 shows the relative change in better perspective.

A second sense in which the concept of good is relative is that the good may be expected to have different meanings in different domains. Figures 4.7 and 4.8 present the location of the word good relative to the set of principle emotions described earlier. Figure 6.1 makes the bipolar pairs more salient, and shows, to an extent, the arbitrariness of the bipolarity of any pair of concepts. Figure 11.1 shows the relative location of the good among the set of concepts used to describe the Dairy Herd Improvement Association Testing Service (the test). In each of these figures, the good is defined as a point in a domain. The procedures adopted here allow each of these goods to be located independently of the others, so that the independence of the location of good in multiple situations becomes an empirical matter.

A third sense in which the good is relative in this system is illustrated in Figure 6.1. Here we see that two separate cultures (males and females) can be seen to have different representations of the good within the same domain. Moreover, each of the selves of the groups is itself at a different orientation from the good of each of the groups. This means that, even within the same domain, different individuals or cultures may disagree among themselves about the location (meaning) of the good.

Thus we can see that the experience of the good is relative in at least three major senses. First, and most fundamentally, the good is relative because it has meaning only in relation to the remaining set of objects of experience. Second, the good is relative in that the meaning of the good for a single person or culture may be domain specific, with a different concept of the good at least possible for each domain of meaning. Third, the good is relative to the groups who hold conceptions of the good, and different groups or persons may locate the good differently within the same general domain.

The Social Good

The notion of the relativity of the good makes it clear that no object or activity may be evaluated on an absolute basis, but rather each object or act must be evaluated relative to a specified set of objects within a specified domain and from the perspective of a designated observer or culture of observers. While some may claim that human knowledge may have access to a universal or absolute notion of the good (as, perhaps, in the sense of Kant's a priori), clearly science cannot make this claim.

Based on the model developed earlier, it is possible to evaluate any object in terms of its measured distance from some good point, or to evaluate any action in terms of whether it results in movement of some self point closer to or further from a good point for some designated observer or set of observers. When multiple observers and multiple domains are involved, science may make an unambiguous determination of the extent to which an object or action is good from the standpoint of each of the observers, but may not make a claim as to the relative merit of the definitions of the good held by each of the observers. But science can inquire into the generating locus of the good for any observer or system of observers.

Origin of the Good

To some extent, evidence is consistent with the notion that at least to an extent human emotions provide a foundation for notions of the good, as the data already examined in Figures 4.7 and 4.8 show. These figures show that the idea of the good for a sample of undergraduate students lies close to the emotional experiences of happiness, joy, and other "positive" emotions, and this represents a linkage of the abstract idea of the good with a set of designatable human experiences. These emotions themselves are suspected by many cross-cultural investigators to be culturally variable, however, and so the link is by no means absolute. In any event, insofar as the cultural definitions of both emotions and the good may be seen to have life expectancies far in excess of a human life span, these cultural notions may be seen to have priority over individual definitions, and in fact may be seen as the source of individual definitions within a single lifetime. Each individual, as Mead (1934) pointed out, is born into a world which is already well formed, and the structure of the culture is then communicated into the individual.

Mobility and the Social Good

The notion of a cultural good which precedes and informs individual notions of the good is consistent with the notion of an average good or golden mean described by Aristotle, and in fact follows directly from Durkheim's notion of the social fact. An individual's moral system may be evaluated from the collective viewpoint of his or her culture not only in principle, but such evaluations are everyday practice. In the theory presented here, each individual learns the notion of the good through communication with other members of the society. In the Platonic model, the good is not learned, but rather remembered from a mythical earlier existence. But in practice Plato will allow that memory may be jogged by living the philosophic life, particularly through participation in dialectic. The dialectic in particular represents a communication of opposing positions, and parties to a dialectical argument must take the position of the other at least in imagination in order to present their own positions. This dialectic transformation of viewpoint bears important resemblances to Mannheim's notion of the role of social mobility in the developing of "true" knowledge of one's society. In a sense, Mannheim's notion advances Plato's, in that it extends the notion of the dialectic from two positions to many positions. In this same sense, it is similar to Mead's notion of taking the role of the other.

Certainly Mannheim's view is more experiential than Mead's more speculative position, since for Mannheim persons actually play multiple roles as a result of social mobility, and thus develop a generalized overview of the social structure, but Mead deals more often with imaginative role playing, in the sense that the member of an athletic team must imagine the role of the other players in order to coordinate his or her activities with those of the others. Aristotle, who views the good act as the golden mean, advises the person who would act well to study the behaviors of others and adopt a position between the extremes. Thus, Aristotle suggests that the good is learned by an active process of studying the acts of others.

Regardless of these differences, all these thinkers argue that the viewpoint developed as a result of taking multiple positions in a society, whether in dialectical argument (Plato), in play or games or imagination (Mead), or through study (Aristotle) or life experience (Mannheim), is a "true" one in some sense. And in all cases, the theory presented in this volume predicts that the viewpoint developed as a result of such communication processes will converge on the average social viewpoint in a statistical and thermodynamic sense, as long as the set of positions sampled is large and random.

The "large and random" stipulations attached to the theory are not out of character with the views of those philosophers, since they imply only that the experiences of a person who sampled information from a biased sample of members of a culture would develop a view which represented those biases, and in this sense would deviate from the "true" or aggregate view. In this statistical sense at least, the good may be seen as hierarchical; that is, the generating locus of the good for any subsystem is the aggregate good of the system of which it is a part. Any individual view of the good is a "false" view from the position of the system, insofar as it differs from the aggregate view. In this sense also, the statistical good represents also an "ulterior good" or "good for which" the other goods are sought and against which they are evaluated. Furthermore, since the overall system "good" is identified with the mean of the structure of that system, the system will evaluate as good those objects and actions which extend and perpetuate the system. Good is thus associated with the maintenance of a system.

This should not be interpreted as an "antiradical" view, since the system to which the good refers for any individual is not the society within which one is embedded and which constitutes the near surround for one's local organizations, but rather to the system of ideas from which the individuals' notions were developed. Thus the good for the radical is the maintenance of the system of (radical) thought from which he or she comes.

Energy

In the long run, systems which communicate their structures to subsequent generations will suffer a decline into increasing entropy in a closed system, since the reversal of entropy in the subsequent generations must be made up by a corresponding increase in the entropy of the older system if the rate of production of entropy is to be conserved. This means that societies which survive will have to exist in open systems which draw in additional energy from the surround in order to maintain their own structures while transmitting information to new generations. Over the long run, therefore, systems which develop capacities to extract energy from the near surround and channel it to the maintenance of structure will maintain a survival advantage until energy sources in the near surround are exhausted.

Recent epochs in human development have been marked by increasing abilities to extract energy from the surround. While printing, for example, led to the development of the possibility of producing multiple copies of masses of information, the act of printing requires inputs of energy, and the costs of manufacturing and distributing multiple facsimiles of a set of information can be calculated in terms of energy. To a large extent, the dominance of Western industrial society over developing nations comes from the availability of energy to transmit information. These processes are actually quite prosaic; broadcasting stations convert chemical or atomic energy into electrical energy which is radiated from a transmitter. Newspapers cut trees and convert chemical or atomic energy into multiple copies which are distributed geographically at the cost of further energy. In developing nations, information is transmitted primarily by means of human energy in the form of voice and audio signals. This difference in the net potential energy is probably sufficient to account for what many have called the "one-way flow" of information from "hot" industrial societies to the developing nations.

Thus the capacity to harness energy from the near surround is a powerful factor in the ability of a society to transmit the information which defines its structure to others.

From the viewpoint of the system with access to the energy, this result is a good one, since it enhances the survival of the system structure, but, of course, from the viewpoint of the systems without such access, this result is not a good one, since it results in the convergence of these systems toward the structure of the energy-rich society.

The System as the Good

The association of the good with the maintenance and expansion of the system, along with the dependence of the system structure on inputs of energy into the system may result in a special relation between energy and the idea of the good. Many writers have suggested that the space of human culture is anisotropic; that is, motion in every direction is not equally likely. Sociologists in particular have long assumed that certain statuses should be considered "higher." Available energy must be spent to move "upward" toward high status positions, but one could "fall" to a lower position without effort (Blau, 1974). If this is so, persons, groups, and societies would accumulate potential energy as a result of moving toward the good. Whether the good is located at a point of high or highest potential is an empirical question within the theory, however. The collective social experience which Durkheim finds at the foundation of the notion of the sacred is characterized within this theory as a period of highly coordinated periodic activity (including ritual chanting, which provides a highly accurate social clock against which behavior can be even more finely coordinated). These kinds of conditions are most likely to produce peaks and resonances due to the coordination in space and time of the periodic functions of the individual consciousness. These events provide both a development and reinforcement of common symbols commonly defined as well as an unusually complete coupling of power across individuals, due to common phase relations, so that flows of energy ought to be very high. Energy plays a role in the creation of the organization of the culture, its symbols, and the idea of the good in same social situations. In the ritual situation, the energy of the event produces a common structure of symbols which form a basis for the collective anchoring of experience in communication.

It is probably also significant that the social situations which generate the common symbols out of which the idea of the society is generated are typified by what might be considered a "harmonious" interaction of the system nodes, since ritual time-keeping, such as chanting, singing, dancing, or other rythmic interchanges, is characteristic of these situations. In this sense the idea of the good ought also to be associated with the idea of organization itself. While Durkheim emphasizes the role of these activities as the ultimate root of the notion of God, it is worth noting the common association between the notions of good and God in most theological systems.

By whatever mechanism the notion of the good may be established, once it is established, the good serves as a standard for the evaluation of any designatable object. Activities can be evaluated on the basis of their consequences, since some actions can have the effect of moving the person or group toward the idea of the good, while other actions may move the self away from the idea of the good. In this sense the idea of the good can serve as a guide to action.

While ultimately and globally, natural selection fixes the character of a culture, over the short range, such a process is too slow to account for what many see as purposeful adaptive behavior of cultures and individuals. Cultures and individuals also exhibit local learning in addition to the process of random generation of random behaviors some of which survive. Local learning, as its is defined here, refers to a selection process whereby some behaviors are selected by an individual or culture over others within short spans of time.

Regardless of whether the movement toward some behaviors and away from others is seen as under the voluntary control of the person or group, most philosophers, rhetoricians, and theologians define the state toward which persons tend as the good. While the notions of guilt and responsibility hinge on whether actors are presumed to be free to choose among acts or not, the idea of the good is independent of ideas of freedom and responsibility. Many philosophers, such as Aristotle and Aquinas, argue that humans are constrained to act toward the perceived good; that is, that all human action is motivated by the good. In the case of Aquinas' theory and Catholic theology, the role of human freedom of choice is viewed as mysterious, since the compulsion toward the good is not contingent, but necessary.

Science and the Good

Social Acts

Activities or behaviors may be thought of as algorithms or methods of acting. Any algorithm A may be described as a sequence of activities a_1,

$a_2, a_3, \ldots , a_n$ arrayed in time. Algorithms themselves may be arrayed in a time sequence to yield higher level algorithms, until very complex long-term activities, such as building a pyramid or becoming a college graduate, have been constructed. Learning to behave involves at early stages mastering the elementary algorithms common to most activities, such as standing, walking, and grasping. At later stages these basic algorithms are sequenced into more complex acts, while at earlier stages still, the basic acts mentioned are themselves composed out of less complex algorithms.

Social acts are those acts which are shared by multiple persons or groups insofar as they have a common social definition. These acts may themselves be constructed of sets of individual acts, as the acts of individual builders are coordinated into the construction of a house. Behavior can be coordinated no more precisely than it can be symbolized, however, since deviations from a specified pattern can be measured only if they can be encoded or recognized. As Wilson (1952) says, every scale or measurement device—including any scale for defining behavior—is always an interval or category scale regardless of its formal structure in the sense that technical limitations of measurement will always result in a smallest interval that can be determined to a given level of certainty. No event or detail smaller than this interval can be noted at a given cost. There will therefore be a practical point at which existing measurement systems provide information sufficient to allow discrimination of an interval of a specific size λ, and, in practice, a culture can specify activities to no tolerance lower than these. While elements larger than λ might be chosen, no activity smaller than λ, where λ represents the smallest interval of any attribute along which the act is described, or briefer than λ_t, where λ_t represents the smallest interval of time that can be measured by the culture, could be used as the unit algorithm.

Science, as in extension of basic human learning processes, increases our collective capacity to execute complex sequences of activity in that its superior coding systems allow for increasingly precise specification of the space–time coordinates of the algorithms. Thus we are able to move from crude descriptions of behavior ("fasten these pieces") to more precise descriptions ("torque these bolts to 1.1 ± .3 kg-m"). This ability to increase the precision which accompanies measures of the space–time coordinates of behavior, leads in turn to the development of more complex behaviors than heretofore. Our collective capacity to specify and enact algorithms is increased by the activities of science.

While science expands the capacity of our cognitive systems to describe acts, technology results in the actual development of such acts or algorithms. Technologies are actual algorithms or ways of doing things, and the range of things it is possible for the technology to do is enhanced by development of its science.

The Selection of Acts

While science clearly increases our collective ability to act precisely and in coordination with others, many thinkers have held that science can have little or nothing to say about which of the array of possible behaviors ought to be performed. Traditionally, this view has held that the realm of ethics or morality could not be scrutinized by science, since its object—human moral principles—is not objectively measurable. Since the relativistic posture of the present book, however, assumes that nothing is "objectively measurable," again the argument segregating ethical or moral objects or experiences from other objects or experiences must be called into question.

On one level, the question of which behaviors will be performed is answered by natural selection. Insofar as certain acts confer a survival advantage on those who perform them, those performers have an increased probability of survival and therefore they and their behaviors will tend to be perpetuated. On a macro-level scale, the natural selection must be reckoned as a powerful factor, confering survival advantage on societies which develop agricultural procedures suited to their locations and so on. Even on a micro level, natural selection forces cannot be ignored, since, for example, the development of certain behavioral skills (such as reading) can lead to enhanced survival potential for individual persons over a single life span. Furthermore, if a behavior is communicated across generations, then the behavior will tend to survive beyond the life span of the individual. In this sense (and in the long run), behaviors which are specifiable (i.e., which can be described precisely) will tend to be selected, since the survival of the algorithm requires it to be communicated across generations.

Moreover, while specifiability or encodability is a necessary condition for communication, it is not itself sufficient, since some potential must also exist. Particularly in this case, where intergenerational communication is involved, differences or potentials ought to be expected to be not so much differences among different structures as differences between highly structured domains (in the adults) and relatively less structured domains (in the children). Intergenerational communication represents then a net decrease in entropy for children at the expense of an increase in entropy for adults (which may be made up by inputs from the near surround). Highly structured states represent low levels of entropy or high levels of information or energy, since they are maximally different from the state of maximum entropy or structurelessness. Natural selection therefore tends to produce behaviors which are specifiable, increasingly structured, and beneficial to those who hold them, where "beneficial" means helpful for survival, at least long enough to be communicated to younger persons. This theory anticipates, therefore, as does Spencer (1897) that natural selection leads to a generalized increase in heterogeneity or complexity of structure, at least when net energy flow from the surround is positive.

The Good as a Goal

Up until now, the only mechanism for the selection of behaviors posited here has been the idea of natural selection, in which behaviors which confer survival advantages on their performers outlast those which do not. But the idea of the good allows for a more rapid and less spontaneous mechanism. Activities which have previously been associated with benefits to the system can become associated with the good, and individuals can be directed by custom and law to learn and perform behaviors which have been judged good (i.e., which are located close to the good). Moreover, the idea of the good can serve as a basis for the evaluation of behaviors in terms of their effects, even if those behaviors have not previously been located with regard to the good.

All human activities may be arrayed along a continuum from highly specified and well known to highly unspecified and novel. Novel, unique, or idiosyncratic behaviors bear an initially unknown relation to the good, but can be judged immediately after their performance by a determination of whether their performance has increased or decreased the separation of the performer from the good. This allows for a more rapid and less drastic selection procedure than natural selection, which requires the performer of a behavior to thrive or die as a consequence of performing the act. Since any system seeks but need not be in an equilibrium condition at any moment, judgments of the location of the good will always remain fallible, and different members of the same society will adjudge different behaviors differentially good. Nonetheless, if the location of the good is not too far off the mark, it serves as a much more rapid way of selecting behaviors with survival value than natural selection itself.

This model can therefore deal as well with the development and selection of novel behaviors. Whenever a behavior is known from past experience of a culture to lead to movements toward the good in a specific situation, then the behavior may be specified in advance and the (known) algorithm for carrying out the act initiated. When no sure pathway to the good is known, however, random activities can be initiated and evaluated in terms of their resulting effects toward or away from the good. Thus trial and error learning becomes more rapid (and safer) when a well-defined notion of the good is available, since otherwise randomly initiated behaviors can be judged only after the system which initiated them prospers or fails. These processes are well understood by applied mathematicians and computer programmers, since they include the two known ways of solving an applied problem. If the algorithm or equation which leads to a desired result is known, it is usually most efficient to apply the algorithm directly. When this is not the case, that is, when an exact solution or path to a solution is not known, a solution can still be found if a criterion for the final solution is known. This criterion can serve as a goal, and the program may be made to perform random or systematic calculations whose results are then compared to the goal. Activities which lead away from the goal (i.e., which do not converge) are then blocked, and activities which lead to reductions in the distance between the result and the goal are retained and repeated until the distance between the result and the goal is as small as desired. When the algorithm is not known, however, and when no goal or criterion can be specified, the problem cannot be solved.

The Good Act

We have argued that the organization of a society gives rise to the notion of the good, which is associated with the structure of the culture itself, and that actions (and all other objects) are subsequently evaluated in terms of their distance from this good. In a real social situation, different subsystems within any system are likely to differ among themselves in their location of the good. Consequently their collective evaluation of any act requires negotiation or communication among the subsystems as they describe to each other the self trajectories they experience with regard to the good as each of them experience it. These negotiations need not be thought of as deliberate, since they are a consequence of differences in potential resulting from difference in system structures brought into synchronization as a result of the act which serves as common object. When their attentions are collectively focused on the act to be evaluated, they will experience a common clock created by the time sequence of the act. This keeping of common time synchronizes the subsystems into a common communication system, and thermodynamic forces press toward readjustments of each of the structures toward a common equilibrium point.

In its most general form, a social act is performed before an audience of individuals or groups, each of whom has an idea of the good, an idea of the self, and an idea of each of the objects in regard to which the act is defined. The performance of the act affects each of the audiences as well as the performer of the act. For any groups, there will be $g + 1$ relative evaluations of the act—one for each group and one for the system constituted of all the groups. The act will result in reorganizations of the structures of each of the cultural systems with resulting motions of the subsystem selves toward or away from the good. Similarly, the act will result in the reorganization of the aggregate structure of all groups pooled together, and this too may be evaluated in terms of its approach toward or recession from the good. (If each group is given an equal weight in an ethical sense, then the overall system structure is determined from the mean of the means of each of the subsystems. If, on the other hand, each individual member of each of the subsystems is weighted equally on an ethical basis, then the mean of the total system is calculated from the mean of the members—that is, each subsystem mean is weighted by its population.)

Moral Perspectives

It is worth recalling that this discussion makes reference to collective social perceptions of the good, and not to any absolute good. In the sense that "man [sic] is the measure of all things," these aggregates can lay some claim to a kind of "truth," insofar as they represent stable, central tendencies or goals toward which large-scale social processes tend. Nonetheless, the capacity of the theory to transform viewpoints across arbitrary perspectives leads to the possibility of examining the good from alternative standpoints.

The Good Advertising Campaign

Figure 12.2 depicts a hypothetical picture of an advertising campaign, which can serve as a useful illustration of the way an act is evaluated from multiple standpoints within this system. In Figure 12.2, three points of view are represented. The position of management is represented by circles, the position of corporate stockholders by squares, and the position of the general public by triangles. (In actual campaign, there are usually more than three groups.) For each of these groups, we have included a concept of the good, a concept of the product to be advertised, and a self point. Also included is a concept called the "message attribute," which represents the campaign strategy itself. For simplicity, we assume that the message strategy is a simple message, and that the message attribute is the single concept representing the best one-pair message. The star near the center of the figure represents the aggregate good for the society within which these three groups are embedded; that is, the grand mean location of the good averaged over all members of the society.

Following the principles described in Chapter 9, the message "product A is message attribute X" will be interpreted differently by each of the three groups, since for each group the product will move from the point at which that group locates it toward the point at which the same group locates the message attribute. This will result in movements of the product as seen by each of the three groups along the three solid vectors in Figure 12.2.

Based on an examination of these vectors it is easy to determine whether or not the message strategy will result in the product being perceived as better or worse by each of the groups simply in terms of whether or not the product as seen by a group moves toward or away from the good as seen by the same group. Thus, for the fictitious data in Figure 12.2, the message campaign results in the product appearing to become worse for stockholders, better from management's viewpoint, and initially better, then worse from the public's viewpoint as the campaign wears on.

Under most circumstances, the extent to which a single product is seen as better or worse as a result of an advertising campaign is not of great importance, although under special circumstances this may be crucial, depending on the centrality and utility of the product to the survival of the society. Generally more important is the extent to which the parties' evaluations of themselves might be affected by the campaign. Assuming of course that the campaign has been well worked out, the product concept will move closer to the self concept for each group involved. (In Figure 12.2, this is true for management and for the public, but not true for stockholders.) This in turn should lead to increased use of the product by the members of the groups involved, which in turn

FIGURE 12.2 Hypothetical representation of results of an advertising campaign for three interest groups. ■, Stockholder's view; ●, management's view; ▲, public's view; ★, average good.

should yield net motions of the selves of the groups toward the new product location (represented in Figure 12.2 by dashed vectors). In the case of management in Figure 12.2, this would clearly yield a net decrease in the distance from self to good as seen by management, representing an improvement in management's opinion of its self-worth. For the public in Figure 12.2, the result is nearly an orthogonal trajectory from the good, resulting in no significant improvement or worsening of the sense of self-worth. It is worth noting, however, that in Figure 12.2, the public self moves directly toward the star which represents the good for the overall society, and so this campaign would result in a net increase in positive evaluation of the consuming public by the general public. For stockholders, the net trajectory of the self in Figure 12.2 is away from the good as they define it, but toward the good as it is defined by the general society.

Many other approaches to measuring the goodness of a public information campaign can be derived within this system, including calculating overall sums of distances on concepts in the domain from the good as described in Table 12.1. In general, however, the key advantage of the system lies in its ability to represent the objects involved in any public information campaign as they are perceived by every relevant group in a single reference frame. This makes it possible to calculate the ethical consequences of any changes in the domain from the perspectives of any of the groups or cultures (or individuals) involved in a precise and unambiguous way. While none of these perspectives is privileged, nonetheless any campaign which results in the worsening of the ethical situation from the viewpoint of some group owes an explanation to members of that group. Moreover, even though the position of no group is privileged, in general there is probably good reason to lend statistical priority to generalized viewpoints over specific component views. This is equivalent to assigning priorities to the general good over the good of special interests.

While these procedures do not solve the ethical problem in an absolute sense, they do make evident the relative notion of the good, and make objective the conflicts which arise in the pursuit of the good across multiple and disparate viewpoints. Viewpoints other than the generalized social view are required in any relativistic theory to provide a standard against which the generalized social standpoint can be evaluated. Such an implication follows from Descartes' notion of comparative measurement and from the principal of relativization. Some of these alternative perspectives might themselves be subsystems of the society or culture, while others may lie outside the social system.

Moral Subsystems

The examples presented so far have all been instantaneous examples, in that they have represented the goodness of objects and actions at a point in time. (Actually, due to the lag inherent in the data collection procedure, these measurements represent averages over a finite interval of time.) Repeated measures over time, however, open the possibility that societies grow by controlling the intake of energy over time—that is, in the integral—rather than instantaneously.

Such a suggestion is equivalent to attributing memory to an organization or society, insofar as such a rule requires minimizing deviations from previous times. For any system measured at intervals of time t_0, t_1, t_2, . . . , t_n, this model implies that the coefficient β_1, β_2, . . . , β_k in the expression

$$X_{t_n} = \beta_0 X_{t_{n-1}} + \beta_1 X_{t_{n-2}} + \cdots + \beta_k X_{t_{n-k}} + e_{t_n}' \qquad (12.1)$$

where $X_{t_{n-i}}$ is the value of any system parameter at t_{n-1} and e_{t_n} the contribution from the system environment, are not all zero. In a system with no memory, all the β_i are uniformly zero, and the state of the system at any time is uninfluenced by its state at any prior time, but is totally determined at each instant by the system environment e.

In the theory elaborated here, the values of the β_i depend directly on values for inertial mass in a culture, and inversely on net forces from the near surround. Cultural systems which exhibit high lags, that is, long memory—should therefore be expected to be relatively massive, isolated structures. These would be systems characterized by high rates of intergenerational communications and low rates of communication with the near surround. Communications with prior generations result in isolation from the near surround reduces exposure to incoming information and hence to unbalanced net forces.

Social organizations of this type—such as for example, monasteries and other cloistered groups—have traditionally been carriers of social values, that is, relatively time-invariant information against which the current state of a culture may be gauged.

Exogenous Measurement Standards

In addition to information stored in designated internal subsystems, standards of reference outside the system may serve as markers against which a culture may evaluate itself. These include other societies as well as "physical" structures. Often cultures invest collective energy into environmental structures such as buildings, books and papers, roads, and other such structures which exert subsequent reactive effects on future information environments for a society. When relatively durable physical structures have been designated by social symbols, those structures exert a defining effect on the symbol for subsequent time periods. To the extent that a culture has invested energy in physical structures in the environment, those structures will stabilize the cultural pattern which informed them. Thus, for example, to the extent that a monastic group invests human energy into inscribing cultural patterns into written form, it stabilizes its pattern. Change in the cultural pattern requires modification of written prescription for the pattern, and the energy required to rewrite the pattern will be proportional to the amount invested in the original structure.

Energy channeled into architecture, such as private and public buildings, produces stabilizing and evaluative results in several ways. In a most obvious sense, the resulting physical structures influence patterns of intercommunication and tend to constrain them to constant values while they endure simply because they control the locations of communicating people in physical space. Any artifacts—including communication media, eating utensils, transportation systems, toys, clothing, and the like—can serve a similar constraining function. Moreover, insofar as the construction of the artifact requires the development of an organized sequence of social acts, the pattern for such an algorithm makes subsequent performances of the same algorithm less energy consuming, since less organizing is required to repeat the algorithm than to develop a new one.

Insofar as such artifacts have been designated by social symbols of an evaluative sort—such as *good* or *beautiful*—then such structures serve as stabilizing influences on the definition of the good, and indeed as standards against which the society may evaluate itself and its actions. Figure 12.3 shows the first principal plane of the domain of automobiles and their attributes as perceived by a small sample of university students. Note that the term "good looking" is included in the domain, and lies at a specific distance from a specific, named automobile (called "car X" in Figure 12.3). While this distance defines the extent to which the car is good looking, it can with equal validity be seen as providing a highly specific meaning for the term "good looking" in reference to a widely distributed, easily accessible standard (and its facsimiles)—that is, car X. Changes in this distance over time can serve as a basis for measuring changes in the standards of the culture, while differences in this distance across cultures can serve as a basis for differentiating the

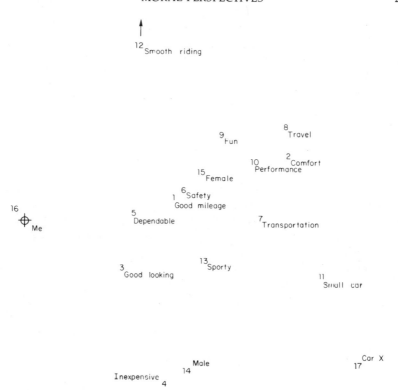

FIGURE 12.3   First principal plane of a neighborhood of a car and its attributes.

standards of different cultures. Moreover, the social energy required to produce, distribute, and maintain multiple facsimiles of the standard (such as the car) can be seen to result in an increase in the mass of the concepts related to the standard, since the existence of the standard in multiple facsimiles stabilizes the meanings of words used to describe them.

Environmental Standards

In any relativistic system, all evaluations have a kind of symmetry in that the attribution of an evaluative word or phrase to an object provides a definition of the object while the object also serves as a definer of the evaluative phrase or word. This mutual defining effect applies not only in the case of artifacts of the culture, but of any designated object, including objects generally considered part of the environment. Flora, fauna, and physical structures may of course be symbolized and evaluated, and then exert a reactive effect on the meanings of the evaluative words. Insofar as physical structures such as plants, animals, or landscape structures, or environmental processes such as snowfalls or evolution are labeled good or bad, they stand as reference symbols which define the experiential meaning of good and bad. These external references serve as standards against which a society may evaluate itself over time.

Extraterrestrial Referents

Ethical writers often make reference to extraterrestrial objects as evaluative standards. Greek authors such as Aristotle defined the notions of celestial bodies as paragons which terrestrial processes could only approach, but not match. In this sense, extraterrestrial processes served as limits on the human conception of the perfect and the perfection achievable by human cultures.

In a more modern treatment, Shklovskii and Sagan (1966) illustrate the capacity of science to enhance and extend human reference frames by their examination of the relative location of human terrestrial life in the cosmic process on an intergalactic scale. Making explicit the evaluative components inherent in such an endeavor, Shklovskii and Sagan introduce the hypothesis of "mediocrity." Since they are interested in inferring from a single case of intelligent life—human life—to the general distribution of intelligent life in the universe, they argue that the most probable hypothesis is that the single case known is mediocre— that is, a typical example. The quantitative evidence they provide about the cosmological processes and likely distribution of thermochemical processes typical of terrestrial processes is consistent with the hypothesis that intelligent life processes are the result of thermodynamic processes (such as those described here) which ought to be relatively widely distributed throughout the universe. Although highly speculative, the discovery of extraterrestrial intelligence would raise the likelihood of nonhuman moral reference frames. In principal, the highly general theory of cross-cultural transformations presented here may provide a basis for establishing initial correspondences with nonhuman life forms.

The Good Science

Science may be thought of as a social object in the same way as any of the other activities we have so far examined, and we may therefore use the same procedures to define and evaluate science as we have used to define and evaluate other social objects in this book. Figure 12.4, for

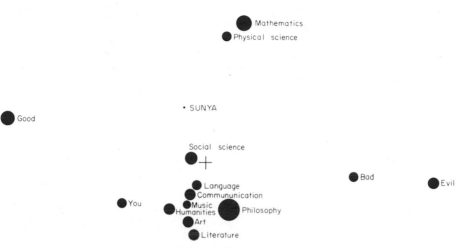

FIGURE 12.4 First three dimensions of the neighborhood of selected human disciplines for a sample of undergraduate humanities students. Diameter of concept $\alpha - d_{(\alpha)} = a + bR^3_{(\alpha)}$, where $a = .24$ and $b = 1.75 \times 10^{-3}$.

example, shows the first three dimensions of a domain within which science has been located as conceived by a sample of university undergraduate students (drawn primarily from the humanities). Table 12.2 shows more precisely the dissimilarity relations between science (both physical and social) from the remaining concepts. The evaluations these students place on science, both physical and social, can be determined primarily from the sets of distances from the three terms *good, bad,* and *evil.*

These data are based on very small samples and are meant only as illustrations of the general procedure in this domain. Nor, regardless of sample size, are the concepts in Figure 12.4 and Table 12.2 exhaustive of the very extensive set of concepts in relation to which science may be defined. Moreover, not all possible samples are usually considered competent to define or evaluate science, and many persons would believe definitions derived from samples of scientists to be more "accurate" than those of populations of nonscientists. The word "science," like any vernacular word, has different meanings within different populations. Like other words which designate activities, it is common that persons involved in (close to) the activity are assumed to be better able to make precise descriptions of the activity. Figure 12.5 shows the same domain as pictured by 12 communication scientists.

Science, however, like other long-range standard-preserving organizations, is a relatively cloistered process with highly selective socialization rituals. Most scientists and students of science agree that there is a

TABLE 12.2

Mean Measured Distances from 14 Selected Concepts to the Concept "Physical Science" for 30 Humanities Undergraduates and 12 Communication Network Researchers

Sample	Philosophy	Literature	Music	Humanities	Arts	Social science	Communication	Language	Mathematics	Good	Bad	Evil	You	Your present university
Researchers	190	313	232	295	304	185	200	245	93	233	310	351	246	163
Students	245	249	247	249	257	236	239	239	68	147	230	255	234	126

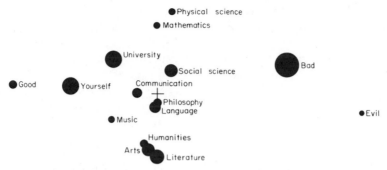

FIGURE 12.5 First three dimensions of the neighborhood of selected disciplines for a sample of 16 communication scientists. Diameter of concept $\alpha = d_{(\alpha)} = a + bR^3_{(\alpha)}$, where $a = .24$ and $b = 1.75 \times 10^{-3}$.

core of knowledge which remains invariant even in the face of scientific development and elaboration, although the nature of this core set has been in dispute. The existence of such a body of information is of course no guarantee that any subset of persons—or less any single person—will know what that subset might be. The information which structures scientific process resides in the minds of all scientists, in libraries, and in the set of expectations nonscientists hold for scientists. To a large extent this book has attempted to elaborate the founding principals of contemporary science, and to produce a theory of human cognitive and cultural processes consistent with those core principals. In this we have been guided by a survey of the writings of many of the most profound scientist of our and other times. We initially (Chapter 1) suggested that the term "science" has been applied in general to a subset of the process by which humans generate systems of symbols for describing, under- standing, and communicating about human experiences.

Implicit in this task has been the notion that science is in some sense "good," and that the development of a scientific model of cultural pro- cesses is also "good." This in turn implies not only that science is evalu- ated as good by some population, but that the consequences of science would be evaluated as good by a significant proportion of humans if they were aware of them.

In this sense, and following from the long-run association between good and the social order, we assume that science provides a social service which enhances the ability of a culture to maintain and expand structures and processes it considers good.

Our best guess as to the founding principles of science are the five principles—relativization, objectivization, empirical verification, max- imum, and minimum information—described in Chapter 1. These principles have been set down in part because they seem to characterize those achievements of science most highly regarded by scientists and described by them as part of their work. Even more so, however, these principles were set out because their implementation seems to lead to a result which most people would consider "good."

Followed to their logical conclusion, we believe these principles are sufficient to lead to the development of the general thermodynamic—information—theoretic model elaborated in this book. To be sure, we believe that the resulting thermodynamic model is not a consequence of the absolute character of experience—such a view is seriously at odds with the philosophy detailed here. Rather we assume that the thermodynamic model is a consequence of the application of these principles to human experience. According to our understanding, the application of different starting principals would yield alternative, nonthermodynamic models. Thus the argument developed in this book has never been that these principles must be applied to human phenomena, but that they should be. At its root, therefore, this book is an ethical argument, which suggests that certain benefits will accrue from the adoption of its conception of science. It is appropriate at this point to reexamine the proposed benefits.

Rationality

The notion of rationality implies that intelligent, goal-seeking agents consider alternative means toward achieving their goals, and base their selection of appropriate means on a calculation of costs and benefits. While many philosophers and social scientists alike have argued that rationality is inherent in every human act, these same writers often note apparent deviations from rationality in everyday human activity. As we noted in Chapter 9, many of the most ingenious and influential theories of human behavior have been developed precisely to deal with apparent deviations from rationality. Thus both Aristotle and Acquinas attribute failures to act rationally—that is, failures to maximize the good through deliberate action—to ignorance of the "true" good or to erroneous conscience. Freud's division of the mind into conscious and unconscious segments is likewise an attempt to save the notion of rationality by placing the locus of the goal in the unconscious mind when none can be found on a conscious level.

In spite of the ingenuity of such theories, many problems in completely rational theories remain. Freud's unconscious motivations, for example, remain unmeasurable and hence his model remains merely plausible. Many conscious activities performed routinely by human individuals—such as cigarette smoking—seem highly destructive and hence irrational. While individual activities which most persons would consider irrational or even stupid are commonly performed, the extent to which organizations of humans behave irrationally is probably even greater. Many humans—including participants—believe that organized social activities in which they engage (such as warfare) are irrational. People often adjudge the collective activities of entire nations to be irrational, as was the case of U.S. activities during the war in Viet Nam.

Many investigators—including the present writers—believe it more plausible that rationality is a state toward which both individuals and intelligent organizations tend but have not yet achieved. From this point of view, science may be seen as a word associated with relatively recent aspects of the development of both individual and particularly collective rationality. We have defined science here (following from the five principles of Chapter 1) as progress toward a precisely articulated thermodynamic model of collective human experiences. Other models can be constructed, but models other than the thermodynamic model all are characterized by "magic" at some junctures. By magic we mean nonthermodynamic models; that is, models in which energy inputs and energy outputs for any process do not match. By this definition, events are magical to the extent that they appear to violate thermodynamic or information theoretic principles.

Development of a thermodynamic model for processes makes rationality possible, since it makes possible the calculation of benefits and rewards. Energy, which is a finite quantity, provides a common currency for the calculation of the cost of activity. Accurate calculations of the relative costs of activities along with quantitative notions of the gains toward some specified goals are prerequisites to rationality. Insofar as these calculations are continuously variable in precision, rationality itself is a continuously variable quantity, increasing as the precision of calculation of costs and returns. Science, then, enhances our collective capacity to define the good on cultural and individual levels, and to estimate the deviations of our course of activity from convergence on the good. Science increases the collective capacity of society to devise strategies for increasing convergence toward the good and for evaluating their relative costs. In this sense, science increases collective rationality.

This benefit, like any good in a relativistic model, is not absolute.

DOCUMENTATION FOR GALILEO VERSION 5.2 COMPUTER PROGRAM

Galileo™ is an integrated programming package for metric mul-tidimensional scaling utilizing paired distance judgment data. Galileo™ will accept data in the form of raw distance scores, aggregate means scores in the form of a square symmetric matrix, or a centroid scalar products matrix.

GALILEO CONTROL CARDS

THE FOLLOWING IS A LIST OF GALILEO CONTROL CARDS.
THESE ARE SIMPLE DESCRIPTIONS OF THE CARDS
IN WHICH -A- STANDS FOR ALPHA OR NUMERIC
CHARACTERS AND -N- STANDS FOR NUMERIC CHARACTERS
ONLY. IF A -N- IS FOLLOWED BY A PERIOD,
THAT PERIOD MUST APPEAR THERE.
USAGE WILL BE DETAILED AT THE END OF THE LIST.
NOTE THAT GALILEO CONTROL CARDS MUST BE
FORMATTED AS INDICATED BELOW:

CARD NAME   VALUE OR LABEL SPECIFICATION
  ⌐   ⌐
(COL.1)   (COL.16)

CARD NAME IS THE NAME INDICATED IN THE LISTINGS
BELOW (AND MUST BE REPRODUCED EXACTLY). THE VALUE OR
LABEL SHOULD BE FORMATTED, STARTING IN COLUMN 16 AS
INDICATED BY THE INFORMATION TYPE IN THE LISTING.

RUN NAME   AAAAAAAAAAAAAAAAAAAAAAAAAAAAAAAAAAAAAAAA

    RUN NAME IS A HEADER AND INITIALIZATION CARD.
    USER MAY SPECIFY ANY NAME UP TO 40 CHARACTERS.
    THIS CARD IS MANDATORY.

N-CONCEPTS   NN

    N-CONCEPTS IS THE RANK OF THE SQUARE MATRIX
    INPUT (OR THE NUMBER OF CONCEPTS IN THE GALILEO SPACE).
    GALILEO V IS LIMITED TO 40 CONCEPTS OR FEWER.
    THIS CARD IS MANDATORY.

N-DATASETS   NN

    N-DATASETS IS THE NUMBER OF INDEPENDENT SETS OF DATA THAT
    THE USER WISHES TO INPUT.
    GALILEO V IS LIMITED TO 50 DATASETS OR FEWER.
    THIS CARD IS MANDATORY.

CRITERION PAIR AAAAAAAAAAAAAAAAAAAAAAAAAAAAAAAAAAAAAAAAAAAA

    CRITERION PAIR IS A HEADER LABEL USED TO INDICATE THE
    STANDARD FOR RATIO JUDGEMENTS ACCORDING TO GALILEO
    PROCEDURES. THE LABEL MAY BE ANY NAME UP TO 40
    CHARACTERS. THIS CARD IS OPTIONAL.

CONLABELS
                AAAAAAAAAAAAAAAAAAAAAAAAAAAAAAAAAAAA

    CONLABELS ARE THE LABELS FOR THE CONCEPTS. THEY ARE USED
    TO LABEL VARIOUS OUTPUTS. A CONLABEL MAY BE ANY NAME UP
    TO 40 CHARACTERS, HOWEVER, ON SOME OUTPUT, ONLY THE FIRST
    10 CHARACTERS WILL BE PRINTED. THERE MUST BE AS MANY
    CONLABELS AS THERE ARE CONCEPTS, ONE CARD PER CONCEPT
    LABEL, BEGINNING ON THE FOLLOWING CARD.
    THESE CARDS ARE OPTIONAL.

OPERATIONS   AAAAAAAAAAAAAAAAAAAAAAAAAAAAAAAAAA

THE OPERATIONS CARD SPECIFIES THE JOB TO BE
PERFORMED. AT PRESENT, GALILEO CAN PERFORM
FIVE DIFFERENT OPERATIONS. ONLY ONE OPERATION
MAY BE SPECIFIED PER RUN. THE USER MAY
SPECIFY THE FOLLOWING:

OPERATIONS   DISTANCES

THIS OPERATION WILL FORM A MATRIX OF
MEAN DISTANCES FROM THE RAW DATA AND COMPUTE
STATISTICS IF SPECIFIED.

OPERATIONS   COORDINATES

THIS OPERATION COMPUTES
COORDINATES FROM A MEAN DISTANCE MATRIX
USING A CENTROID SCALAR PRODUCTS ROUTINE
AND A DIRECT ITERATIVE PROCEDURE.

OPERATIONS   COMPARISONS

COMPARISON OF SPACES WILL ROTATE
A SERIES OR GROUP OF SPACES TOGETHER.
ROTATION IS TO A LEAST-SQUARES BEST FIT.
THEORETICAL CRITERIA FOR ROTATION MAY BE SPECIFIED

OPERATIONS   PLOT ONLY

PLOT ONLY ALLOWS THE USER TO PLOT THREE
DIMENSIONAL DATA IN A GALILEO REPRESENTATION
USING OUTPUT FROM PREVIOUS RUNS.

OPERATIONS   AMG ONLY

AMG ONLY ALLOWS THE USER TO CALL THE
AUTOMATIC MESSAGE GENERATOR USING
COORDINATES GENERATED FROM PREVIOUS RUNS.
PRE-GENERATED COORDINATES (COORDINATE INPUT).

SPECIFICATIONS

SPECIFICATIONS ALLOWS THE USER TO MODIFY A
PARTICULAR OPERATION BY ALTERING DEFAULT
VALUES. THESE CARDS MAY FOLLOW IN ANY ORDER.
THE FOLLOWING SPECIFICATION CARDS ARE
AVAILABLE:

MAXVAL   NNNNN

USED WITH RAW DATA INPUT TO ANY OPERATION.
ALLOWS THE USER TO SPECIFY A MAXIMUM
DISTANCE VALUE TO BE ACCEPTED BY
THE PROGRAM. LARGER VALUES WILL BE
DELETED FROM MEANS COMPUTATION.
AN INFORMATIVE MESSAGE IS ALSO PRINTED.

EXTREME VALUE   NNNNN

    USED WITH RAW DATA INPUT TO INFORM USER
    OF EXTREMELY LARGE VALUES .   VALUES
    ARE NOT DELETED FROM COMPUTATION.
    THE DEFAULT VALUE IS 1000.

SELECT
EXCLUDE

    ALLOWS USER TO SPECIFY SUBSETS OF THE
    RAW DATA INPUT BY THE CONTENTS OF THE
    IDENTIFICATION FIELD. DEFAULT IS
    NO SELECTION (ALL CASES ACCEPTED)
    REGARDLESS OF IDENTIFICATION FIELD.
    EXAMPLES OF THE SELECT CARD FOLLOW:
      THE EXCLUDE CARD DOES THE EXACT OPPOSITE
    ACTION OF THE SELECT CARD.   IE, INSTEAD OF
    USING ONLY THOSE CASES WITH CERTAIN CHARACTERS
    IN THE ID FIELD, EXCLUDE USES ALL BUT THOSE CASES.

        SELECT   **1*****
        ⌐   ⌐
        (COL. 1)   (COL. 16)
                THE ABOVE SELECT CARD ACCEPTS ONLY
                THOSE WITH A "1" IN COLUMN 3 OF THE
                IDENTIFICATION FIELD.

        EXCLUDE   **1**3**
        ⌐   ⌐
        (COL. 1)   (COL. 16)
                THE ABOVE EXCLUDE ACCEPTS ALL CASES EXCEPT
                THOSE WITH A "1" IN COLUMN 3 OR A "3"
                IN COLUMN 6 OF THE IDENTIFICATION FIELD.

MAINSPACE   N

    ALLOWS THE USER TO SPECIFY SPACE N FOR
    USE AS THE CRITERION SPACE FOR ROTATIONS.
    IF THIS CARD IS NOT USED, EACH SPACE ROTATES TO
    THE PREVIOUS SPACE IN TIME.

MIDPOINT   NN

    ALLOWS THE USER TO SPECIFY THE CENTROID OF
    A SPACE TO BE AT THE CONCEPT INDICATED.
    IF NOT USED, THE SPACE IS LEFT UNTRANSLATED
    UNLESS A STABLE CONS, FREE CONS, OR STABLE ROTATE CARD
    IS USED.

SCONS   NN,NN,NN,NN,NN,NN,NN...
SCONS   NN,NN,NN,NN,NN,NN,NN...

    STABLE CONS ALLOWS THE USER TO SPECIFY A
    CONCEPT NUMBER OR SERIES OF CONCEPT NUMBERS FOR
    THE LEAST-SQUARES ROTATION. THE ROTATION WILL
    BE PERFORMED ONLY ON THESE CONCEPTS. THE REMAINING
    CONCEPTS WILL BE ADJUSTED ACCORDINGLY. UP TO 20
    STABLE CONS MAY BE SPECIFIED.

FCONS   NN,NN,NN,NN,NN,NN,NN...

FREE CONS WORKS JUST AS A STABLE CONS CARD DOES,
EXCEPT, INSTEAD OF SPECIFYING THOSE CONCEPTS WHICH
ARE TO BE HELD STABLE DURING ROTATION, THE
USER SPECIFIES THOSE CONCEPTS WHICH ARE FREE
TO MOVE DURING ROTATION. ALL OTHERS ARE STABLE.

SROT   NN,NN,NN,NN,NN,NN,NN...

STABLE ROTATE ALLOWS THE USER TO SPECIFY
DIFFERENT SETS OF STABLE CONCEPTS FOR
USE IN THE ROTATION OF DIFFERENT POINTS
IN TIME. THERE MUST BE A STABLE CONS OR FREE
CONS CARD (FOLLOWING THE STABLE ROTATE CARD)
FOR EACH STABLE ROTATE VALUE SPECIFIED.
SEE EXAMPLE 4 FOR FURTHER DETAILS.

THETA   NN.NN

THETA ALLOWS THE USER TO SPECIFY THE TOLERANCE
TO WHICH THE ROTATER IS ACCURATE. LARGER VALUES
GIVE QUICKER, CHEAPER ROTATIONS;SMALLER VALUES
GIVE GREATER ACCURACY. DEFAULT IS 1 DEGREE.

TOLERANCE   N.NNNNNNN

TOLERANCE ALLOWS THE USER TO INCREASE OR DECREASE
THE ACCURACY OF ITERATION WHEN COMPUTING THE
COORDINATE MATRIX SOLUTION. DEFAULT TOLERANCE IS
0.0001. ROUNDING ERROR MAY BE DETERMINED FROM
THE EIGENVECTOR ASSOCIATED WITH THE ZERO ROOT.

MAXITER   NN

MAXITER ALLOWS THE USER TO SPECIFY THE MAXIMUM NUMBER
OF ITERATIONS USED TO DERIVE A GIVEN ROOT BEFORE
BEFORE THE TOLERANCE FOR THAT ROOT IS DECREASED.
IF THE ITERATION COUNTER GOES ABOVE MAXITER, TOLERANCE
IS REDUCED BY A FACTOR OF 10 AND THE ITERATION
COUNTER IS RESET TO 0. IF THE TOLERANCE GOES BELOW
1, THE PROGRAM ABORTS WITH A MESSAGE THAT IT IS UNABLE
TO FACTOR THE GIVEN ROOT IN THE GIVEN MATRIX.

ADDRESSED
FORMAT   (XXXXXXXXXXXXX)
UNADDRESSED
FORMAT
ID LENGTH   NN
PAIRS   NN

THE FOUR SPECIFICATIONS ABOVE ARE USED TOGETHER TO
ALLOW THE USER TO INPUT NON-STANDARD RAW DATA TO THE PROGRAM.
ADDRESSED IMPLIES THAT THE RAW DATA HAS CELL ADDRESSES
IF THE DATA HAS NO CELL ADDRESSES, THE UNADDRESSED CARD
SHOULD BE USED. IF THE DATA HAS CELL ADDRESSES, BUT HIS/HER
DATA IS IN SOME FORMAT OTHER THAN(A8,8(2I2,F5.0)), THE ADDRESSED
CARD SHOULD BE USED WITH APPROPRIATE FORMAT. NOTE THAT THIS
FORMAT IS A FORTRAN-TYPE FORMAT AND IS USED DIRECTLY
BY THE PROGRAM W/OUT ANY CHECKING. THE DEFAULT IS ADDRESSED
IN THE FORMAT (A8,8(2I2,F5.0)).
THE MAXIMUM LENGTH OF THE FORMAT IS 16 CHARACTERS.

ALSO NOTE THAT UNADDRESSED INPUT IS ASSUMED TO BE IN FULL
MATRIX ORDER, THAT IS, 0102,0103,0104,0105,...
THE IDLENGTH CARD SPECIFIES THE LENGTH OF THE IDENTIFICATION
FIELD USED BY THE PROGRAM. THE DEFAULT IS 8 AND THE
MAXIMUM IS 10.
THE PAIRS CARD TELLS HOW MANY PAIRED COMPARISONS THERE ARE
ON ONE "CARD" OF THE DATA. THE DEFAULT
IS 8 AND THE MAXIMUM IS 30, HENCE, THE
DEFAULT ADDRESSED INPUT IF EXPRESSED IN THESE SPECIFICATION
CARDS WOULD LOOK LIKE:

```
      (COL 1)              (COL 16)
      :                    :
      ADDRESSED            (A8,8(2I2,F5.0))
      IDLENGTH             8
      PAIRS                8
```

NOW, SUPPOSE YOUR RAW DATA IS PUNCHED IN 3 COL FIELDS,
WITH A 5 COLUMN ID FIELD AND 25 PAIRS PER CARD W/OUT ADDRESS
YOUR SPECIFICATION CARDS WOULD LOOK LIKE:

```
      UNADDRESSED          (A5,25F3.0)
      IDLENGTH             5
      PAIRS                25
```

END OF SPECIFICATIONS

THIS CARD IS USED TO TERMINATE THE
LIST OF SPECIFICATION CARDS.

THE FOLLOWING CONTROL CARDS ARE USED TO
CALL SPECIAL "SUB PROCEDURES" NOT DIRECTLY
INVOLVED WITH THE FORMATION AND COMPARISON
OF GALILEO COORDINATES. IF USED, THEY MUST
FOLLOW THE END OF SPECIFICATIONS CARD
AND PRECEDE THE OPTIONS CARD.

PLOTTER

PLOTTER ALLOWS THE USER TO GENERATE PLOTS
USING THE RPI CALCOMP PLOTTER.
THE FOLLOWING ARE PARAMETER CARDS WHICH MAY FOLLOW
THE "PLOTTER" CARD IN ANY ORDER OR NUMBER:

TIME FRAME   AAAAAAAAAA

THE TIME FRAME CARD PERMITS THE USER TO
INDICATE EITHER STATIC OR DYNAMIC REPRESENT-
ATIONS OF THE DATA MATRIX. IF THE USER
DESIRES A SINGLE SPATIAL CONFIGURATION
FOR EACH DATA MATRIX, THIS CARD SHOULD
SPECIFY "STATIC". IF THE USER DESIRES
A TIME SERIES TO BE REPRESENTED
(WITH TRAJECTORIES), THEN THIS CARD SHOULD

SPECIFY "DYNAMIC". IF THE USER DESIRES
BOTH REPRESENTATIONS, THIS CARD SHOULD
SPECIFY "BOTH". THE DEFAULT IS "STATIC".

BOXD   **N.NNNN**

BOXD IS THE DIMENSION OF THE CONCEPT MARKER
IN THE REPRESENTATION. THE DEFAULT IS 0.10

SIZE   **N.NNNN**

SIZE IS A SCALING CONSTANT WHICH ALLOWS THE
USER TO ALTER THE SIZE OF THE OVERALL PLOT.
IF SIZE IS SET TO 1.0 (WHICH IS THE DEFAULT),
THEN THE VERTICAL DIMENSION OF THE PLOT
WILL BE 10 INCHES.
COMMON SIZE PARAMETERS ARE: 0.5 (FOR CONVENTION
PAPERS), 0.34375 (FOR THESIS MARGINS), AND
1.25 (FOR LARGE DISPLAY). NOTE THAT "SIZE" LESS
THAN OR EQUAL TO 1.0 WILL BE PLOTTED ON NARROW
WIDTH PAPER, "SIZE" LARGER THAN 1.0 WILL BE PLOTTED
ON WIDE PAPER.
SIZES GREATER THAN 1.5 ARE NOT RECOMMENDED.

COLOR   **N**

COLOR ALLOWS THE USER TO SPECIFY MULTI-
COLOR OR SINGLE COLOR PLOTS. IF COLOR IS
SET TO 1, PLOTS WILL BE DRAWN ENTIRELY WITH
BLACK INK. IF COLOR IS SET TO 2, STATIC
PLOTS WILL HAVE BLACK REFERENCE PLANES,
RED CONCEPT MARKERS AND LABELS, AND BLUE
PROJECTIONS TO THE X-Z PLANE; DYNAMIC
PLOTS WILL HAVE BLACK REFERENCE PLANES, RED
CONCEPT MARKERS AND LABELS, AND BLUE TRAJEC-
TORIES. DEFAULT IS 1.

VIEW   **N,N,N,N**

VIEW ALLOWS THE USER TO SPECIFY WHICH REPRESENTATIONS
ARE PLOTTED.

VIEW	REPRESENTATION
1	3-D CUBE
2	X-Y PLANE
3	Y-Z PLANE
4	X-Z PLANE

WHERE X, Y, AND Z CORRESPOND
TO DIMENSIONS 1, 2, AND 3, UNLESS
AN AXIS CARD IS USED.
DEFAULT IS 3-D VIEW ONLY.

AXIS   **NN,NN,NN**
THE AXIS CARD ALLOWS THE USER TO ALTER THE
DEFAULT AXIS ASSIGNMENTS TO X, Y, AND Z AS PRESENTED
IN THE VIEW CARD.

CARD USED		FACTORS PLOTT5400000
COL 1	COL 16	X Y Z
:	:	
AXIS	I	1,2,I
AXIS	I,J	1,I,J
AXIS	I,J,K	I,J,K

NAME   AAAAAAAAAA

    NAME ALLOWS THE USER TO PLACE A LABEL OF UP TO
    10 CHARACTERS ON THE PLOT DRAWINGS.

QUEUE   NN

    ALLOWS THE USER TO SELECT NON-STANDARD
    INKS AND PAPERS FOR SPECIALIZED OUTPUTS.
    DEFAULT QUE IS SELECTED BY THE PROGRAM
    ACCORDING TO SIZE AND COLOR DESIRED.

XEYE   N.NN
YEYE   N.NN
ZEYE   N.NN
ROTATION   N.NN

    THESE CARDS ALLOW THE USER TO SELECT
    AN ALTERNATIVE PERSPECTIVE POINT
    (AN EYE POINT, OR WHERE THE 3-D VIEW IS
    OBSERVED FROM) AND ANGLE OF ROTATION
    ABOUT THE Z-AXIS. DEFAULTS ARE:
        XEYE = 1.0
        YEYE = 15.0
        ZEYE = 50.0
        ROTATE = -45.0 DEGREES

LETTERSIZE   .NN

    ALLOWS USER TO SET THE HEIGHT OF THE
    LETTERING (PRIMARILY, THE CONCEPT NUMBERS)
    MULTIPLES OF .21 ARE ADVISED TO ENSURE
    PROPERLY PROPORTIONED LETTERING.
    DEFAULT IS .42

END OF PLOT

    THE "END OF PLOT" CARD IS THE LAST CARD OF
    THE PLOT PARAMETER LIST. THIS CARD MUST BE
    USED WHENEVER PLOTTER IS SPECIFIED, EVEN
    IF THE USER DOES NOT ALTER ANY PARAMETERS.

AMG

    AMG--AUTOMATIC MESSAGE GENERATOR. SEE
    "A MULTIDIMENSIONAL SCALING BASED PROCEDURE
    FOR GENERATING PERSUASIVE MESSAGES AND MEASUR
    ING THEIR EFFECTS" BY WOELFEL, HOLMES, CODY
    AND FINK (1976). SEE EXAMPLES 6,7 AND 8.

START   NN

    SPECIFIES THE START CONCEPT OF THE SPACE.
    THIS IS THE CONCEPT THAT IS TO BE MOVED.

TARGET   NN

           SPECIFIES THE TARGET CONCEPT, I.E.,
           THE "IDEAL POINT" TOWARD WHICH THE
           START CONCEPT IS INTENDED TO MOVE.

APPROACH   NN.NN

           THE APPROACH CARD SPECIFIES WHETHER MESSAGES
           TO MOVE THE START CONCEPT TOWARD OR AWAY FROM
           THE TARGET CONCEPT ARE DESIRED. NN.NN IS THE
           PERCENTAGE OF THE STARTING DISTANCE BETWEEN
           THE START AND TARGET CONCEPTS TO WHICH THE
           START CONCEPT IS TO BE MOVED. IF NN.NN IS
           EQUAL TO OR LESS THAN 1, AMG WRITES MESSAGES
           WHICH WILL APPROACH THE TARGET TO WITHIN NN.NN
           PERCENT OF THE TARGET DISTANCE OR CLOSER. IF
           NN.NN IS GREATER THAN 1, AMG WRITES MESSAGES
           THAT MOVE THE START CONCEPT NN.NN PERCENT OF
           THE START-TO-TARGET DISTANCE OR FURTHER AWAY
           FROM THE TARGET. THUS APPROACH   .75
           WILL CAUSE AMG TO WRITE ONLY MESSAGES TO
           BRING THE START CONCEPT TO WITHIN 75% OF THE
           PRESENT START-TO-TARGET DISTANCE OR CLOSER.
           APPROACH   2   WILL CAUSE AMG TO WRITE
           ONLY MESSAGES WHICH CALL FOR MOVING THE START
           CONCEPT TO TWICE ITS PRESENT DISTANCE FROM
           THE TARGET CONCEPT OR FURTHER. DEFAULT IS 1.

PAIRS   N,N,N,N

           SPECIFIES WHICH SET(S) OF MESSAGES ARE
           TO BE GENERATED. MULTI-CONCEPT MESSAGES
           OF UP TO 4 CONCEPTS MAY BE REQUESTED.

EFFECTS   NN,NN,NN,NN
           USED TO MEASURE THE EFFECTIVENESS OF A
           SINGLE OR MULTI-CONCEPT MESSAGE GIVEN TWO
           OR MORE DATASETS. NN,NN,NN,NN ARE THE
           CONCEPTS WHICH FORMED THE INITIAL MESSAGE.
END OF AMG

           SIGNALS THE END OF THE AMG CONTROL CARDS.
           THE USER IS WARNED THAT THE AMG CONTROL
           CARDS HAVE **NO DEFAULT** VALUES AND
           THEREFORE, EACH ONE MUST BE SPECIFIED.
           ALSO, THE USER IS REMINDED THAT A
           -PAIRS- CARD CAUSES MESSAGES TO BE GENERATED,
           AND AN -EFFECTS- CARD GIVES MEASURES OF
           EFFECTIVENESS OF PREVIOUSLY GENERATED (AND
           ISSUED) MESSAGES, GIVEN TWO OR MORE SETS OF
           DATA. THEREFORE, USE ONLY ONE OF THESE TWO
           CARDS IN A SINGLE RUN.

OPTIONS   N,N,N,N,N...
           OPTIONS ARE USED TO SELECT PRINTING AND PUNCHING
           OF VARIOUS TYPES OF OUTPUTS SO THE USER GETS ONLY
           WHAT IS NEEDED. IF AN OPTION IS NOT SELECTED, ITS CORRESPONDING
           ACTION IS NOT DONE.

```
OPTION      ACTION
1           RAW DATA INPUT
2           SCALAR PRODUCTS INPUT
3           COORDINATE MATRIX INPUT
            (THE DEFAULT INPUT IS MEANS MATRIX)
4           PRINT MEANS AND N-S OF CELLS
5           PUNCH MEANS OF CELLS
23          LIST PAIRS WITH N LESS THAN 30
22          PRINT ERRORS FOUND IN RAW DATA INPUT
18          COMPUTE AND PRINT STATISTICS.  STATISTICS ARE:
            STANDARD DEVIATION, STAND ERROR, SKEWNESS, COEFFICIENT
            OF VARIATION, KURTOSIS, MINIMUM, MAXIMUM, %ERROR,
            ARITHMETIC MEAN AND CELL SIZE FOR EACH CELL.
            MEAN, AND CELL SIZE FOR EACH CELL.
            (EFFECTIVE ONLY WITH RAW DATA INPUT)
6           PRINT SCALAR PRODUCTS MATRIX
7           PUNCH SCALAR PRODUCTS MATRIX
            (EFFECTIVE ONLY WITH RAW DATA OR MEANS INPUT)

8           PRINT NORMAL EIGEN COORDINATES
9           PUNCH NORMAL EIGEN COORDINATES
10          PRINT TRANSLATED EIGEN COORDINATES
11          PUNCH TRANSLATED EIGEN COORDINATES
19          RE-GENERATE MEAN DISTANCE MATRIX FROM NORMAL
            EIGEN COORDINATE MATRICIES
20          RE-GENERATE MEAN DISTANCE MATRIX FROM TRANSLATED
            EIGEN COORDINATE MATRICIES
            (EFFECTIVE ONLY WHEN COORDINATES OR
             COMPARISONS OF SPACES IS CALLED)

12          PRINT ROTATED COORDINATES
13          PUNCH ROTATED COORDINATES
14          PRINT DISTANCE MOVED SUMMARY TABLE
15          CORRELATE ROWS OF ADJACENT ROTATED DATASETS
16          CORRELATE COLUMNS OF ADJACENT ROTATED DATASETS
21          RE-GENERATE MEAN DISTANCE MATRIX FROM
            ROTATED COORDINATE MATRICIES
            (EFFECTIVE ONLY DURING COMPARISON OF SPACES)
17          PRINT PLOT-FACTORS TABLE
            (EFFECTIVE ONLY DURING PLOTTER OR PLOT ONLY)
```

READ DATA

THE "READ DATA" CARD IS THE LAST GALILEO
CONTROL CARD BEFORE THE INPUT DATA. FAILURE
TO INCLUDE THIS CARD WILL CAUSE GALILEO TO
TERMINATE.

INPUT AND OUTPUT FORMATS

1) RAW DATA SHOULD BE INPUT ACCORDING TO THE
FOLLOWING CARD FORMAT: (A8,8(I2,I2,I5)). THE FIRST
EIGHT COLUMNS ARE THE IDENTIFICATION FIELD FOR THE
USER AND WILL BE USED BY THE PROGRAM IF IT IS
NECESSARY TO PRINT A DIAGNOSTIC OR FOR
SELECTION PURPOSES. THE REMAINING 72
COLUMNS CONTAIN EIGHT GALILEO RESPONSES WITH
MATRIX ADDRESSES. EACH VALUE FIELD HAS 9 COLUMNS
WITH THE FORMAT (I2,I2,I5). THE FIRST VALUE IS
THE COLUMN ADDRESS (LOW VALUE), THE SECOND VALUE
IS THE ROW ADDRESS, (HIGH VALUE), AND THE THIRD
VALUE IS THE RESPONSE. NOTE THAT ZERO IS A

LEGITIMATE VALUE. ALSO NOTE THAT MISSING VALUES (DATA)
ARE DENOTED BY LEAVING THE DISTANCE FIELD BLANK. NUMBERS
OF 100,000 AND LARGER SHOULD BE INDICATED BY THE
VALUE OF 99999. MULTIPLE SETS OF RAW DATA
ARE SEPARATED BY **ENDOFSET** CARDS.
AN **ENDOFSET** CARD STARTS IN COL. 1.

2) MEANS MATRIX OUTPUT (MEANS INPUT FOR COORDINATES
AND COMPARISON ROUTINES) IS FORMATTED AS (8F10.4).
THE BEGINNING OF A NEW ROW IS INDICATED BY A NEW
CARD. MULTIPLE MATRIX OUTPUT IS SEPARATED BY HEADER
CARDS.

3) SCALAR PRODUCTS MATRIX OUTPUT (WHICH IS
OPTIONAL INPUT FOR THE COORDINATES ROUTINE)
IS FORMATTED AS (6F12.3). THE BEGINNING OF A
NEW ROW IS INDICATED BY A NEW CARD. MULTIPLE
MATRIX OUTPUT IS SEPARATED BY HEADER CARDS (WHICH
MUST BE REMOVED FOR INPUT TO SUBSEQUENT ROUTINES).
THIS OUTPUT (INPUT) IS OBTAINABLE BY USING "OPTIONS".

4) COORDINATE MATRIX OUTPUT (WHICH IS
OPTIONAL INPUT FOR COMPARISON ROUTINE) IS
FORMATTED AS (6F12.4). THE BEGINNING OF A
NEW ROW IS INDICATED BY A NEW CARD. MULTIPLE
MATRIX OUTPUT IS SEPARATED BY HEADER CARDS
**(WHICH MUST NOT BE REMOVED FOR INPUT TO SUBSEQUENT
ROUTINES).** THIS OUTPUT IS DEFAULT FOR THE
COORDINATES ROUTINE AND THE COMPARISON
ROUTINE, HOWEVER, IT MAY BE SUPPRESSED FOR
THE COMPARISON OPERATION BY USING "OPTIONS".

5)COMPARISON OF SPACES AND AMG ONLY INPUT FORMAT
IS (FORMAT) XX. THE FORMAT STATEMENT BEGINS WITH
"(" IN COLUMN 1. IN COLUMNS 13 14 PUT THE NUMBER
OF REAL DIMENSIONS. THIS HEADER CARD MUST PROCEED
EACH MATRIX OF INPUT DATA.

THE FOLLOWING ARE SAMPLE JOB SETUPS FOR GALILEO WITH
BASIC DESCRIPTIONS OF THEIR FUNCTIONS:

1) AN INITIAL MEANS COMPUTATION FOR EXAMINING RAW DATA

```
RUN NAME          FIRST CHECK ON RAW DATA
N-CONCEPTS        8
N-DATASETS        3
OPERATIONS        DISTANCES
OPTIONS           1,4,23,22,18
READ DATA
 ***
 *** DATA SET 1
 ***
ENDOFSET
 ***
 *** DATA SET 2
 ***
ENDOFSET
```

```
***
*** DATA SET 3
***
ENDOFSET
```

THIS JOB WILL READ THREE SETS OF RAW DATA,COMPUTE STATISTICS
FOR EACH SET, AND PRINT OUT, FOR EACH SET, THE STATISTICAL
DATA, A MEAN DISTANCE MATRIX, AND A SAMPLE SIZE MATRIX. PUNCH
OUTPUT HAS BEEN SUPPRESSED. ALSO, ERRORS IN RAW DATA WILL
BE PRINTED.

    2) COMPUTATION OF MEANS AND COORDINATES FOR ABOVE EXAMPLE

```
RUN NAME            SAMPLE COMPUTATION OF SPACES
N-CONCEPTS          8
N-DATASETS          3
CRITERION PAIR  RED AND WHITE - 10 UNITS
                    CAPTAIN KANGAROO
                    VIOLENT SEX
                    RICHARD NIXON
                    GEORGE WALLACE
                    SEXUAL EQUALITY
                    STERILITY
                    PASSION
                    ME
OPERATIONS          COORDINATES OF GALILEO SPACES
SPECIFICATIONS
MAXVAL              10000
EXTREME VALUE       2000.
TOLERANCE           0.000001
END OF SPECIFICATIONS
OPTIONS             1,4,18,6,8
READ DATA
  ***
  *** DATA SET 1
  ***
ENDOFSET
  ***
  *** DATA SET 2
  ***
ENDOFSET
  ***
  *** DATA SET 3
  ***
ENDOFSET
```

THIS JOB WILL COMPUTE STATISTICS, MEANS MATRICES AND
COORDINATE MATRICES FOR EACH OF THREE SETS OF DATA WITH
DISTANCE JUDGEMENTS FOR 8 CONCEPTS. VALUES LARGER
THAN 10000. HAVE BEEN DELETED FROM COMPUTATIONS AND
VALUES LARGER THAN 2000. WILL BE LISTED WITH AN INFORM-
ATIVE MESSAGE. TOLERANCE WAS INCREASED TO GIVE EXTRA
PRECISION TO THE COORDINATE VALUES. OPTION 6 WILL
CAUSE SCALAR PRODUCTS TO BE INCLUDED IN THE PRINTOUT.

    3) ROTATION AND PLOTTING OF SEVERAL MATRICES

```
RUN NAME            SAMPLE ROTATED SOLUTIONS
N-CONCEPTS          6
N-DATASETS          8
CONLABELS           MICKEY MOUSE
                    NELSON ROCKEFFELLER
                    INTELLIGENT
                    HUMBLE
```

```
                    SINCERE
                    CREDIBLE
OPERATIONS          COMPARISON OF SPACES
SPECIFICATIONS
STABLE CONS    03,04,05,06
END OF SPECIFICATIONS
PLOTTER
TIME FRAME     DYNAMIC
COLOR          2
NAME           DUMMIES
END OF PLOT
READ DATA
 ***
 *** MEAN DATA MATRICES
 *** ONE - EIGHT
 ***
```

THIS JOB WILL COMPUTE COORDINATES AND ROTATE THE SOLUTIONS
TO LEAST-SQUARES BEST FIT IN TIME SEQUENCE. CONCEPTS
03 - 06 HAVE BEEN ROTATED SO THAT MOTIONS OF 01 AND 02 WILL
BE OBSERVABLE RELATIVE TO A STABLE CONFIGURATION. A 3-D PLOT
OF THE TRAJECTORIES WILL BE INCLUDED WITH THE OUTPUT.

          4) ROTATION OF SEVERAL MATRICES USING STABLE ROTATION

```
RUN NAME       STABLE ROTATE EXAMPLE
N-CONCEPTS     6
N-DATASETS     6
CONLABELS      PERFECT TEACHER
               PERFECT STUDENT
               PERMISIVENESS
               NUMBER OF TESTS
               OUT-OF-CLASS WORK
               SCALE OF GRADING
OPERATIONS     COMPARISON OF SPACES
SPECIFICATIONS
STABLE ROTATE  03,05
STABLE CONS    01,02,03
STABLE CONS    04,05,06
END OF SPECIFICATIONS
READ DATA
 ***
 *** MEAN MATRICES
 *** ONE - SIX
 ***
```

THIS JOB WILL COMPUTE COORDINATES AND ROTATE THE
SOLUTIONS IN TIME-FRAME ORDER (2-1, 3-2, 4-3, ETC.).
CONCEPTS 1, 2, AND 3 ARE HELD STABLE DURING ROTATION
OF TIME 3. CONCEPTS 4, 5, AND 6 ARE HELD STABLE
DURING ROTATION OF TIME 5.

5) A PLOT RUN USING SPECIAL FEATURES AND OTHER CONTROL CARDS

```
RUN NAME       FULL-BLOWN RUN
N-CONCEPTS     10
N-DATASETS     2
CONLABELS      BOOKS
               STUDENTS
               GRADES
               PROFS
               GIRLS
               BEER
```

```
                 JOBS
                 DEGREES
                 ME
                 SEX
OPERATIONS       COMPARISON OF SPACES
SPECIFICATIONS
EXTREME VALUE    999.
SELECT           **2***3*
END OF SPECIFICATIONS
PLOTTER
TIME FRAME       BOTH
VIEW             4
SIZE             .6875
COLOR            1
NAME             MOO-U
QUEUE            05
LETTERSIZE       .42
END OF PLOT
OPTIONS          1,4,8,12,14,15,16,17
READ DATA
  ***
  *** RAW DATA SET 1
  ***
ENDOFSET
  ***
  *** RAW DATA SET 2
  ***
ENDOFSET
```

THIS INVOLVED JOB DOES THE BASIC ROTATION OF TWO
SPACES IN TIME-ORDER, BUT DOES STRANGE PLOTTER TRICKS.
QUEUE 5 INFORMS THE PROGRAM TO SEND THE PLOT TO A SPECIAL
QUEUE THAT PLOTS IN LIQUID BLACK INK ON STANDARD PAPER,
THIS GIVES A PLEASING EFFECT OF HIGH CONTRAST, ALLOWING
PHOTO-REDUCTION TO 8 1/2 X 11 INCH SIZE. LARGE NUMERALS
WERE CHOSEN FOR VISIBILITY. THE SIZE .6875 JUST FILLS
THE PAPER DIMENSIONS CHOSEN FOR SMALL PLOTS. PLOTS ARE
BOTH STATIC AND DYNAMIC, AND VIEWS OF EACH SEPARATE PLANE
AS WELL AS A 3-D BOX ARE PRODUCED.

THIS RUN ALSO COMPUTES ROW AND COLUMN CORRELATIONS
BETWEEN TIME FRAMES. ROW CORRELATIONS INDICATE THE RELATIVE
ORIENTATIONS OF THE CONCEPT VECTORS OVER TIME. COLUMN
CORRELATIONS GIVE AN INDICATION OF THE STABILITY OF THE
FACTOR OVER TIME.

FINALLY, THIS RUN MAKES USE OF THE -SELECT- SPECIFI-
CATION. IF THE ID FIELD OF THE RAW DATA WAS CODED WITH
THE SEX IN COLUMN 3 (1 IS MALE, 2 IS FEMALE) AND THE CLASS
IN COLUMN 7 (1 IS FRESH., 2 IS SOPH., ETC.), THEN THIS RUN
WOULD ONLY INCLUDE FEMALES IN THE JUNIOR CLASS.

6) GENERATING MESSAGES FROM RAW DATA

```
RUN NAME         SELLING SOAP
N-CONCEPTS       10
N-DATASETS       1
CONLABELS        IVORY *
                 MILDNESS
                 LASTING LATHER
                 LEAVES SKIN SOFT
                 SCENT
                 LEAVES SKIN CLEAN
                 SOAP FILM
                 ZEST *
                 SAFEGARD *
                 ME
```

```
OPERATIONS      COORDINATES OF SPACES
SPECIFICATIONS
MIDPOINT        10
END OF SPECIFICATIONS
AMG
START           10
TARGET          01
PAIRS           1,2,3,4
END OF AMG
OPTIONS         1
READ DATA
  ***
  *** ONE SET OF RAW DATA
  ***
ENDOFSET
```

THIS JOB WILL FIRST COMPUTE COORDINATES REPRESENTING
THE AGGREGATE OF THE DISTANCES REPORTED. THEN, IT WILL
GENERATE ONE-, TWO-, THREE-, AND FOUR-PAIR MESSAGE SOLUTIONS
THAT MAY BE USED TO MOVE THE PEOPLE (-ME-) TO THE PRODUCT
(-IVORY-). PUNCHED OUTPUT HAS BEEN SUPRESSED.

7) GENERATING MESSAGES FROM PRE-GENERATED COORDINATES

```
RUN NAME        SELLING DENIM JEANS
N-CONCEPTS      9
N-DATASETS      1
CONLABELS       LEVIS *
                SEAR'S BEST *
                H.I.S. *
                FADED LOOK
                BREAK-IN TIME
                WEAR AND TEAR
                COST
                LOOKS
                ME
OPERATIONS      AMG. ONLY
AMG
START           09
TARGET          03
PAIRS           2,3
END OF AMG
OPTIONS         3
READ DATA
  ***
  *** COORDINATES (ONE SET)
  ***
```

THIS JOB TAKES THE COORDINATE INPUT AND CENTERS THE
SPACE ON THE START CONCEPT (SEE THE PAPER MENTIONED)
THEN, THE PROGRAM GENERATES TWO- AND THREE-PAIR MESSAGE
SOLUTIONS TO MOVE THE PEOPLE (-ME-) TO THE JEAN COMPANY
(-H.I.S.-). THE USER WILL NOTE THAT IN THIS OPERATION,
DIFFERENT -START- AND -TARGET- CONCEPTS MAY BE USED WITH
THE SAME SET OF COORDINATES, WITHOUT REGENERATION. THIS
IS, THEREFORE, THE CHEAPEST WAY TO RUN THE A.M.G.

DOCUMENTATION PAU.   UPDATES WILL BE FORTHCOMING.

* TRADEMARKS OF RESPECTIVE COMPANIES ARE USED
  FOR ILLUSTRATIVE PURPOSES ONLY. THE EXAMPLES ARE
  PURELY FICTITIOUS: NOTHING IS EXPRESSED OR IMPLIED
  BY THE USE OF THESE TRADE NAMES.

PAU   MAHALO

APPENDIX B

SAMPLE
QUESTIONNAIRES

Human Knowledge Study

DESIGN: J. Woelfel
State University of New York
at Albany
Department of Rhetoric and Communication
September 1978

Administration Date _____

Site _____

Respondent Sex _____

Department _____

Age _____ ·   Time _____ AM/PM

Instructions to Respondents

The following questionnaire asks you to give us your opinions on a set of ideas. We would like you to give your opinions by telling us how different pairs of concepts are. Distance between concepts is measured in units, so that the more different two concepts are, the more units apart they are for each other.

To give you a "yardstick" to enable you to express how far apart two concepts are, we will say that Philosophy is 100 units different from Literature, or Philosophy and Literature are 100 units apart. In other words, all the differences between Philosophy and Literature together account for 100 units of difference.

The idea is for you to tell us *your* opinion of how many units apart the concepts which follow are from each other. Remember, the *more different* two concepts are from each other, the larger the number of units apart they are. If you think any pair of concepts are more different than Philosophy and Literature, you would write a number larger than 100. If you think they are twice as large, write 200. If you think that they are less different than Philosophy and Literature, you would write a number smaller than 100. For example, if you perceived them as one-half as large, write 50. If you think two concepts are identical, that is, they are the same thing, you would write a "0." You can write any number you want.

Emotions Study

DESIGN:	Michigan State University Department of Communication East Lansing, Michigan 48823 U.S.A. Spring 1978
ADMINISTRATION:	Michigan State University Department of Communication Spring, Summer 1978

Dear Participant,

We are currently engaged in a project to determine the perceived difference between various emotions. It is our opinion that persons such as yourself are in an excellent position to accurately make these distinctions. Therefore, we are asking you to assist us in this task. Your coopeartion will greatly contribute to the project's success.

On the following pages we will present you with a list of emotions and ask you to tell us *how different* each one is from the other according to *your opinion*. If you think that two items are very different, then you could say that they are *far apart*. If you think they are very similar, then you could say that they are very close *together*. Instead of using words like "very far apart" to say how different two items are from one another, you could use a *number*.

Take PRIDE and SORROW, for example. If you think that these two aspects of life are similar, seem to go together, or are often associated with each other, then you would write a *small* number. On the other hand, if you think that they are very different, do not seem to go together, or are seldom associated with one another, then you would use a *large* number.

Thus, a *large* number would mean two items are very *different;* a small number would mean that two items are very *similar*. Zero (0) would mean they are the same or that there is no difference between them.

On the following pages we will present you with several pairs of items. To help you make your estimates, we'll give you a mental ruler. Think of the difference between ANGER and EXCITEMENT. Call this difference 10.0. Keep the number 10.0 in mind when you make the other comparisons. You will compare each pair of items to the difference between ANGER and EXCITEMENT, which is now *10.0* units on your mental ruler. On each page you will be shown several pairs of items like ANGER and EXCITEMENT, followed by a space to write how many units apart *YOU* think they are.

Instructions

Please estimate how different or "far apart" each of the following
words or phrases is from each of the others. The more different,
or further apart they seem to be, the larger the number you should
write. To help you know what size number to write, remember
   Philosophy and Literature are 100 units apart.
If two words or phrases are not different at all, please write
zero (0). If you have no idea, just leave the space blank.

   Thank you very much for your help.

Duplicate 1-6
Card 00   7-8

	col.	How Far Apart Are			Units
0102	09-17	Philosophy	and	Literature	-----
0103	18-26	Philosophy	and	Music	-----
0104	27-35	Philosophy	and	Humanities	-----
0105	36-44	Philosophy	and	Arts	-----
0106	45-53	Philosophy	and	Physical Science	-----
0107	54-62	Philosophy	and	Social Science	-----
0108	63-71	Philosophy	and	Communication	-----
0109	72-80	Philosophy	and	Language	-----

Duplicate 1-6
Card 01   7-8

	col.	How Far Apart Are			Units
0110	09-17	Philosophy	and	Mathematics	-----
0111	18-26	Philosophy	and	Good	-----
0112	27-35	Philosophy	and	Bad	-----
0113	36-44	Philosophy	and	Evil	-----
0114	45-53	Philosophy	and	You	-----
0115	54-62	Philosophy and Your Present University			-----
0203	63-71	Literature	and	Music	-----
0204	72-80	Literature	and	Humanities	-----

Duplicate 1-6
Card 02   7-8

	col.	How Far Apart Are			Units
0205	09-17	Literature	and	Arts	-----
0206	18-26	Literature	and	Physical Science	-----
0207	27-35	Literature	and	Social Science	-----
0208	36-44	Literature	and	Communication	-----
0209	45-53	Literature	and	Language	-----
0210	54-62	Literature	and	Mathematics	-----
0211	63-71	Literature	and	Good	-----
0212	72-80	Literature	and	Bad	-----

```
Duplicate 1-6
Card 03    7-8
```

	col.	How Far Apart Are			Units
0213	09-17	Literature	and	Evil	
0214	18-26	Literature	and	You	-----
0215	27-35	Literature			-----
	and	Your Present University			
0304	36-44	Music	and	Humanities	-----
0305	45-53	Music	and	Arts	-----
0306	54-62	Music	and	Physical Science	-----
0307	63-71	Music	and	Social Science	-----
0308	72-80	Music	and	Communication	-----

```
Duplicate 1-6
Card 04    7-8
```

	col.	How Far Apart Are			Units
0309	09-17	Music	and	Language	
0310	18-26	Music	and	Mathematics	-----
0311	27-35	Music	and	Good	-----
0312	36-44	Music	and	Bad	-----
0313	45-53	Music	and	Evil	-----
0314	54-62	Music	and	You	-----
0315	63-71	Music			-----
	and	Your Present University			
0405	72-80	Humanities	and	Arts	-----

```
Duplicate 1-6
Card 05    7-8
```

	col.	How Far Apart Are			Units
0406	09-17	Humanities	and	Physical Science	
0407	18-26	Humanities	and	Social Science	-----
0408	27-35	Humanities	and	Communication	-----
0409	36-44	Humanities	and	Language	-----
0410	45-53	Humanities	and	Mathematics	-----
0411	54-62	Humanities	and	Good	-----
0412	63-71	Humanities	and	Bad	-----
0413	72-80	Humanities	and	Evil	-----

```
Duplicate 1-6
Card 06    7-8
```

	col.	How Far Apart Are			Units
0414	09-17	Humanities	and	You	
0415	18-26	Humanities			-----
	and	Your Present University			
0506	27-35	Arts	and	Physical Science	-----
0507	36-44	Arts	and	Social Science	-----
0508	45-53	Arts	and	Communication	-----
0509	54-62	Arts	and	Language	-----
0510	63-71	Arts	and	Mathematics	-----
0511	72-80	Arts	and	Good	-----

```
Duplicate 1-6
Card 07   7-8

          col.   How Far Apart Are                                    Units
          ------------------------------------------------------------------
0512   09-17   Arts                         and   Bad                 _____
0513   18-26   Arts                         and   Evil                _____
0514   27-35   Arts                         and   You                 _____
0515   36-44   Arts
         and   Your Present University                                _____
0607   45-53   Physical Science             and   Social Science      _____
0608   54-62   Physical Science             and   Communication       _____
0609   63-71   Physical Science             and   Language            _____
0610   72-80   Physical Science             and   Mathematics         _____
          ------------------------------------------------------------------

Duplicate 1-6
Card 08   7-8

          col.   How Far Apart Are                                    Units
          ------------------------------------------------------------------
0611   09-17   Physical Science             and   Good                _____
0612   18-26   Physical Science             and   Bad                 _____
0613   27-35   Physical Science             and   Evil                _____
0614   36-44   Physical Science             and   You                 _____
0615   45-53   Physical Science
         and   Your Present University                                _____
0708   54-62   Social Science               and   Communication       _____
0709   63-71   Social Science               and   Language            _____
0710   72-80   Social Science               and   Mathematics         _____
          ------------------------------------------------------------------

Duplicate 1-6
Card 09   7-8

          col.   How Far Apart Are                                    Units
          ------------------------------------------------------------------
0711   09-17   Social Science               and   Good                _____
0712   18-26   Social Science               and   Bad                 _____
0713   27-35   Social Science               and   Evil                _____
0714   36-44   Social Science               and   You                 _____
0715   45-53   Social Science
         and   Your Present University                                _____
0809   54-62   Communication                and   Language            _____
0810   63-71   Communication                and   Mathematics         _____
0811   72-80   Communication                and   Good                _____
          ------------------------------------------------------------------

Duplicate 1-6
Card 10   7-8

          col.   How Far Apart Are                                    Units
          ------------------------------------------------------------------
0812   09-17   Communication                and   Bad                 _____
0813   18-26   Communication                and   Evil                _____
0814   27-35   Communication                and   You                 _____
0815   36-44   Communication
         and   Your Present University                                _____
0910   45-53   Language                     and   Mathematics         _____
0911   54-62   Language                     and   Good                _____
0912   63-71   Language                     and   Bad                 _____
0913   72-80   Language                     and   Evil                _____
          ------------------------------------------------------------------
```

```
Duplicate 1-6
Card 11    7-8

        col.  How Far Apart Are                                    Units
        --------------------------------------------------------------
0914   09-17  Language                  and   You
0915   18-26  Language                                              -----
        and   Your Present University
                                                                    -----
1011   27-35  Mathematics              and   Good
1012   36-44  Mathematics              and   Bad                    -----
1013   45-53  Mathematics              and   Evil                   -----
1014   54-62  Mathematics              and   You                    -----
1015   63-71  Mathematics                                           -----
        and   Your Present University
                                                                    -----
1112   72-80  Good                     and   Bad
                                                                    -----
Duplicate 1-6
Card 12    7-8

        col.  How Far Apart Are                                    Units
        --------------------------------------------------------------
1113   09-17  Good                     and   Evil
1114   18-26  Good                     and   You                    -----
1115   27-35  Good                                                  -----
        and   Your Present University
                                                                    -----
1213   36-44  Bad                      and   Evil
1214   45-53  Bad                      and   You                    -----
1215   54-62  Bad                                                   -----
        and   Your Present University
                                                                    -----
1314   63-71  Evil                     and   You
1315   72-80  Evil                                                  -----
        and   Your Present University
                                                                    -----
Duplicate 1-6
Card 13    7-8

        col.  How Far Apart Are                                    Units
        --------------------------------------------------------------
1415   09-17  You
        and   Your Present University
                                                                    -----
        --------------------------------------------------------------
```

Instructions

Please estimate how different or "far apart" each of the following words or phrases is from each of the others. The more different, or further apart they seem to be, the larger the number you should write. To help you know what size number to write, remember
Love and Hate are 100 units apart.
If two words or phrases are not different at all, please write zero (0). If you have no idea, just leave the space blank.

Thank you very much for your help.

Duplicate 1-6
Card 01   7-8

	col.	How Far Apart Are			Units
0102	09-17	Love	and	Hate	-----
0103	18-26	Love	and	Anger	-----
0104	27-35	Love	and	Joy	-----
0105	36-44	Love	and	Envy	-----
0106	45-53	Love	and	Fear	-----
0107	54-62	Love	and	Jealousy	-----
0108	63-71	Love	and	Happiness	-----
0109	72-80	Love	and	Sadness	-----

Duplicate 1-6
Card 02   7-8

	col.	How Far Apart Are			Units
0110	09-17	Love	and	Anxiety	-----
0111	18-26	Love	and	Excitement	-----
0112	27-35	Love	and	Indifference	-----
0113	36-44	Love	and	Depression	-----
0114	45-53	Love	and	Selfish	-----
0115	54-62	Love	and	Guilt	-----
0116	63-71	Love	and	Strong	-----
0117	72-80	Love	and	Bad	-----

Duplicate 1-6
Card 03   7-8

	col.	How Far Apart Are			Units
0118	09-17	Love	and	Active	-----
0119	18-26	Love	and	Weak	-----
0120	27-35	Love	and	Good	-----
0121	36-44	Love	and	Passive	-----
0122	45-53	Love	and	Yourself	-----
0203	54-62	Hate	and	Anger	-----
0204	63-71	Hate	and	Joy	-----
0205	72-80	Hate	and	Envy	-----

```
Duplicate 1-6
Card 04    7-8
         col.  How Far Apart Are                                    Units
         -------------------------------------------------------------------
0206    09-17   Hate                    and  Fear              -----
0207    18-26   Hate                    and  Jealousy          -----
0208    27-35   Hate                    and  Happiness         -----
0209    36-44   Hate                    and  Sadness           -----
0210    45-53   Hate                    and  Anxiety           -----
0211    54-62   Hate                    and  Excitement        -----
C212    63-71   Hate                    and  Indifference      -----
0213    72-80   Hate                    and  Depression        -----
         -------------------------------------------------------------------
Duplicate 1-6
Card 05    7-8

         col.  How Far Apart Are                                    Units
         -------------------------------------------------------------------
0214    09-17   Hate                    and  Selfish           -----
C215    18-26   Hate                    and  Guilt             -----
0216    27-35   Hate                    and  Strong            -----
0217    36-44   Hate                    and  Bad               -----
0218    45-53   Hate                    and  Active            -----
0219    54-62   Hate                    and  Weak              -----
0220    63-71   Hate                    and  Good              -----
0221    72-80   Hate                    and  Passive           -----
         -------------------------------------------------------------------
Duplicate 1-6
Card 06    7-8

         col.  How Far Apart Are                                    Units
         -------------------------------------------------------------------
0222    09-17   Hate                    and  Yourself          -----
0304    18-26   Anger                   and  Joy               -----
0305    27-35   Anger                   and  Envy              -----
0306    36-44   Anger                   and  Fear              -----
C307    45-53   Anger                   and  Jealousy          -----
0308    54-62   Anger                   and  Happiness         -----
C309    63-71   Anger                   and  Sadness           -----
0310    72-80   Anger                   and  Anxiety           -----
         -------------------------------------------------------------------
Duplicate 1-6
Card 07    7-8

         col.  How Far Apart Are                                    Units
         -------------------------------------------------------------------
0311    09-17   Anger                   and  Excitement        -----
0312    18-26   Anger                   and  Indifference      -----
C313    27-35   Anger                   and  Depression        -----
0314    36-44   Anger                   and  Selfish           -----
0315    45-53   Anger                   and  Guilt             -----
0316    54-62   Anger                   and  Strong            -----
0317    63-71   Anger                   and  Bad               -----
0318    72-80   Anger                   and  Active            -----
         -------------------------------------------------------------------
```

```
Duplicate 1-6
Card 08    7-8

       col.  How Far Apart Are                                              Units
             -----------------------------------------------------------------
0319   09-17 Anger                          and  Weak                       -----
0320   18-26 Anger                          and  Good                       -----
0321   27-35 Anger                          and  Passive                    -----
0322   36-44 Anger                          and  Yourself                   -----
0405   45-53 Joy                            and  Envy                       -----
0406   54-62 Joy                            and  Fear                       -----
0407   63-71 Joy                            and  Jealousy                   -----
0408   72-80 Joy                            and  Happiness                  -----
             -----------------------------------------------------------------
Duplicate 1-6
Card 09    7-8

       col.  How Far Apart Are                                              Units
             -----------------------------------------------------------------
0409   09-17 Joy                            and  Sadness                    -----
0410   18-26 Joy                            and  Anxiety                     -----
0411   27-35 Joy                            and  Excitement                 -----
0412   36-44 Joy                            and  Indifference               -----
0413   45-53 Joy                            and  Depression                 -----
0414   54-62 Joy                            and  Selfish                     -----
0415   63-71 Joy                            and  Guilt                       -----
0416   72-80 Joy                            and  Strong                      -----
             -----------------------------------------------------------------
Duplicate 1-6
Card 10    7-8

       col.  How Far Apart Are                                              Units
             -----------------------------------------------------------------
0417   09-17 Joy                            and  Bad                        -----
0418   18-26 Joy                            and  Active                      -----
0419   27-35 Joy                            and  Weak                        -----
0420   36-44 Joy                            and  Good                        -----
0421   45-53 Joy                            and  Passive                     -----
0422   54-62 Joy                            and  Yourself                    -----
0506   63-71 Envy                           and  Fear                        -----
0507   72-80 Envy                           and  Jealousy                    -----
             -----------------------------------------------------------------
Duplicate 1-6
Card 11    7-8

       col.  How Far Apart Are                                              Units
             -----------------------------------------------------------------
0508   09-17 Envy                           and  Happiness                  -----
0509   18-26 Envy                           and  Sadness                    -----
0510   27-35 Envy                           and  Anxiety                     -----
0511   36-44 Envy                           and  Excitement                 -----
0512   45-53 Envy                           and  Indifference               -----
0513   54-62 Envy                           and  Depression                 -----
0514   63-71 Envy                           and  Selfish                     -----
0515   72-80 Envy                           and  Guilt                       -----
             -----------------------------------------------------------------
```

```
Duplicate 1-6
Card 12    7-8

        col.  How Far Apart Are                                          Units
        ------------------------------------------------------------------------
0516    09-17  Envy                       and  Strong                    -----
0517    18-26  Envy                       and  Bad                       -----
C518    27-35  Envy                       and  Active                    -----
0519    36-44  Envy                       and  Weak                      -----
C520    45-53  Envy                       and  Good                      -----
0521    54-62  Envy                       and  Passive                   -----
C522    63-71  Envy                       and  Yourself                  -----
0607    72-80  Fear                       and  Jealousy                  -----

Duplicate 1-6
Card 13    7-8

        col.  How Far Apart Are                                          Units
        ------------------------------------------------------------------------
0608    09-17  Fear                       and  Happiness                 -----
C609    18-26  Fear                       and  Sadness                   -----
0610    27-35  Fear                       and  Anxiety                   -----
0611    36-44  Fear                       and  Excitement                -----
0612    45-53  Fear                       and  Indifference              -----
0613    54-62  Fear                       and  Depression                -----
0614    63-71  Fear                       and  Selfish                   -----
C615    72-80  Fear                       and  Guilt                     -----

Duplicate 1-6
Card 14    7-8

        col.  How Far Apart Are                                          Units
        ------------------------------------------------------------------------
C616    09-17  Fear                       and  Strong                    -----
0617    18-26  Fear                       and  Bad                       -----
C618    27-35  Fear                       and  Active                    -----
0619    36-44  Fear                       and  Weak                      -----
0620    45-53  Fear                       and  Good                      -----
0621    54-62  Fear                       and  Passive                   -----
0622    63-71  Fear                       and  Yourself                  -----
0708    72-80  Jealousy                   and  Happiness                 -----

Duplicate 1-6
Card 15    7-8

        col.  How Far Apart Are                                          Units
        ------------------------------------------------------------------------
0709    09-17  Jealousy                   and  Sadness                   -----
C710    18-26  Jealousy                   and  Anxiety                   -----
0711    27-35  Jealousy                   and  Excitement                -----
C712    36-44  Jealousy                   and  Indifference              -----
0713    45-53  Jealousy                   and  Depression                -----
C714    54-62  Jealousy                   and  Selfish                   -----
0715    63-71  Jealousy                   and  Guilt                     -----
0716    72-80  Jealousy                   and  Strong                    -----
```

```
Duplicate 1-6
Card 16   7-8
```

	col.	How Far Apart Are			Units
0717	09-17	Jealousy	and	Bad	
0718	18-26	Jealousy	and	Active	-----
0719	27-35	Jealousy	and	Weak	-----
0720	36-44	Jealousy	and	Good	-----
0721	45-53	Jealousy	and	Passive	-----
0722	54-62	Jealousy	and	Yourself	-----
0809	63-71	Happiness	and	Sadness	-----
0810	72-80	Happiness	and	Anxiety	-----

```
Duplicate 1-6
Card 17   7-8
```

	col.	How Far Apart Are			Units
0811	09-17	Happiness	and	Excitement	-----
C812	18-26	Happiness	and	Indifference	-----
0813	27-35	Happiness	and	Depression	-----
0814	36-44	Happiness	and	Selfish	-----
0815	45-53	Happiness	and	Guilt	-----
0816	54-62	Happiness	and	Strong	-----
0817	63-71	Happiness	and	Bad	-----
C818	72-80	Happiness	and	Active	-----

```
Duplicate 1-6
Card 18   7-8
```

	col.	How Far Apart Are			Units
0819	09-17	Happiness	and	Weak	-----
0820	18-26	Happiness	and	Good	-----
0821	27-35	Happiness	and	Passive	-----
0822	36-44	Happiness	and	Yourself	-----
C910	45-53	Sadness	and	Anxiety	-----
C911	54-62	Sadness	and	Excitement	-----
C912	63-71	Sadness	and	Indifference	-----
0913	72-80	Sadness	and	Depression	-----

```
Duplicate 1-6
Card 19   7-8
```

	col.	How Far Apart Are			Units
0914	09-17	Sadness	and	Selfish	-----
0915	18-26	Sadness	and	Guilt	-----
0916	27-35	Sadness	and	Strong	-----
0917	36-44	Sadness	and	Bad	-----
0918	45-53	Sadness	and	Active	-----
0919	54-62	Sadness	and	Weak	-----
C920	63-71	Sadness	and	Good	-----
0921	72-80	Sadness	and	Passive	-----

```
Duplicate 1-6
Card 20   7-8
```

col.	How Far Apart Are			Units
0922	09-17	Sadness	and	Yourself	
1011	18-26	Anxiety	and	Excitement	-----
1012	27-35	Anxiety	and	Indifference	-----c
1013	36-44	Anxiety	and	Depression	-----
1014	45-53	Anxiety	and	Selfish	-----
1015	54-62	Anxiety	and	Guilt	-----
1016	63-71	Anxiety	and	Strong	-----
1017	72-80	Anxiety	and	Bad	-----

```
Duplicate 1-6
Card 21   7-8
```

col.	How Far Apart Are			Units
1018	09-17	Anxiety	and	Active	
1019	18-26	Anxiety	and	Weak	-----
1020	27-35	Anxiety	and	Good	-----
1021	36-44	Anxiety	and	Passive	-----
1022	45-53	Anxiety	and	Yourself	-----
1112	54-62	Excitement	and	Indifference	-----
1113	63-71	Excitement	and	Depression	-----
1114	72-80	Excitement	and	Selfish	-----

```
Duplicate 1-6
Card 22   7-8
```

col.	How Far Apart Are			Units
1115	09-17	Excitement	and	Guilt	
1116	18-26	Excitement	and	Strong	-----
1117	27-35	Excitement	and	Bad	-----
1118	36-44	Excitement	and	Active	-----
1119	45-53	Excitement	and	Weak	-----
1120	54-62	Excitement	and	Good	-----
1121	63-71	Excitement	and	Passive	-----
1122	72-80	Excitement	and	Yourself	-----

```
Duplicate 1-6
Card 23   7-8
```

col.	How Far Apart Are			Units
1213	09-17	Indifference	and	Depression	
1214	18-26	Indifference	and	Selfish	-----
1215	27-35	Indifference	and	Guilt	-----
1216	36-44	Indifference	and	Strong	-----
1217	45-53	Indifference	and	Bad	-----
1218	54-62	Indifference	and	Active	-----
1219	63-71	Indifference	and	Weak	-----
1220	72-80	Indifference	and	Good	-----

```
Duplicate 1-6
Card 24   7-8
```

col.	How Far Apart Are			Units
1221	09-17	Indifference	and Passive	-----
1222	18-26	Indifference	and Yourself	-----
1314	27-35	Depression	and Selfish	-----
1315	36-44	Depression	and Guilt	-----
1316	45-53	Depression	and Strong	-----
1317	54-62	Depression	and Bad	-----
1318	63-71	Depression	and Active	-----
1319	72-80	Depression	and Weak	-----

```
Duplicate 1-6
Card 25   7-8
```

col.	How Far Apart Are			Units
1320	09-17	Depression	and Good	-----
1321	18-26	Depression	and Passive	-----
1322	27-35	Depression	and Yourself	-----
1415	36-44	Selfish	and Guilt	-----
1416	45-53	Selfish	and Strong	-----
1417	54-62	Selfish	and Bad	-----
1418	63-71	Selfish	and Active	-----
1419	72-80	Selfish	and Weak	-----

```
Duplicate 1-6
Card 26   7-8
```

col.	How Far Apart Are			Units
1420	09-17	Selfish	and Good	-----
1421	18-26	Selfish	and Passive	-----
1422	27-35	Selfish	and Yourself	-----
1516	36-44	Guilt	and Strong	-----
1517	45-53	Guilt	and Bad	-----
1518	54-62	Guilt	and Active	-----
1519	63-71	Guilt	and Weak	-----
1520	72-80	Guilt	and Good	-----

```
Duplicate 1-6
Card 27   7-8
```

col.	How Far Apart Are			Units
1521	09-17	Guilt	and Passive	-----
1522	18-26	Guilt	and Yourself	-----
1617	27-35	Strong	and Bad	-----
1618	36-44	Strong	and Active	-----
1619	45-53	Strong	and Weak	-----
1620	54-62	Strong	and Good	-----
1621	63-71	Strong	and Passive	-----
1622	72-80	Strong	and Yourself	-----

```
Duplicate 1-6
Card 28    7-8
```

	col.	How Far Apart Are			Units
1718	09-17	Bad	and	Active	
1719	18-26	Bad	and	Weak	-----
1720	27-35	Bad	and	Good	-----
1721	36-44	Bad	and	Passive	-----
1722	45-53	Bad	and	Yourself	-----
1819	54-62	Active	and	Weak	-----
1820	63-71	Active	and	Good	-----
1821	72-80	Active	and	Passive	-----

```
Duplicate 1-6
Card 29    7-8
```

	col.	How Far Apart Are			Units
1822	09-17	Active	and	Yourself	
1920	18-26	weak	and	Good	-----
1921	27-35	Weak	and	Passive	-----
1922	36-44	weak	and	Yourself	-----
2021	45-53	Good	and	Passive	-----
2022	54-62	Good	and	Yourself	-----
2122	63-71	Passive	and	Yourself	-----

REFERENCES

American Psychological Association. *Standards for educational and psychological tests and manuals.* Washington, D.C.: American Psychological Association, 1966.

Aronson, E., & Carlesmith, J. Experimentation in social psychology. In G. Lindsey and E. Aronson (Eds.), *Handbook of social psychology.* Reading, Mass.: Addison-Wesley, 1968.

Barnett, G. *Reliability and metric multidimensional scaling.* Unpublished manuscript, Michigan State University, East Lansing, 1972.

Barnett, G., & Woelfel, J. On the dimensionality of psychological processes. *Quality and Quantity,* 1979, *13,* 215–232.

Barnett, G., Serota, K., & Taylor, J. Campaign communication and attitude change: A multidimensional analysis. *Human Communication Research,* 1976, 2(3), 227–244.

Berger, P., & Luckman, S., *The social construction of reality.* Garden City, N.Y.: Anchor Books, 1967.

Blalock, H. M. Jr. *Theory construction.* Englewood Cliffs, N.J.: Prentice-Hall, 1969.

Blau, P. *On the nature of organizations.* New York: Wiley, 1974.

Blumenthal, L. *Theory and applications of distance geometry.* Bronx, N.Y.: Chelsea, 1970.

Born, M. *Einstein's theory of relativity.* New York: Dover, 1965.

Brillouin, L. *Scientific uncertainty and information.* New York: Academic Press, 1964.

Bronowski, J. *The ascent of man.* Boston: Little and Brown, 1974.

Brophy, M. *A study of the interrelationships between the social structure and the cognitive belief system or "culture" of a social unit.* Unpublished M.A. thesis, Michigan State University, East Lansing, 1976.

Bruner, J. Social psychology and perception. In E. Maccoby, T. Newcomb, & E. Hartley (Eds.), *Readings in social psychology.* New York: Holt, 1958.

Capra, F. *The Tao of physics.* Boulder, Col.: Shambhala, 1975.

Cliff, N. Adverbs as multipliers. *Psychological Review,* 1959, *66,* 27–44.

Cliff, N. Orthogonal rotation to congruence. *Psychometrika,* 1966, *31,* 33–42.

Cody, M. The validity of experimentally induced motions of public figures in a multidimensional scaling configuration. In D. Nimmo (Ed.), *Communication Yearbook* (Vol. 4). New Brunswick, N.J.: Transaction Press, 1980.

Cody, M., Marlier, J., & Woelfel, J. D. *An application of the multiple attribute measurement model: Measurements and manipulation of source credibility.* Paper presented to the Annual Meeting of the Mathematical Psychology Association, Lafayette, Ind., 1976.

Coleman, J. *Introduction to mathematical sociology.* New York: The Free Press of Glencoe, 1964.

Cushing, J. *Applied analytical mathematics for physical scientists.* New York: Wiley, 1975.

Cushman, D. P., & Pierce, W. B. Generality and necessity in three types of theory about human communication, with special attention to rules theory. *Human Communication Research,* 1977, *3,* No. 4, Summer.

Cushman, D. P., & Tompkins, P. K. A theory of rhetoric for contemporary society and Implications of an open systems cybernetic analysis of paradoxical communication for the development of a contemporary rhetorical theory. In D. P. Cushman (Ed.), *Communication, attitudes, and behavior.* New York: Academic Press, 1980.

Danes, J., Hunter, J., & Woelfel, J. Belief change as a function of accumulated information. *Human Communication Research,* Spring, 1978.

Danes, J., & Woelfel, J. *An alternative to the "traditional" scaling paradigm in mass communication research: Multidimensional reduction of ratio judgments of separation.* Paper presented to the International Communication Association Annual Meeting, Chicago, April 1975.

Descartes, R. *Philosophical essays discourse on method, meditations rules for the direction of the mind,* L. J. Lefleur (Trans.). New York: Bobbs-Merrill, 1964.

Durkheim, E., *Elementary forms of the religious life: A study in religious sociology.* J. W. Simon (Trans.). New York: Macmillan, 1915.

Durkheim, E. *Suicide.* Glencoe, Ill.: The Free Press, 1951.

Durkheim, E. *The rules of sociological method,* S. Solovay (Trans.). New York: The Free Press, 1966.

Edwards, H. W. *Analytic and vector mechanics.* New York: McGraw-Hill, 1933.

Einstein, A. The foundation of the general theory of relativity. *The principle of relativity.* New York: Dover, 1952.

Einstein, A. *The meaning of relativity* (5th ed.). Princeton, N.J.: Princeton University Press, 1956.

Einstein, A. *Relativity: The special and general theory.* New York: Crown, 1961.

Festinger, L. *A theory of cognitive dissonance.* Evanston, Ill.: Row Peterson, 1957.

Fink, E., Serota, L. K., Woelfel, J. D., & Noell, J. *Communication, ideology and political behavior: A multidimensional analysis.* Paper presented to the Political Communication Division of the International Communication Association, Chicago, April 1975.

Foote, N. N. Identification as the basis for a theory of motivation. *American Sociological Review,* 1951, Feb., 10–21.

Garfinkel, H., *Studies in ethnomethodology.* Englewood Cliffs, N.J.: Prentice-Hall, 1967.

Gellert, W., Kustner, H., Hallwich, M., & Katner, H. (Eds.). *The VNR concise encyclopedia of mathematics.* (1st American ed.). Princeton, N.J.: Van Nostrand Reinhold, 1977.

Gillham, J., & Woelfel, J. The Galileo system of measurement. *Human Communication Research,* 1977, *3*(3), Spring.

Goffman, E. *Frame analysis: An essay on the organization of experience.* New York: Harper & Row, 1974.

Goldstein, H. *Classical mechanics.* Reading, Mass.: Addison-Wesley, 1950.

Gordon, T. *Subject abilities to use MDS: Effects of varying the criterion pair.* Unpublished research paper, Temple University, Philadelphia, Pa., 1976.

Gordon, T., & Deleo, H. C. *Structural variation in "Galileo" space: Effects of varying the criterion pair in multidimensional scaling.* Paper presented at the Annual Meeting of the International Communication Association, Portland, Ore., 1976.

Green, P., & Carmone, F. Marketing research applications of nonmetric multidimensional scaling methods. In A. Romney, R. Shephard, & S. Nerlove (Eds.), *Multidimensional scaling: Theory and applications in the behavioral sciences*. New York: Academic (Seminar) Press, 1972.

Green, P., Maheshwari, A. & Rao, V. Self-concept and brand preference. *Journal of Market Research Society*, 1969, 2, 343–360.

Haller, A. O., & Miller, I. W. *The occupational aspiration scale: Theory, structure and correlates*. New York: Shenkman, 1971.

Haller, A. O., & Woelfel, J. D. *The Wisconsin significant other battery*. U.S. Office of Education Report, 1969.

Halliday, M. A., and Resnick, R. *Physics*. New York: Wiley, 1966.

Hamblin, R. Social attitudes: Magnitude measurement and theory. In H. Blalock, Jr. (Ed.), *Measurement in the social sciences*. Chicago: Aldine, 1974.

Heider, F. *The psychology of interpersonal relations*. New York: Wiley, 1958.

Heise, D. *Causal analysis*. New York: Wiley, 1975.

Heisenberg, W. *Physics and beyond*, A. J. Pomerans (Trans.). New York: Harper & Row, 1971.

Hertz, H. *The principles of mechanics*. New York: Dover, 1956.

James, G., & James, R. C., *Mathematics dictionary*, Princeton, N.J.: Van Nostrand Reinhold, 1976.

Jones, L., & Young, F. Structure of a social environment: Longitudinal individual differences scaling for an intact group, *Journal of Personality and Social Psychology*, 1972, 24, 102–121.

Kincaid, D. L. The convergence model of communication. *Communication institute monograph*, No. 18, East-West Center, Honolulu, Hawaii, 1980.

Kokinakis, C. *A pilot study for the National Organization for Women: Attitudes toward the women's movement*. Unpublished M.A. Thesis, Michigan State University, East Lansing, 1979.

Korzenny, F., Ruiz, M., & Ben David, A., *Metric multidimensional scaling and automatic message generation applied to the tourism industry: The case of Israel*. Paper presented at the International Communication Association Annual Meeting, Chicago, April 1978.

Kuhn, M. H. Major trends in symbolic interaction theory in the past twenty-five years. *Sociological Quarterly*, 1964, 5, 61–84.

Kuhn, T. *The structure of scientific revolutions*. Chicago: University of Chicago Press, 1970.

Lemert, E. *Social pathology*. New York: McGraw-Hill, 1951.

Mach, E. *The science of mechanics* (5th English ed.). LaSalle, Ill., Open Court, 1942.

Mannheim, K. *Essays on sociology and social psychology*, P. Kecskemeti (Ed.). New York: Oxford University Press, 1953.

McConnell, A. *Applications of tensor analysis*. New York: Dover, 1933.

McKeon, R. *The basic works of Aristotle*. New York: Random House, 1941.

McPhail, C. *The description and analysis of some elementary patterns of collective behavior*. Unpublished paper, University of Illinois at Urbana, Champaign, 1974.

McPhail, T. L., and Barnett, G. A. *Broadcasting, culture and self: A multidimensional pilot study*. Report prepared for the Ministry of the Secretary of State, Canada, 1977.

Mead, G. H. *Mind, self and society from the standpoint of a social behaviorist*, C. Morris (Ed.). Chicago: The University of Chicago Press, 1934.

Mettlin, C. *Assessing the effects of interpersonal influence in the attitude formation process*. Unpublished Ph.D. dissertation, University of Illinois, 1970.

Mettlin, C. Smoking as behavior: Applying a social psychological theory. *Journal of Health & Social Behavior*, 1973, 14, 144–152.

Meyer, S. L. *Data analysis for scientists and engineers*. New York: Wiley, 1975.

Michels, W. C., Malcolm, C., & Patterson, A. L. *Foundations of physics*. Princeton, N.J.: Van Nostrand Reinhold 1968.

Mills, C. W. Situated actions and vocabularies of motive. *American Sociological Review, 5,* 1940, 904–913.

Nels-Frumkin, M. *Handbook for research on attitudes toward health maintenance organizations*. Unpublished MA thesis, Michigan State University, East Lansing, 1978.

Newcomb, T. M. An approach to the study of communication acts. *Psychological Review,* 1953, *60,* 393–404.

Nisbett, R. E., & Wilson, T. D. Telling more than we can know: Verbal reports on mental processes. *Psychological Review,* 1977, *84,* 231–259.

Osgood, C., Tannenbaum, P., & Suci, G. *The measurement of meaning*. Urbana: University of Illinois Press, 1957.

Poincaré, H. *The foundations of science*. Lancaster, Pa.: Science Press, 1946.

Poole, M. S. *A test of some mathematical models of change in hierarchies of attitudes*. Unpublished M.A. thesis, Michigan State University, East Lansing, 1977.

Prigogine, O. Time, structure, and fluctuations. *Science,* 1978, *201*(4358), 777–785.

Reichenbach, H. *Space and time*. New York: Dover, 1958.

Saltiel, J. *Predicting occupational choice*—A multidimensional scaling approach. Paper presented at the First Annual "Metric Multidimensional Scaling Workshop," International Communication Association, Chicago, April 1978.

Saltiel, J., & Woelfel, J. D. Inertia in cognitive process: The role of accumulated information in attitude changes. *Human Communication Research,* 1975, *1,* 333–344.

Sarbin, T. R., & Allen, V. L. Role theory. In G. Lindsey & E. Aronson (Eds.), *Handbook of Social Psychology* (2nd ed., Vol.1). Reading, Mass.: Addison-Wesley, 1968.

Schönemann, P. A generalized solution of the orthogonal procrustes problem. *Psychometrika,* 1966, *31,* 1–10.

Schwartz, M. *Communication network design and analysis*. Englewood Cliffs, N.J.: Prentice-Hall, 1977.

Serota, K., *et al*. Precise procedure for optimizing campaign communication. In R. Brent (Ed.), *Communication yearbook* (Vol. 1). New Brunswick, N.J.: Transaction Books, 1977. Pp. 475–494.

Serota, K., Cody, M., Barnett, G., & Taylor, J. Precise procedures for optimizing campaign communication. In B. Ruben (Ed.), *International communication association communication yearbook*. New Brunswick, N.J.: Transaction Books. 1978. Pp. 425–442.

Shinn, T. Relations between scales. In H. M. Blalock (Ed.), *Measurement in the social sciences: Theories and strategies*. Chicago: Aldine, 1974.

Shklovskii, V., & Sagan, C. *Intelligent life in the universe*. San Francisco: Holden-Day, 1966.

Simpson, G. *Emile Durkheim: Selections from his work*, with an introduction and commentaries by G. Simpson. New York: Crowell, 1963.

Sorokin, P. A. *Contemporary sociological theories*. New York: Harper & Row, 1928.

Spencer, H. *The principles of sociology*. New York: Appleton, 1897.

Stefflre, V. J. Some applications of multidimensional scaling to social science problems. In A. Romney, R. Shephard, & S. Nerlove (Eds.), *Multidimensional scaling: Theory and applications in the behavioral sciences*. New York: Academic (Seminar) Press, 1972.

Stevens, S. S. Mathematics, measurement and psychophysics. In S. Stevens (Ed.), *Handbook of experimental psychology*. New York: Wiley, 1951.

Sullivan, H. S. *The interpersonal theory of psychiatry*. New York: Norton, 1953.

Suppes, P., & Zinnes, J. L. Basic measurement theory. In R. D. Luce, R. R. Bush, & E. Golanter (Eds.), *Handbook of mathematical psychology*. New York: Wiley, 1963.

Thurstone, L. L. *Multiple factor analysis development and expansion of the vectors of the mind.* Chicago: The University of Chicago Press, 1947.

Torgerson, W. S. *Theory and method of scaling.* New York: Wiley, 1958.

Tribus, M., & McIrvine, E. C. Energy and information. In *Energy and power.* San Francisco: Freeman, 1971.

Tucker, L., & Messick, S. Individual difference model for multidimensional scaling. *Psychometrika,* 1963, *28,* 333–367.

Van de Geer, J. P. *Introduction to multivariate analysis for the social sciences.* San Francisco: Freeman, 1971.

Wallace, R. *A study of Michigan dairymen's attitudes toward the Dairy Improvement Association's testing programs.* Unpublished MA thesis, Michigan State University, East Lansing, 1979.

Weber, M. *The theory of social and economic organization,* A. M. Henderson and T. Parsons (Trans.). New York: The Free Press, 1947.

Whitehead, J. H., & Veblen, O. *The foundations of differential geometry.* Cambridge, England: The University Press, 1932.

Whorf, B. L. In J. B. Carroll (Ed.), *Language, thought, and reality: Selected writings.* Cambridge: Technology Press of Massachusetts, Institute of Technology, 1956.

Wilson, E. B. *An introduction to scientific research.* New York: McGraw-Hill, 1952.

Woelfel, J. C. *The relative contribution of mothers and fathers to the political socialization of their children.* Unpublished manuscript, University of Michigan, Ann Arbor, 1976.

Woelfel, J. D. A theory of occupational choice. In J. S. Picou and R. Campbell (Eds.), *Career patterns of minority youth.* Columbus, Ohio: Charles E. Merrill, 1975.

Woelfel, J. D. The western model. In D. L. Kincaid, C. Y. Cheng, & J. D. Woelfel (Eds.), *Eastern and western communication theory.* Unpublished manuscript. Honolulu, Hawaii: The East-West Center, 1979.

Woelfel, J. D. Foundations of cognitive theory. In D. P. Cushman and R. McPhee (Eds.), *Message-attitude-behavior relationship.* New York: Academic Press, 1980.

✓ Woelfel, J. D., Barnett, G. A., & Dinkelacker, J. W. *Metric multidimensional scaling in Riemann space.* Paper presented at the Annual Meeting of the Psychometric Society, Hamilton, Ontario, August 1978.

Woelfel, J., Cody, M., Gillham, J., & Holmes, R. Basic premises of attitude change theory. *Human Communication Research,* 1980, *6,* No. 2, Winter, 153–168.

Woelfel, J. D., Danes, J. Multidimensional scaling models for communication research. In P. Monge and J. Capella (Eds.), *Multivariate techniques in human communications research.* New York: Academic Press. 1980.

Woelfel, J. D., & Haller, A. O. Significant others, the self-reflexive act, and the attitude formation process. *American Sociological Review,* 36(1), Feb., 1971.

Woelfel, J. D., Holmes, R. A., Cody, M., & Fink, E. L. *Message strategies in Riemann space.* Paper presented before Joint Sessions of the Psychometric Society and the Mathematical Psychology Group, Durham, North Carolina, April 1976.

Woelfel, J. D., Holmes, R., & Kincaid, D. L. *Rotation to congruence for general Riemann surfaces under theoretical constraints.* Paper presented at the Second Annual Workshop in "Multidimensional Scaling," International Communication Association, Philadelphia, May 1979.

Woelfel, J. D., Newton, B., Kincaid, D. L., & Holmes, R. *Perceptions of occupation names.* Unpublished manuscript. Honolulu, Hawaii: The East-West Center, 1979.

Woelfel, J. D. & Saltiel, J. Cognitive processes as motions in a multidimensional space. In F. Casimer (Ed.), *International and intercultural communication.* University Press, New York, 1978.

Woelfel, J. D., & Werner, E. *Attitude research in the future, annual review of attitude research.* American Marketing Association, 1979.

Woelfel, J. D., Woelfel, J. C., & Woelfel, M. L. *Standardized vs. unstandardized matrices: Which type is best for factor analysis?* Paper presented to the Annual Meeting of the American Sociological Association, San Francisco, August 1977.

Young, G., & Householder, A. Discussion of a set of points in terms of their mutual distances. *Psychometrika*, 1938, 3, 19–22.

INDEX